When All
Roads Led To

Tucson about 1880, as Gray would have seen it passing through en route to Tombstone.

Tombstone

A Memoir

by
John Plesent Gray

*All my best
W. Lane Rogers*

Edited and Annotated by
W. Lane Rogers

With Foreword by
John Duncklee

First Edition: January, 1998

10 9 8 7 6 5 4 3 2 1

ISBN: 1–886609–13–6

Cover design by Kathleen Petersen

Published by:

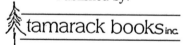 tamarack books inc.

PO Box 190313
Boise, ID 83719–0313
800/962-6657, 208/387-2656, fax 208/387-2650
e-mail: admin@tamarackbooks.com
website: http://www.tamarackbooks.com

Printed in the United States of America

This book is warmly dedicated to historian
Wallace E. Clayton,
who was, is, and will forever be the heart and soul of the
Tombstone Epitaph,
and whose association is sorely missed.

TABLE OF CONTENTS

by
John Duncklee

The discovery of the manuscript, *When All Roads Led To Tombstone,* is to Tombstone and southern Arizona history, what finding the Dead Sea Scrolls was to theology.

Resting in the archives of the Arizona Historical Society, this remarkable memoir written by John Plesent Gray, waited for an historical researcher with an eye for significant primary source material. Not only did W. Lane Rogers find the manuscript in the archives, read it and recognize its importance, but he also added much value to Gray's writing with his thoroughly-researched, enlightening annotation.

Gray's eyewitness account of the gunfight near the OK Corral offers a view much at odds with the commonly accepted version and ought to be a terminator to the nonsense written about it. Hollywood and others have proceeded *ad nauseam* with romanticized tales of the Earp/Clanton squabble ever since it happened. All sorts of historical writing, fiction and nonfiction, amateur and otherwise, has spawned controversy over who shot whom, and who shot first, and who did not shoot at all, until the entire affair has been blown completely out of historical significance. Gray's memoir, with Rogers' insightful annotation, helps set the record straight.

Beyond events in Tombstone, Gray's account of the cattle business in the latter part of the nineteenth century is particularly significant. He captures the essence of the business and the way of life of raising cattle on the frontier, and how it was challenged by Mexican and American cattle thieves, smugglers, Apache raiders, drought, overgrazing, and railroad freight rates.

J.J. Wagoner's, *History of the Cattle Industry in Southern Arizona: 1540–1940,* is recognized by scholars as the classic study for anyone interested in cattle-raising history in southern Arizona. However, Gray's memoir adds a flavor not possible in such a work as Wagoner's. Gray was there. Gray was a cowman during the 1880s and 1890s. He not only wrote about his personal experiences in the cattle business, but also recognized and commented about what was happening to southern Arizona ranges because of the influx of too many cattle.

Gray was a survivor in the truest sense of the word. He was ranching from a headquarters in Rucker Canyon, east of Tombstone, in the Chiricahua Mountains, a place frequented by rustlers, outlaws, and Apache raiders. Yet he survived and prospered.

As a resident of Tombstone, Gray witnessed events and was acquainted with many of the town's notables: merchants, stage robbers, sheriffs, and bar owners. He praises Nellie Cashman as a charitable, unselfish soul of the frontier. He rode with Geronimo after the surrender. Gray extended his hospitality to anyone who rode into his ranch headquarters, including the likes of the rustler gang of Curly Bill Brocius.

Mike Gray, John Gray's father, established the now well-known Gray Ranch in the Animas Valley, across the Arizona border in New Mexico, after going bust on a litigated mining claim in Tombstone. As a result of the threat both from Mexicans retaliating against attacks on their smuggling operations, and from Apache raiders, the Grays moved their ranching operation to Rucker Canyon where the US Cavalry had once maintained a base for excursions against the renegades. Later, the Gray Ranch in New Mexico was acquired by the Kern County Land and Cattle Company of Bakersfield, California. In later years, the Nature Conservancy took over the operation of the ranch.

Gray sprinkles his memoir with a number of opinions garnered from his experiences. Using examples, he praises good watch dogs and cow horses; he may have been one of the first to advocate gun control. He draws from a number of episodes to substantiate why he and other cattlemen thought the cavalry was inept in its campaigns against the Apache, when the Indians fled the reservations and established headquarters in the Sierra Madres in Mexico.

When All Roads Led To Tombstone is an enrichment to the history of southern Arizona and the Southwest.

John Duncklee
Oracle, Arizona

Author John Duncklee fields questions from the audience following a reading at Eastern Arizona College, November 11, 1997.

It was with wonderment that I read the Gray manuscript, a most important document that had lain dormant in the archives of the Arizona Historical Society nearly sixty years. Snippets of its text had been quoted here and there in a handful of books, but never had a book been made of it. It occurred to me that one ought to be, that the material was too important to history to collect dust another sixty years. Here, after all, was a man who witnessed the shootout near the OK Corral in Tombstone, who rubbed shoulders with Geronimo and the Apache Kid, who knew generals Miles and Crook; a man who lived at a time when momentous history was being made in the West.

What we know of John Plesent Gray, aside from information shared with us in his colorful and most compelling narrative, comes largely from a three-page biographical sketch given to the Arizona Pioneers' Historical Society (today's Arizona Historical Society), written September 16, 1940.

From it we learn that he was born in Sacramento, California, February 29, 1860, to Michael and Sarah Ann Gray. He attended the University of California at Berkeley, from which he graduated in 1880. Upon graduation, he set out for Tombstone to join his family, who had settled there at its inception in 1879.

"At Tombstone worked in mines," he wrote in abbreviated form, "in post office under P.M. Fred Emerson Brooks for two years. In 1882 located cattle ranch at old Camp Rucker in Chiricahua Mts. Followed cattle business for next twenty years."

Inelegant as that brief paragraph may be, Gray had a flair for the written word, and he understood that history—however inconsequential it might seem to be at the moment—ought to be preserved. And that is what he did. By doing so, this and future generations will have a more complete understanding of events that occurred in Tombstone during its turbulent boom days; of the complexity of the Apache wars; of the challenge of operating a cattle ranch in a rugged, hostile land.

In bringing this book to print, my greatest debt is owed to John Plesent Gray, for he was the man who put pen to paper. Gratitude is due my friend and colleague John Duncklee—a brilliant wordsmith and former cattleman who knows the business from the hoof up, and who has written two excellent books about the industry—who in the early stages, reviewed the manuscript, at once recognized its value, and encouraged me to edit, annotate, and find a publisher. I found one in Kathy Gaudry, a warm, gentle person who possesses a razor-sharp mind and is a pleasure to work with. My appreciation is extended to friend and colleague

Robert Kirby who, on many occasions, has taken time from a busy writing schedule to research various items for me. Wendy Lawton was most helpful in providing me with otherwise elusive information; and to James R. Smith is owed an enormous debt of gratitude for his dogged effort in researching a variety of California items. And a warm thank you is extended to my colleague Kay Macfarlane for drawing maps of Tombstone and Camp Rucker. Countless hours were spent in the archives of the Arizona Historical Society, the University of Arizona Library, and the Tucson Public Library. I am indebted to the many professionals who aided in my research. And, as always, a loving thank you is extended to my wife Patricia, who has gotten to understand why, now and again, writers leave unwashed dishes in the sink and forget to take out the trash.

W. Lane Rogers
Tucson, Arizona

A Memoir

by
John Plesent Gray

Edited and Annotated by
W. Lane Rogers

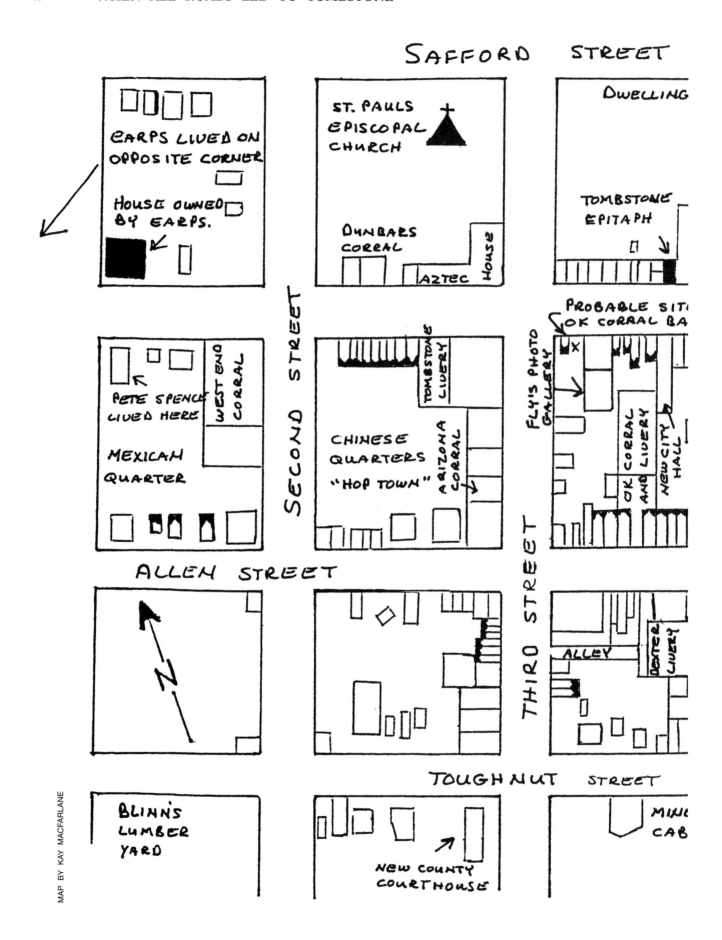

MAP BY KAY MACFARLANE

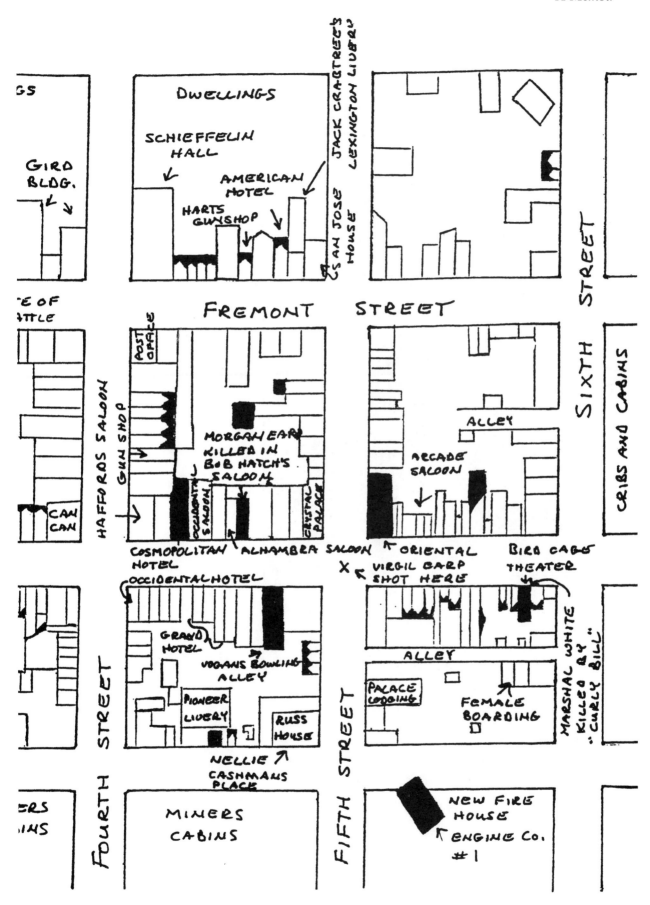

TOMBSTONE, ARIZONA
EARLY 1880's

*John Plesent Gray
photographed in
San Francisco in 1894,
at age thirty-four.*

*"If my viewpoint in these memoirs seems to belittle
some of these men who lived by their guns instead of
by honest toil, I can only say I have tried to state the
case as I saw and knew it, and if time has glossed
over some of their deeds, my memory tells only of
those old days as they appeared at the time and they
are not being viewed as a distant era, which seems
inclined to make heros out of desperadoes."*

A steam locomotive passes through Pantano, which in June 1880, was the end of the Southern Pacific track.

(1) Located some thirty miles southeast of Tucson and once an important ranch and stage station, Pantano was originally called La Cienega (Spanish for marsh or swamp), and later Tullyville for Pickney Randolph Tully, twice mayor of Tucson who, with partner Estevan Ochoa, ran the successful freighting firm of Tully and Ochoa. Mrs. Granville H. Oury, wife of Arizona Territory's delegate to the Confederate Congress in 1861, wrote of the Pantano area in her diary: "We are traveling through country which has always been infested by Indians, and very recently they have committed depredations and horrible atrocities on this very road. Our party is very small and there would be no escape for us if a party of Apaches were to attack us. We all realize this and are trusting to some good fortune or fate to get us through safely." The old cemetery at Pantano is filled with graves of pioneers who were killed by Apaches.

Workers of the Writers' Program of the Work Projects Administration. *Arizona, The Grand Canyon State: A State Guide.* NY: Hastings House, 1940, pp. 382–83.

Sonnichsen, C.L. Tucson: *The Life and Times of an American City.* Norman: University of Oklahoma Press, 1982, p. 94.

A FEW MILES EAST of Tucson, Arizona is the Southern Pacific railway station at Pantano,[1] and that point marked the end of the Southern Pacific Railroad in June of 1880.

There were about thirty passengers on the train arriving at Pantano the morning of June 4th of that year, all headed for the promised land of Tombstone. That mournful name did not seem to dampen the ardor of any of the thirty, of which I was one. If it had borne the name "Hell," it is probable our enthusiasm would have been none the less.

I remember how eager we were to pile out of the train and into the stage coach standing ready by the track with its six-horse team that seemed as impatient as we were to get away. Our railroad ride from California had been very tiresome, for in those days the roadbed was new and despite the slow speed of the train caused much jolting of the passengers. The dust crept in through window casings and every conceivable place, even when the car windows were all closed, and that with the desert heat, which was a new and trying experience, had about exhausted all of us.

That last morning on the train we had stopped for breakfast at Tucson and we were told they had just finished celebrating "the arrival of the iron horse" and had wired the Pope at Rome that "the Ancient and Honorable Pueblo of Tucson" was now in touch with the rest of the world.[2] Signed by Mayor Bob Leatherwood,[3] the cablegram put Tucson on the map as "the Ancient and Honorable Pueblo"—afterward abbreviated to "the A. and H. Pueblo," a title still preserved by old-timers.

That day's stage ride will always live in my memory, but not for its beauty spots. Jammed like sardines on the hard seats of an old-time leather spring coach— a Concord—we left Pantano and crept much of the way, letting the horses walk through miles of alkali dust. The wheels rolled it up in thick clouds, of which we received the full benefit. We couldn't then see much romance in the old stage method of traveling. But the driver said that was his daily job, which made us ashamed of our weakness. We still wondered, however, why the Concord coach was ever invented as it seemed such a crude creation, especially now that we look back and compare it to later horse drawn vehicles. But there was no question about its ability to withstand rough usage. It was evidently built for mountain travel, and many a Concord stage has gone off the grade and still held together to continue in use. It is always a mystery to the passenger how many people can be wedged into and on top of a stage coach. If it had not been for the long stretches when the horses had to walk, enabling most of us to get out and "foot it" as a relaxation, it seems we could never have survived the trip.

It had been rather a disappointing sight we had experienced of the flat little town of drab adobe houses—Tucson. Because in age it is close to being the oldest town in the United States, we naturally expected something different. With its square-built adobe houses standing flush with the narrow, treeless streets—apparently bare of any sort of plant life, it had made us still more homesick than before for the bright flower gardens and cheerful paint that graced

AHS #1842

R.N. (Bob) Leatherwood, mayor of Tucson, who is said to have wired the Pope upon the arrival of the railroad.

(2) Moving east from the California border at Yuma, the Southern Pacific Railroad arrived at Tucson, March 20, 1880. This long-awaited event was heralded with much fanfare and plans were laid for a village-wide celebration. On March 17, Mayor Robert N. (Bob) Leatherwood telegrammed the mayors of Yuma, Los Angeles, and San Francisco inviting them to attend the festivities. In a much-told story that may be apocryphal, it is said that Leatherwood wired the Pope as well. During the gala, clerks delivered a telegram to the mayor which read:

"His Holiness the Pope acknowledges with appreciation receipt of your telegram informing him that the ancient city of Tucson at last has been connected with the outside world and sends his benediction, but for his own satisfaction would ask, where the hell is Tucson?"

Sonnichsen, *Tucson*, pp. 102–04.

Harte, John Brett. *Tucson: Portrait of a Desert Pueblo.* CA: Windsor Publications, 1980, p. 54.

Trimble, Marshall. *Arizona: A Cavalcade of History.* Tucson: Treasure Chest Publications, 1989, pp. 186–87.

(3) A Confederate veteran, Robert N. (Bob) Leatherwood was born in North Carolina in 1844 and came to Tucson in 1869. He was proprietor of Leatherwood's Stables at the corner of Church and Pennington streets; served on the city council; was a member of the territorial legislature; was Pima County Sheriff;

". . . [a] flat little town of drab adobe houses," is how Gray characterized Tucson in 1880.

county treasurer; and captain of the Arizona Rangers, an elite but short-lived law enforcement body. Leatherwood was thirty-six-years-old when, on January 1, 1880, he became mayor of Tucson.

Sonnichsen, *Tucson*, p. 102.

Hart, p. 54.

(4) The "flat little town" to which Gray refers was, in reality, the center of commerce of Arizona Territory as well as much of the Southwest. Between 1870 and 1880, the population of Tucson had more than doubled, from some 3,500 inhabitants to 7,007. Still, however, Mexican influence (Tucson had been the northern-most outpost of Sonora, Mexico until the Gadsden Purchase of 1853) was largely dominant and, as Gray notes, its' architecture was mostly square-built mud adobe structures. Will C. Barnes, noted Arizona soldier-cowboy-turned-historian, referred to Tucson in 1880 as a "sorry-looking Mexican town with narrow, crooked streets lined with one-story houses built of sun-dried adobe, and mostly with dirt floors and dirt roofs."

Mabry, Jonathan, B. *Tucson at the Turn of the Century: The Archaeology of a City Block.* Tucson: Center for Desert Archaeology, 1994, p. 4.

Giebner, Robert C., ed. *Armory Park 74ff.* Tucson: University of Arizona, College of Architecture, 1974, p. 16.÷

California towns. But in time we discovered that many of these rough-looking mud houses had an inside court or patio with flower gardens pretty as any California home could boast of.[4]

Our railroad tickets billing us to Tombstone had cost us ninety-eight dollars apiece and most of the party, including myself, would land in Tombstone practically broke. So we didn't waste too much time getting the blues over what we didn't like in Tucson. We had a good dinner at our first stop, a stage stand near where Benson was afterward founded, and this revived us and saved the day. This was our initiation to the frontier, and often since I have found that a good, hearty meal is the best cure-all for weariness of mind and body. I can hardly believe a suicide could occur following a good dinner.

In our company that day were at least two men destined to figure in Tombstone's future. One of them was Sol Israel, whose book store became a well known business on Allen Street, and another, Bob Crouch, who started the Sandy Bob Stage Line and in time absorbed the entire stage business between Tombstone and the railroad.

I will always remember our thrilling entry into Tombstone about sundown. Our driver cracked his long whip over the six weary horses and forced them into a gallop up Allen Street. Then, with a grand flourish, brought

A 4-4-0-locomotive, like this one, would have pulled Gray's train over the newly laid Southern Pacific tracks to southern Arizona.

the coach to a stop in front of the Cosmopolitan Hotel owned and operated by A.C. Bilicke and son,[5] who founded there the fortune that grew to millionaire proportions later in Los Angeles.

Tombstone was new then, less than one year old. That was before the coming of the Earps, Doc Holliday,[6] and the late discordant elements. It seemed everybody had gathered on the street, as was the custom, to meet the incoming stage. The glad hand extended us made us feel at home at once. I looked in vain for any guns or so-called gunmen. I learned later that it was one of the town's first ordinances that no guns were to be permitted in any public place, and Tombstone always was a quiet, safe town for the man who minded his own business.

Sandy Bob Crouch started his opposition stage line almost at once after his arrival in Tombstone. On July 4th, 1880, he drove his first stage, pulled by four gray horses, out of Tombstone for the new town of Benson,[7] which was making its debut into the world that day. I was one of his passengers and his "mud-wagon,"[8] as that style of stage was commonly termed, was well loaded, for Sandy Bob was starting his opposition to the Walker Stage Line at reduced fare.

Our driver, Sandy Bob himself, tried desperately to pass the big six-horse stage, but the latter had the lead and we had to take his dust all the way. That was a red letter day in more ways than one.

(5) A.C. (Albert) Bilicke was, in fact, the son of Chris Bilicke, proprietor of the Cosmopolitan Hotel. The latter once filed a mining claim with Wyatt Earp and, following the gunfight near the OK Corral, contributed to his bail. A.C. later testified in Earp's defense.

Marks, Paula Mitchell. *And Die in the West: The Story of the OK Corral Gunfight.* Norman: University of Oklahoma Press, 1996, pp. 288–89.

(6) The Earps and Doc Holliday arrived in Tombstone late November or early December, 1879; Holliday apparently preceded the Earps. Historians differ, some claiming the brothers Earp—Wyatt, Virgil, Morgan, James—traveled as a group; others that Wyatt arrived first, followed by the rest.

Breakenridge, William M. Richard Maxwell Brown, ed. *Helldorado: Bringing the Law to the Mesquite.* Lincoln: Bison Books, 1992, p. 154.

Burrows, Jack. *John Ringo: The Gunfighter Who Never Was.* Tucson: University of Arizona Press, 1996, pp. 16–18.

Myers, John Myers. *Tombstone's Early Years.* Lincoln, Bison Books, 1995, p. 64.

Chaput, Donald. *Virgil Earp: Western Peace Officer.* Norman: University of Oklahoma Press, 1996, pp. 52–53.

Marks, p. 89.

(7) Situated on the banks of the San Pedro River, twenty-five miles northwest of Tombstone, Benson was established by the Southern Pacific Railroad as the shipping point for mines of the Tombstone District. As early as 1860, however, the site was a river crossing for the Butterfield Overland Stage. The area surrounding Benson has been inhabited for centuries. In 1697, a Spanish officer wrote of ranches along the San Pedro River and noted that they were habitually raided by Apaches.

Barnes, Will C. *Arizona Place Names.* Tucson: University of Arizona Press, 1988, p. 44.

Workers, *Arizona,* p. 382.

(8) A mud wagon was a small, lightweight coach.

THE SOUTHERN PACIFIC Railway Company was auctioning off town lots in Benson, and it was there we met a big excursion train from Tucson. It looked as if all the inhabitants of Tucson had come to the sale. I was on my way to Tucson and had to wait at Benson till the sale was over and the excursion train ready to return to its starting point.

In Benson there was not yet a single house erected, but a few tents were up, these being used for saloons and restaurants, which were doing a good business. Anyway, they were that day. I expect, however, that Benson was a livelier place that 4th of July than at any other time of its career. And it was astounding the prices lots were bid up to that day. I venture to say that at no time since has Benson real estate ever risen to the peak prices of that day. The main bidders were Tucson people and the bidding was an amazing thing to witness out on that desert spot along the railroad track—a spot which apparently had no redeeming features as to location except, as the auctioneer stressed, it being a possible junction point for a future branch line to Guaymas, Mexico. I feel sure that auctioneer never did a better business for the railroad company, and if Benson had lived up to that day's promise it would be a thriving city today instead of just another railroad station. But maybe it has moved up a step since I knew it.

From that time on the order was to take the stage at Benson for Tombstone. All roads led to that Mecca—the promised land for the toiler, the down-and-outer, the confidence man and, last but not to be ignored, the gunman, who seemed to figure always in our frontier outposts.

A stagecoach drawn by six white horses awaits passengers at Tombstone in 1880.

Wyatt Earp in his prime as a gambler, womanizer, and sometimes-lawman. May have been photographed in Tombstone.

Virgil Earp, lawman who often deputized his brothers.

Morgan Earp, wounded in the shootout near the OK Corral; later murdered.

THE EARP BROTHERS—notorious gunmen—came, and it was no time it seemed until Wyatt was deputy sheriff, Virgil was town marshal, and Morgan was shotgun messenger of the Wells Fargo Express. The only Earp brother without a fighting job was Jim Earp, who always seemed to be a quiet fellow, keeping out of the limelight.

Another member of the "Earp clan," probably the most capable and noted for his coolness under fire as well as his skill as a dead shot, and who always seemed to be on hand when trouble brewed with the Earps, was Doc Holliday. A slim, frail-looking man, a gambler by profession who, like Wyatt Earp, was a graduate of Dodge City, Kansas' turbulent school of frontier scraps. And so it might be said, the scene was set for trouble.

I was in Tombstone on the afternoon that the Earps, in their official capacity as peace officers, engineered the killing of Billy Clanton and the McLaury brothers, Tom and Frank.

Our home was on Fremont[9] at Sixth and the battle—or rather murder—took place on Fremont Street between Fourth and Fifth. My father had told us early in the day that trouble was brewing between the Earps and the McLaurys, advising us to keep off the street as a shooting scrape was often as dangerous to an innocent spectator as to the actors

(9) Named for renowned explorer John C. Fremont, then governor of Arizona Territory, Fremont Street was intended to be Tombstone's main street. It was not to be. Business gravitated a block south to Allen Street, which became the town's principal thoroughfare, the hub of activity centered at the intersection of Allen and Fifth streets.
    Myers, p. 37.

Doc Holliday, who preferred drinking and gambling to dentistry.

(10) Gray is mistaken. Virgil Earp's arm was crippled by a bullet, but the incident occurred more than two months following the gunfight near the OK Corral—during which he was shot through the calf.

At about 11:30 on Wednesday night, December 28, 1881, Virgil was enroute to his room at the Cosmopolitan Hotel, when he was ambushed in the street. The Los Angeles *Herald* provides details of the shooting: "Last night about half-past 11 o'clock, as the United States Deputy Marshal was crossing Fifth street, between the Oriental saloon and Eagle brewery (later the Crystal Palace Saloon), and when in the middle of the street, he was fired upon with double-barreled shotguns, loaded with buckshot, by three men concealed in an unfinished building diagonally across Allen street. Five shots were fired in rapid succession. Marshal Earp was wounded in the left arm just above the elbow, producing a longitudinal fraction of the bone. One shot struck him above the groin, coming out near the spine. the wounds are very dangerous, possibly mortal. The men ran through the rear building and escaped in the darkness, back of the Vizina hoisting works."

According to historian Paula Mitchell Marks, sixteen stray shots peppered the awnings of the Eagle Brewery; three shots penetrated the saloon's windows; another lodged itself in the office wall of Dr. George Goodfellow, located above the drinking and gaming establishment.

Ike Clanton and Frank Stillwell were the prime suspects in the shooting. Other names were bandied about as well, but it is unlikely that the identity of the shootist, or shootists, will ever be known.

Virgil survived his wounds. He died at age 62, October 19, 1905, in Goldfield, Nevada.

Marks, p. 317.

Chaput, pp. 148–149, 220.

Los Angeles *Herald,* December 30, 1881.

(11) As long as ink meets paper, the gunfight near the OK Corral (it occurred in a vacant lot behind—not at—the OK Corral) will be written about; countless retellings are in print worldwide. And as long as the famous—or infamous, depending on one's point of view—gun battle is written about, it will be shrouded in controversy (a most balanced account appears in Paula Mitchell Marks, *And Die in the West: The Story of the OK Corral Gunfight*). Writers *ad nauseam* have dissected each second (some thirty seconds in all) of the action, and rarely does one agree with another. Gray's re-telling warrants serious consideration, however, for of the hundreds of accounts written about the incident, his is one of a mere handful penned by an actual eye witness.

involved. When I heard the first sound of rapid firing I knew the fight was on and from our front door I saw the one-sided battle. The three Earps—Wyatt, Virgil, and Morgan—and Doc Holliday, had stepped suddenly out on to Fremont Street from the rear entrance of the OK stable lot and immediately commenced firing on the three cowboys, who were preparing to leave town. In fact, Frank McLaury was sitting on his horse and at first fire fell mortally wounded, but game to the last he returned the fire, wounding Virgil in the arm, leaving that member useless for any further gunplay in the life of Virgil Earp.[10] The other cowboys lay dead in the street. Tom McLaury had his hands up when a load of buckshot cut him down. It was all over almost as soon as begun. A play enacted by the Earps to wipe out those cowboys under the pretense of enforcing the law, and carried out under the manner of shooting first and reading the warrant to the dead men afterward. But in this case I doubt if there was ever a warrant issued.[11]

Now Tombstone was definitely on the map as the bad town of the West, and as the crowd gathered after the smoke of battle had cleared—the dead bodies of the cowboys still lying in the street where they fell—in came the six-horse stage with its load of passengers. One wonders what their thoughts were. It was reported that several of them left town on the next out-going coach.

*Tombstone's OK Corral,
date unknown.*

Just a short time before this killing took place I had been at the McLaury boys' camp in Sulphur Springs Valley.[12] I had ridden there hungry and tired, making the long trip from the Animas Valley,[13] New Mexico, on horseback. Both Tom and Frank were home and they treated me to the best they had: a good meal and a fresh horse for my remaining twenty-five mile ride to Tombstone. They had asked me to stay all night, but it was urgent that I ride home that night. So when I saw these young men lying wounded to death there on Fremont Street, I felt a terrible mistake had been made. These boys were plain, good-hearted, industrious fellows. They may have harbored passing rustlers at their ranch, but what rancher did not? And it would have been little of a man who would have turned away any traveler in that land of long trails and hard going.

I think few, if any, ever tried to justify the cold-blooded killing of those three boys on that Tombstone

(12) Extending from Willcox south to Douglas, the Sulphur Springs Valley—or "Sufferin' Springs," as some residents call it—is roughly twenty miles wide and sixty miles long. It is known in early Spanish records as "Playas de las Pimas" or "The Beaches of the Pimas." The two springs from which it takes its name are heavy in sulphur content. Lush native grasses lured cattlemen to the area in the early 1870s, and many considered it the richest cattle country in the West. In February, 1873, Henry Clay Hooker located his legendary Sierra Bonita Ranch in the valley, grazing 10,000 head of Texas cattle. Abundant as the grasses were, however, within two decades droughts and overgrazing ravaged the valley turning it to near desert.

Wilson, John P. *Islands in the Desert: A History of the Uplands of Southeastern Arizona.* Albuquerque: University of New Mexico Press, 1995, p. 188.

Barnes, p. 429.

Trimble, Marshall. *Roadside History of Arizona.* Missoula: Mountain Press Publishing Company, 1986, p. 27.

(13) The Animas Valley is situated in the southwest corner of New Mexico bordering Arizona and Mexico.

Hilliard, George. *A Hundred Years of Horse Tracks: The Story of the Gray Ranch.* Silver City, NM: High-Lonesome Books, 1996, p. 10.

Issac (Ike) Clanton, who precipitated the shootout, but did not participate in it.

(14) Wyatt Earp tells quite a different story. See Appendix D.

(15) Located at the northeast corner of Allen and Fourth streets, the Grand Hotel was directly across Allen from Hatch's Saloon, which was reputedly headquarters of the Earp faction following the shootout near the OK Corral. The Grand and its rival, the Cosmopolitan Hotel, were Tombstone's finest. The building stands today, refitted as a saloon.
Marks, pp. 8–9.
Myers, p. 55.
Breakenridge, pp.176, 265.

(16) Alder (not George) Randall was a most controversial mayor of Tombstone. Part of the anti-Earp faction, he was an associate of Gray's father.
Marks, pp. 57, 98, 112, 117.

(17) The Contention was one of three discoveries that made Tombstone the richest mining district in the West. Prospectors Hank Williams and John Oliver made an arrangement with Richard Gird to assay their findings in return for a split of any claims they might locate. As time passed, the men forgot about the arrangement and, when valuable claims were made, had to be reminded. An argument erupted, but Gird and his partners—Ed and Al Schieffelin—prevailed. It seemed to the trio that the Contention was an appropriate name for their new mine.
Myers, p. 32.

(18) Superintendent of the Grand Central and Contention Mines, E.B. Gage was a leading citizen of Tombstone and an enthusiastic supporter of the Earps. "I know personally," he once stated, "that whatever Virgil Earp did in Tombstone was at the request of the best men in Cochise County." One of only a handful of prominent men to remain in Tombstone after the boom, Gage was nearly lynched when, on May 1, 1884, miners went on strike. The strike later was quelled by soldiers brought in from Fort Huachuca.
During the summer of 1881, Endicott Peabody came to Tombstone to build a church. Seeking funds, he interrupted Gage in a poker game in the back room of a hotel. Much to Peabody's surprise, the mining man counted out about $150 from his pile of winnings and donated it to the minister's cause. Not to be outdone, the other poker players followed suit.
In 1902, Gage was instrumental in forming the Tombstone Consolidated Mines Company, which introduced a new pumping system, and reopened the flooded mines. By 1909, the enterprise had failed.
Marks, pp. 288, 327, 416.
Breakenridge, pp. 187, 216–19, 239.

street. In a few moments they would have been on their way home had not the Earps and Holliday suddenly appeared from the rear of the OK stable lot, calling out "hands up" and firing almost simultaneously.[14]

Many of the better citizens deplored this notoriety given to Tombstone and too late realized the blunder made in giving the Earps the upper hand of authority. They were in power, and many were giving serious thought to the question of how to put them out. The Earps ruled as they saw fit for quite a while and things happened in the name of the law which were very injurious to the welfare and good name of Tombstone. All this ended only with the exit of the Earps when they finally knew their game was up.

There were many worthy men in business in Tombstone in those discordant days. The Bilickes of the old Cosmopolitan Hotel who figured prominently later in the history of Los Angeles; Comstock of the new Grand Hotel;[15] George Randall, the mayor;[16] White of the Contention mine;[17] Gage of the Grand Central;[18] Ed Schieffelin and Dick

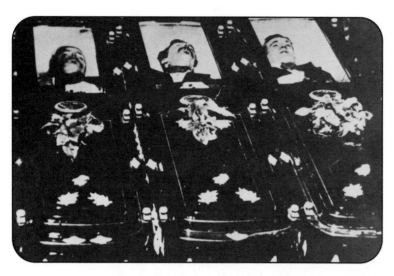

*According to Gray's account, these men were murdered
by the Earp brothers and Doc Holliday in what
has come to be called the Shootout at the OK Corral.*

Gird of the Tombstone M&M Company;[19] P.W. Smith, merchant;[20] Jim Vizina;[21] M.E. Joyce;[22] Alex Robertson, later the well known bookstore man and publisher of San Francisco whose little store in Tombstone was the haven for many lonesome moments. Many more could be named in the list of pioneers—all men who have stood the test of time, and many who have well proved their worth in the later world of business. But it was the old, old story of most mining and frontier towns; the so-called gunman seeks and gets control. We have yet to learn how to keep the corrupt element from ruling even our largest towns and cities.

MY FATHER WAS AMONG THE FIRST to arrive on the ground after Ed Schieffelin's discovery of the Tombstone mines, and early in 1879 he had located and filed on a 320-acre townsite plot which lay mostly on a comparatively level mesa just east of the hills in which the mines were located. To give the new town a start, father gave to the business houses already at the camp their choice of lots on Allen Street, which became the center of Tombstone's busy years. But as a real estate venture the townsite business did not pay. My father was granted a U.S. patent for the townsite and his title was without flaw, but it was the old story of most all mining camps. Lot jumping was considered a legitimate business. A hastily constructed shack would be hauled onto, or erected on a vacant lot by night, and the jumper would be in possession the next morning.

(19) Born in Pennsylvania in 1847, Edward L. (Ed) Schieffelin had prospected the West before recording, on September 3, 1877, his first silver discovery in what would become the Tombstone Mining District. Schieffelin and his brother Albert (1849–1887) sold their Tombstone holdings March 14, 1880, to a Philadelphia syndicate headed by Hamilton Disston for $600,000. Despite his wealth, Schieffelin could not resist the lure of prospecting. He died in 1897 near Canyonville, Oregon.

Wrote Schieffelin of his Tombstone discovery, "Whenever I went into Camp Huachuca for supplies on one of my trips, some of the soldiers would frequently ask me if I had found anything. The answer was always the same, that I had not found anything yet, but that I would strike it one of these days in that country. The Indians at that time were very troublesome, and many settlers were killed previous to and during the year. Several times in reply to my remark that I would eventually find something in that country, the soldiers said, 'Yes, you'll find your tombstone;' and repeated that several times. The word lingered in my mind, and when I got into the country where Tombstone is now located, I gave the name to the first location I made. On the organization of the district it was called Tombstone from that location."

Underhill, Lonnie E., ed. "The Tombstone Discovery: The Recollections of Ed Schieffelin and Richard Gird." *Arizona and the West,* Vol. 20, No. 1 (Spring, 1979), pp. 44–67.

Born in New York state in 1836, miner, civil engineer, and assayer Richard (Dick) Gird migrated to California in 1852. With the exception of two years spent in Chile, he remained there until 1861, when he relocated to Arizona Territory. Gird assayed Schieffelin's silver discovery and formed a lucrative partnership with the brothers. As head of the Tombstone Mining and Milling Company, Gird became a wealthy man. Later, his fortune increased through land development, sugar beet production, and cattle ranching during the 1880s and 1890s near Chino, California, and in northern Mexico.

Faulk, Odie B. *Tombstone: Myth and Reality.* NY: Oxford University Press, 1972, pp. 36–46, 164–65, 188–89.

(20) Little has been recorded about P.W. Smith and the historical record is scant. It is known that he was a successful merchant, banker, and mine operator in Tucson, later at Tombstone, and was among the founding partners of the *Tombstone Epitaph.* Wrote a reporter for the *Arizona Weekly Star,* "The *Tombstone Epitaph.* is now published by a stock company. The incorporators are P.W. Smith, M.B. Clapp, E.B. Gage, John P. Clum and Charles D. Reppy, all of whom are directors. . . . The *Epitaph* has been a pronounced success from the first day of its publication [May 1, 1880] and has done much to advance the interests of [the] Tombstone district. The names of the incorporators of the new company are those of representative men and large property owners of Tombstone and are a guarantee of the financial stability of the enterprise. . . ." The *Arizona Enterprise* wrote of the ". . . great commercial house of P.W. Smith & co., on the corner of Allen and Fourth streets . . . . the success of this adventurous firm has been as phenomenal as has been the growth and prosperity of the district to which it is a credit. On the same day that witnessed the permanent re-establishment of the firm to Tombstone also witnessed the establishment of a stable commercial banking department in connection with its wholesale and retail merchandising business. . . ."

Arizona Weekly Star, August 11, 1881.
Arizona Enterprise, November 10, 1881.

(21) Mining mogul and Earp supporter Jim Vizina, in partnership with Benjamin Cook, developed a city block of connecting store buildings at the northeast corner of Allen and Fifth streets, Tombstone's most bustling intersection. Housed there were the Oriental Saloon, Safford, Hudson & Company Bank, a men's haberdashery, and a dry goods store.

Traywick, Ben T. *John Henry: The "Doc" Holliday Story.* Tombstone: Red Marie's Bookstore, 1996, p. 88.

(22) M.E. (Milt) Joyce (variously spelled Joice) was owner of the Oriental Saloon, Tombstone's finest. "Last evening," wrote the *Tombstone Epitaph,* "the portals were thrown open and the public permitted to gaze upon the most elegantly furnished saloon this side of the favored city of the Golden Gate." Common it was for hotels, saloons, restaurants, etc., to compare themselves with their San Francisco counterparts. Nevertheless, this bar and gambling house was an elegant affair sporting crystal chandeliers and Brussels carpets.

Despite the fact that Wyatt Earp owned a quarter interest in the Oriental's gambling concession, Joyce—a Democrat who served as chairman of the Cochise County Board of Supervisors—was part of the anti-Earp, Doc Holliday faction. And he had good reason to be, as evidenced by this item from the *Tombstone Epitaph:*

"About 12:30 on Sunday night last [October 10, 1880] a shooting affray took place at the Oriental Saloon . . . between M.E. Joyce . . . and a man, named Doc Holliday, during the course of which Joyce was shot in the right hand and his partner, Mr. Parker, received a stray bullet in the big toe. The particulars, as we gather them from an eye-witness, are about as follows: During the early evening Holliday had an altercation with Johnny Tyler which boded a shooting scrape. Shortly before the shooting referred to occurred, Holliday and Joyce came into the Oriental. Joyce went to Tyler and told him to leave the saloon, as he didn't want trouble. Tyler complied and Joyce then made the same request to Holliday. Holliday demurred, and Joyce and he got into an altercation, during which Joyce put Holliday out of the saloon. Holliday, shortly afterward, returned, and as Joyce was coming out from behind the bar, opened fire on him with a self cocker, firing two shots in quick succession. The first shot struck Joyce in the pistol hand, disabling it, the second missed him and passing through the bar, struck Parker on the foot. Joyce kept advancing all the time, and it is said, fired one shot. Closing with Holliday, he struck him on the head with his six-shooter and finally threw him on the floor. While the men were struggling, Officer Bennett appeared upon the scene and separated the combatants, taking Joyce out of the saloon. Holliday was picked up and placed in a chair, it being generally thought, from his bloody appearance, that he was severely, if not fatally, hurt. Such, however, proved not to be the case, and he was arrested by Deputy Marshal Earp. A warrant was subsequently issued for his arrest, on the charge of assault with a deadly weapon, with intent to kill. His bail was fixed by Judge Reilly at $200, which we understand, he furnished. Joyce and Parker are both getting along nicely."

The day this story appeared, Holliday appeared in court in the custody of town marshal Fred White. He pleaded guilty to a charge of assault and battery; no prosecution witnesses appeared, thus the charge of assault with a deadly weapon was dismissed. Holliday was fined $20 and court costs of $11.25. Joyce and Parker recovered from their wounds.

Tombstone Epitaph, July 22, 1880; October 12, 1880.

Marks, pp. 64–65, 156–57.

Ed Schieffelin, who was told that by prospecting in hostile Apache country, all he would find would be his Tombstone.

Endless lawsuits for the ejection of squatters followed and as soon as the squatter found that he was to be dispossessed, he would pick up his shack, always by night, and next morning he would be sitting snugly on some other lot. Then a new ejection suit would have to be started. Much bad feeling resulted and "Townsite" Gray, as my father was called, became the object of much abuse, unjustly so, by the lot jumpers. At one time the lot jumpers made a desperate effort to have my father's U.S. patent rescinded. Carl Shurz was then Secretary of the Interior and he was appealed to. The patent had already been mailed at Washington and the document was located en route at the Chicago post office. Secretary Shurz asked the Chicago postmaster to return it to Washington, but this he refused to do. His action was upheld at Washington, as it was decided that a mailed letter or parcel must go unmolested to its destination.

John P. Clum, founder of the Tombstone Epitaph, *mayor of Tombstone, and avid Earp supporter. Photographed with Apache Scouts when he was agent of the San Carlos Reservation.*

The patent came through to the Tombstone Townsite Company and the squatters were left without any lawful rights, but by the time lawsuits were settled the glory of Tombstone began to fade and real estate values vanished almost in a night.[23]

IN THE EARLY DAYS of Tombstone it was all Pima County,[24] extending south of Tucson to the Mexican border and east to the New Mexico line. Tombstone had a unique place among the mining camps of the West. In its prime, it stood alone as the newest going discovery, and for awhile all roads led to Tombstone. Bodie, California had blown up. The Comstock had seen its best days, and the big strikes at Cripple Creek and Leadville, Colorado were as yet uncovered to the world. Thus all the adventurers, prospectors, gamblers, and other wanderers pulled up stakes wherever they were at the moment and headed for Tombstone. And it might be close to the truth to say that Allen Street was the meeting place for all the world's wandering population—the flotsam and jetsam of civilization in the Eighties.

(23) A most controversial figure in Tombstone's history, Michael (Mike) Gray is rarely afforded the sympathetic treatment given him by his son. At a date uncertain, but prior to October, 1879, Gray was appointed justice of the peace. In that capacity an alliance was formed with Mayor Alder Randall. Whether or not Gray had applied for a land patent, he and James Clark formed the Tombstone Townsite Company and laid claim to town lots. At the same time, however, the Gilded Age Mining Company claimed the land on which Tombstone was built, and filed a lawsuit against Gray and Clark. Wrote the *Weekly Nugget,* ". . . there is a great deal of feeling in the community [about the case], and as it is to be brought before the district court at the present session, we hope it will be summarily disposed of. As a controversy, it has done no little damage in retarding business improvements in that locality, as those who purchase ground don't care to buy a lawsuit also."

While the suit was pending, Gray and Clark allegedly convinced Mayor Randall—legal holder of the town patent—to deed the patent over to them. Rumors circulated about town that Randall would do just that and, on November 6, 1880, a public protest was held at the corner of Fifth and Allen streets.

The following day, Randall promised a hastily-formed citizens' committee that he would follow the wishes of the town council, but a dissident council member warned that the mayor could not be trusted; that he was dealing privately with Gray and Clark.

Later, in a brief filed by lawyers seeking redistribution of property, it was alleged that on November 9, just three days after the public demonstration, Randall had conveyed the townsite deed to Gray and Clark.

Townsfolk, worried that their property would illegally be gobbled up, formed the Tombstone Citizens League, headed by such staunch Republican businessmen as John P. Clum, publisher of the *Tombstone Epitaph.*

The situation came to a head when, on December 4, Gray and Clark employed a force of men to move a house sitting on disputed property into the street. Marshal Ben Sippy intervened and, before firearms came into play, put a stop to it.

John Clum (who later became mayor) forced an injunction against the townsite company. In time, lawsuits worked their way through the Territorial courts—Gray and Clark losing virtually every one—but by then the boom was over and the disputed properties were all but worthless.

Weekly Nugget, October 5, 1879.
Marks, pp. 112–15.
Myers, pp. 107–09.

(24) On February 1, 1881, the Territorial Assembly carved 4,003,840 acres out of eastern Pima County and designated it Cochise County after the legendary Chiricahua Apache leader. Tombstone was named county seat.

Dreyfuss, John J., ed. *A History of Arizona's Counties and Courthouses.* Tucson: The National Society of the Colonial Dames of America in the State of Arizona, 1978, p. 61.

Allen Street looking west from 5th Street. Tombstone, 1880, about the time Gray arrived.

There were no restrictions on nationality, color, or reputation, but the city marshal was on hand as the loaded stages came in, and saw to it that all exposed firearms were deposited away from view.

The man who ventured on Allen Street wearing a derby or high hat would soon lose sight of said head-covering. Off it would fall, and first one and then another would bunt it along with kicks, soon making it an object not worth recovering. But the owner generally took this playfulness good naturedly, soon falling in line by wearing the regulation soft or cowboy headgear. Often the crowd would chip in the price of a new hat for the tenderfoot.

Many men of doubtful occupation drifted in to ply their trade upon the innocent or gullible citizens. But most of these soon found the climate was not suitable and, as quickly, drifted out. I remember a man was brought up before my father, then justice of the peace, on a charge of passing counterfeit money. The evidence positively showed his guilt, but my father thought the light jail sentence he could give the man would not serve much good, so he appealed to the audience, consisting mostly of hard-boiled miners, to give the offender a severe lesson. That meant that the guilty party must immediately leave town and keep going. So a lane was formed, and at the given word, the criminal was ordered to start going. As he hurried down the line he was helped along by kicks and slaps, which left him almost a wreck before he managed to disappear down the highway leading to elsewhere. So far as known, he never came back and passing bad money was not considered a paying business thereafter.

In its rush days Tombstone's Allen Street presented an interesting jumble of humanity. Even the stranger would be carried away by the constant hurry with something doing every minute. Saloons, restaurants, hotels, well stocked stores, and barber shops—all brightly lighted for those pre-electric days—kept open house on both sides of Allen Street away into the night. The music from dance halls, and all the hubbub that a crowd of men away from their home ties and seeking excitement, can make—all of this filled the air with a confused roar of the crowd. It could be heard miles away by the lonely cowboy or prospector wandering in to join the gang.

In daytime Allen Street was generally like an ordinary street in a country crossroads town, but at nightfall everybody was milling about and giving vent to all their suppressed feelings and good fellowship. It was like a jolly crowd of grown boys out for a night of fun, and most business houses did a better business at night than in the daytime.

Some of the early eating places gained fame beyond the confines of the city limits. A sheriff of Cochise County took a trip to New York City and upon his return to Tombstone asserted that no place in New York City—not even Delmonico's—could set a better meal than the old Can Can Restaurant. The Can Can was well named, for in those days in a place like Tombstone, the can opener was about the only way of arriving at dinner.[25]

The beef was the toughest thing in the camp. Cattle ranching had not been started and the butchers got their cattle mostly from rustlers who rushed them in from fifty or more miles away, as a rule from across the border in Mexico—and the poor cattle were surely rushed. The rustlers would bring in the old longhorns which were good travelers and able to get a move on, and the butcher had time to get the hides off and hidden away before the proper owner had time to trail up the "lost" animals. This was cheap beef for the butcher and when an animal was found so poor that the meat had a bluish tinge to it, he put that particular beef on the market as "veal." The Tombstone

(25) Notwithstanding Gray's tongue-in-cheek reference to a can opener, Tombstone was replete with fine restaurants, the Can Can among them. Wrote the *Arizona Star* in 1880, ". . . the restaurants are models of neatness, and supplied bounteously with the choicest meats and such other danties as the markets afford." Notable were Cafe Francais and the Maison Doree, the latter about which diarist George W. Parsons wrote, ". . . an enjoyable repast. . . . rather expensive one too when imported oysters and imported claret and champagne are on the list."
Tombstone Epitaph, May, 1980.

butchers and the rustlers had the time of their lives, but of course, this was only at the beginning—but Tombstone hardly had a beginning before the end of prosperity came.

No doubt, much the same story can be told of all mining camps, even though they produced millions. About as much money has been invested in hunting vainly for riches as has ever been taken out of the ground. But even at that, the benefit to the world is substantial. Many rich men spent vast sums during Tombstone's boom era to find for themselves some easy money. Holes were sunk and many men were given work. In fact, nothing serves to loosen up the pursestrings quicker than a prospector's discovery of hidden treasure. Even today, if someone discovered a new Comstock, our worried statesmen could sit back and watch with interest the sudden solution of the unemployed problem, and bid goodbye to the depression. After all is said, it is the hope of success which must come to us, for without that hope we become just a led ox. The old grizzly prospector never loses that hope, and I never knew one who was a failure—to himself. They are all "Colonel Sellers" and "there's millions in it."

The Bird Cage Theatre long after the boom had turned to bust.

AHS #26661

Dos Cabezas, Arizona, date unknown.

Old-timers remember the story of the Casey brothers of Dos Cabezas.[26] They had a mining claim and had worked it for years with an old Mexican *arastra* made by themselves, and they had managed to extract a small quantity of gold, enough to buy what little grub they needed. And though many cash offers had been made to them for their claims, they had refused to sell. Their price was sixty thousand or nothing, and it was said they could have sold many times for half that sum. But in the end these two old brothers died in their lowly and lonely cabin on their claim in dire poverty, always refusing the fortune that might have been theirs for the asking.

IN ITS PALMY DAYS, a nervous man would not have been happy with the methods of life in Tombstone. If you sought a peaceful sleep at night you might be suddenly awakened by some unearthly noise, musical or otherwise, from "Promenade to the Bar" at some dance hall, a yell of "Keno" from some rejoicing gambler, to a pistol shot by some shoot-'em-

(26) Located some fifteen miles east of Willcox in Cochise County, Dos Cabezas—Spanish for "two heads"—was settled in 1878 and took its name from nearby Dos Cabezas Mountains where gold and silver were discovered. Originally called Ewell Spring, a station was established there in 1857 for the San Antonio-San Diego Stage Line, more commonly called the "Jackass Mail." It is said that Ewell Spring had the first school in Cochise County. By the mid 1880s, the community sported three stamp mills, a brickyard, hotel, three saloons, a brewery, and a population of about 300.

Workers, *Arizona*, p. 438.

Sherman, James E. and Barbara H. Sherman. *Ghost Towns of Arizona.* Norman: University of Oklahoma Press, 1969, p. 50.

Varney, Philip. *Arizona Ghost Towns and Mining Camps.* Phoenix: Arizona Highways Books, 1994, p. 129.

up Dick just to keep things moving. But you could sleep on in the midst of this if you could simply consider it as harmless as the noise of a boiler factory.

As to danger from holdup men, even the name itself was unknown. A man's roll was perfectly safe unless he spent it of his own will. In those days many carried their money in a neat roll made by shaping greenbacks like a roll of ribbon kept intact by a rubber band. I wonder how long one could keep his bankroll nowadays in his inside coat pocket.

One summer evening, Allen Street was stirred by the appearance of a Gypsyish-looking man wearing big hoop earrings and leading a huge cinnamon colored bear by a short chain. In a few minutes these stray visitors absorbed the attention of the whole population of Tombstone, and all other business was definitely at a standstill.

The Gypsy-man was not there for his health, however, and soon he had the sturdy miners interested by offering to bet five dollars a side—the bear against anyone in a wrestling match—the winner being the one who could lay the other down on the street. At first it looked easy for a husky miner but when the bear stood on his hind legs his head reached more than a foot above the tallest miner, and no man's arms were long enough to encircle his cinnamon-colored highness around the middle. One miner after another took his turn, but the bear hardly moved from his tracks, no matter what tactics were used against him. Some thought they could pick up one of the bear's feet and thus throw him off balance, but the monster stood like a statue, and none was able to lift the bear's leg even the least little bit from the ground.

The bear showed wonderful patience, as if he were sure of his power, and after prolonged effort of an opponent to no avail, his owner would speak one word and Mr. Bear would place his paws around his opponent's body, gently lift the man off the ground, and as gently lay him down in the dust of the street.

Nearly every miner wanted a turn at it and the five dollar bills fell on the Gypsy like rain. It was more fun to the crowd than anything that ever happened in Tombstone. Even when it got too dark to continue with the performance, the crowd kept urging the bear's owner to come back the next day for more. But Gypsy and bear disappeared that night for good and it was rumored that the saloons, gambling joints, and dance halls had bestowed a good sized purse on the Gypsy in order to get him to beat it out of town with his bear game.

THERE WAS A PASSENGER who rode into Tombstone on that hot day of June, 1880, who later made quite a stir on busy Allen Street.

Most people looked upon Duke Fields of the Gilded Age Mine as something of a nut, but maybe we were all wrong and he was but playing a part. The Duke was a rather small, stocky-built man, bald headed, always smooth shaven, and always nattily dressed. In fact, he was by far the best dressed man who ever walked the dusty streets of Tombstone.

Without fail, he always appeared in the mornings in a well tailored, dark business suit. In midday, the Duke's form would be clothed in an immaculate white coat and trousers, and he would be wearing a straw hat. His evening attire was the regulation dark blue or black cutaway and striped pants.

"Make way for his Royal Highness, the Duke!" was often heard on Tombstone streets, but he was always good natured. He had a way of heading off any attempts at familiarity, however, and I never heard of anyone working the Duke for a friendly loan or any investment scheme. It was soon apparent that the Duke, on his part, did have some big fish on the line, for overnight, as it were, he became a mining magnate.

A mining claim had been located across the townsite of Tombstone which had been named the Gilded Age, and

Members of the G.A.R. strut their stuff in front of the Epitaph Building on Fremont Street.

on this claim the Duke started to sink a shaft. In those days mining shafts were liable to appear anywhere, as money was spent lavishly in sinking a hole, even though the surface showed no sign of a mineral ledge or any suggestion of mineral wealth hidden below.

No one at his mine thought much of Duke. Needless to say, no sign of pay dirt was ever found at the Gilded Age, though the shaft was sunk several hundred feet. There were times when the Duke would lay off his crew of miners and he would disappear for a month or more. Then he would be back again, apparently flush with money, to start up the mine. Meanwhile, with no one delegated to look out for the work already done, the shaft was used by that section of town as a dumping place for all kinds of refuse and rubbish. On Duke's return to resume work, he had to pay ten dollars a day for men until the shaft was put back in condition.

It was a mystery for quite a while where the Duke got his money. This intermittent mining went on for several years, but in time it was apparent that the Duke's resources were at a low ebb. The mining work was stopped and in a desperate effort, evidently to recoup his finances, the Duke tried to collect rent from the residences within the boundaries of the surface line of the Gilded Age. In fact, the Tombstone townsite patent was dated before the Gilded Age had been located, hence the court eventually ruled in favor of the townsite titles—but the Duke had run a bluff anyhow.

Our home place was partly on Gilded Age surface. The line of the mining location just cut off one room, but the hallway leading to this room was outside the Gilded Age lines. So, one day when I was alone at home, my folks being away on a trip to the country, there appeared at the front door the county sheriff and a deputy to serve a court order to give the sheriff possession as a receiver of our one room, claimed by Duke Fields. It was rather an odd situation. My father had anticipated this trouble and told me not to allow the sheriff any possession rights, so I told the officer I would resist any attempt to take possession and that he must stay out.

I guess it was lucky for me that the sheriff seemed a little doubtful about his authority when I convinced him that the door to the room was not on the mining claim, and his only entrance would be through the window. He retreated and in a few days the court ruled against the Duke's surface rights to any land, except the small piece necessary for working the mine. And so the Duke had made his last stand and he disappeared for the last time from the Tombstone scene.

A short time later there came to Tombstone old Doctor Ayres of well known pill fame. This old patent medicine man was no doubt the source of Duke Fields' money. But if Duke Fields had worked the Ayres pill factory to a finish, the old doctor himself fell to the lure of the faro banks as well. He lingered in Tombstone for several weeks and, from all accounts, he dropped a small fortune trying to beat the faro game. General rumor placed Doctor Ayres' gambling loss in Tombstone at sixty thousand dollars. This was probably a much larger sum than Duke Fields had received from him.

The old professional gambler, Napa Nick, was in the dealer's chair during most of the attack on his faro bank by Doctor Ayres, and the table was always surrounded by an interested crowd of spectators. Napa Nick was an interesting study. A professional gambler of the old school, he looked more like a sedate judge and was often addressed as "Judge" by men. He was white haired, wore Uncle Sam chin whiskers, and was always dressed in a proper black suit. But in a way, Judge Nicholls was a man of mystery.

At that time, I worked as clerk in the Tombstone post office, and one day a couple of new arrivals by stage asked me concerning the whereabouts and business of one Judge Nicholls of Napa City, California. They thought he must have a law office. The only Nicholls I knew was the old gambler, so I directed them to Napa Nick's faro bank and saloon, where sure enough they recognized their man dealing cards at a faro table.

They were much taken aback, and came around to tell me about it. They said the Nicholls residence at Napa was one of the town's show places, and that the judge's wife and two pretty daughters moved in the best circles. They said that, although the judge was away most of the time, he was a liberal contributor to many worthy functions of social welfare.

I never heard how Napa Nick explained his life to these friends from the old home town, but I venture to say nothing could phase the sedate appearance of the old judge. When sitting opposite old Doctor Ayres, slowly turning the top card that could mean either a small fortune to him, or the breaking of his bank, he seemed indifferent to the result.

I imagine Napa Nick was dreaming of the day when he could retire and again be Judge Nicholls of California, and it is probable that the dream came true.

Soon after my father's arrival in Tombstone in 1879, he located and secured title to the Way-Up Mine.[27]

Ed Schieffelin had located a number of claims to cover his find in the Tombstone hills when he wandered in there in 1878, finding his fortune where his friends had predicted he would find only his tombstone. But between one of the claims, called the Tough Nut Mine,[28] and the big ravine, always known as Tombstone Gulch, lay a small, irregular-shaped hillside. And it was on Ed Schieffelin's advice that my father got hold of this. He named it the Way-Up Mine hoping it would prove a way up to us from the many lean years of the past to a better future.

Mule drawn ore wagons could haul as much as 18,000 pounds across the Arizona desert.

It was not until the following year, 1880, that we were able to start development of the Way-Up. A shaft was started near the west end of the claim where it joined the Tough Nut surface line, where lay some limestone outcroppings. No mineral was in sight, but we followed a small crack running through the crust of limestone in sinking the shaft, hoping it might lead to pay ore. And so it did.

At a depth of 105 feet, the crack we were following suddenly widened into a large pocket of silver chloride ore, assaying as high as $300 to the ton.

We had struck it rich. And what a glorious feeling to see sudden wealth of unknown proportions lying before us, deep in the ground awaiting only the act of digging it out—a wealth that was ours by the right of discovery; a wealth that no man could accuse us of obtaining by fraud, or by

(27) Gray's narrative, although written from his own bias, reveals otherwise elusive information about the Way Up Mine.

Garbani, James H. *Arizona Mines and Mining Companies: 1854–1954.* Tucson: Sunrise Graphics, 1993, p. 254.

(28) Discovered by Ed Schieffelin, the Tough Nut was one of the three richest mines in the Tombstone District. It was so named because a mining claim could be only 600 by 1500 feet. Wrote Schieffelin in a contemporary account, "The Grand Central and the Contention and the Tough Nut were the best mines in the district, and remain so to the present time."

Myers, p. 32.
Underhill, pp. 44–67.

any so-called illegitimate manner or business deal with our fellow man. No title to riches seems quite so sure as that of discovery—finding wealth never before known to man.

But strange as it seems, a strike of riches buried for centuries has been the cause of most desperate contentions, interminable lawsuits, and often murder. So, although we started the Way-Up Mine with every sign of peace and the most hopeful of prospects, almost at once, like a bolt of lightening from a clear sky, trouble fell upon us in the form of a lawsuit and injunctions which compelled us to stop working our claim. We already had taken out and milled at a local custom mill, ore that returned us some $30,000—and the fight was on.

It proved to be a right royal battle of high priced lawyers and higher priced experts, and it was a case of the poor man being squeezed dry in a death struggle to hold what was his by right of discovery. It was that old question of "the dip of the ledge."

Our mining laws allow the location of a mining claim as a piece of land 1,500 feet in length and 300 feet on each side of a ledge containing minerals, but subsequent court rulings allow the location to follow a ledge on its lateral dips without regard to where it might lead. It is a law that has caused endless litigation and confusion about rights, and has given cause for tying up valuable properties. In fact, it has often resulted in the absolute ruin of both litigants.

The original owners of the big Tombstone Mill and Mining Company properties were its discoverer Ed Schieffelin and Dick Gird, the latter having backed Ed in his prospecting trip. But they had sold out to a Pennsylvania group of capitalists[29] who had sent out to take charge of the property a Professor Church. It was this man who proved to be our evil spirit. He claimed our Way-Up strike was only a dip of the Tombstone ledge, and though well outside his boundaries, that the summit of our ledge was rightly on his side of our dividing line.

This was a far fetched theory, but in law was considered a sufficient cause to enjoin the Way-Up from working. My father was enraged at this legal outrage, and it was difficult for us to restrain him from personal attack on Church, who had started what proved to be almost interminable strife. We fought back with every legal weapon available, hiring Garber and Thornton of San Francisco, then the most noted mining attorneys of the Pacific Coast, and securing the expert services of Professor Blake of Pennsylvania, then a leading geologist—and the court fight was on.

(29) Ed Schieffelin wrote that in March, 1880 ". . . A party was on the way from Philadelphia to buy our property; they were Messrs. Disston, Corbin, Ashbury, Hart, and Sheriff Wright, who had chartered a special car and come down to the mines. They made Mr. Disston the spokesman of the party, and he came to me and asked what we would take for our interest in Tombstone, in the two companies, the Tough Nut Mill and Mining Company, and the Corbin Mill and Mining Company. We answered six hundred thousand dollars for our remaining interest in the two companies; our proposition was reported to the other parties and they accepted it."
Underhill, pp. 44–67.

For weeks, the little courtroom in Tombstone was the crowded scene of our legal battle, and the learned discourses of geologists about fossil remains and all imaginable kinds of rock formations. They explained that the Tombstone hills were once the bottom of an ocean, and the resultant limestone created by fossil's shells. But strange to relate, the expert geologists agreed on but few points when it came to formation of ledges and ore deposits. And in this, the main point at issue, it seemed a purely partisan affair involved in earning a big fee.

Despite the riches of the Tombstone Mining Company, spent lavishly in the fight, and in spite of every subterfuge used to crush the Way-Up defense, our Professor Blake was simply superb in his learned exposition of the Tombstone hills; that no well-defined ledge could exist in such a formation, stating that all deposits were simply pockets deposited in cracks and caves that were left by a volcanic

Cochise County Courthouse, Tombstone.

upheaval of the limestone from its ocean bed, and, in a word, that the "dip of the ledge" theory had no possible standing in the case.

With this defense by Professor Blake, and the ability of Mr. Thornton, of Garber and Thornton, the Way-Up Mine won. If that had been the end of it, all would have been well with us. But this man Church had started something and was determined to go the limit. In those days, Arizona was a Territory and the district judges were appointees from Washington. What kind of influence was brought to bear on Washington it is needless to speculate upon, but a new judge was appointed to replace the one who had tried our case. The Territorial Court of Appeals was then composed of all the district judges, one of whom was the new judge lately appointed.

But even with this substitution, which had the appearance of providing a stuffed court against the Way-Up, the Appellate Court upheld the trial court, and the case went to the Supreme Court at Washington. In those days, as today, the Supreme Court was looked upon as the court of "wise old men" who were the bulwark of justice, and we felt confident they would uphold the trial court—which they did in the course of time.

But time, as the lawyers say, is the essence of most human trials, and the two long years before our case was heard by the Supreme Court were our undoing. With our mine in enforced idleness, our opponent, Church, had tapped our ore deposit from below, and when the Supreme Court finally cleared our title, it left us only a gutted mine and an attachment suit for damages. Unfortunately, such an attachment can be levied only on the improvements and property on the surface of the mine. And in this case, such property consisted of a hoisting works and some elevated tramways, which were of no value now that the Tombstone Mill and Mining Company had been worked out. And then all businesses closed down.

Nothing is more worthless and dead than an abandoned mine, and at the time of our Supreme Court decision, all the once busy mines of Tombstone were closed and the bottom had dropped out of the once busy camp. All but a few hundred people had gone to other fields, and you couldn't give away a house and lot.[30]

Since then, Tombstone has revived to the point that a population of about 800 people make a living there and still find enough paying ore by chloriding and working over old dumps, but at the time of the big shut down the stampede to get away became almost a panic. The Way-Up

(30) Tombstone's boom was short lived. In 1884, water in the mines was struck at the 500 foot level and massive pumping operations begun. Then in 1886, fires at the Contention and Grand Central Mines destroyed the pumps. It was the beginning of the end. By 1890, the town was nearly deserted.
Myers, p. 235.
Trimble, *Roadside*, p. 65.
Workers, *Arizona*, p. 245.

*Tombstone in 1880,
the year of Gray's arrival.*

Mine had won the right to take the $30,000 which had been mined and milled from its depths, and divide it between Professor Blake, the law firm of Garber and Thornton, and cover sundry other expenses incurred in fighting Professor Church, who had long since lost his job—that occurring when he lost his case before the Supreme Court.

Left with a worthless writ of attachment and a hole in the ground as our only consolation for empty pockets, we had the feeling that we had fought and won—but lost again. "Of all sad words of tongue or pen, the saddest are these, 'it might have been.'" But life must go on—and there is always *manana*.

I REMEMBER OUR FIRST COUNTY ELECTION in Tombstone. Shibell[31] of Tucson was running for sheriff on the Democratic ticket and his opponent was Bob Paul,[32] a Republican. In those days, every man of age could vote, and many a bunch of illiterate Mexicans was herded to the polls, handed the ballot of the right party and directed to drop it into the ballot box. If any objections arose, or the voter was challenged in any way, it was a simple matter to

(31) It was Pima County Sheriff Charlie Shibell who appointed Wyatt Earp a deputy. Forced to resign when Cochise County was formed, Earp was replaced by John Behan.
    Myers, pp. 104, 126–27.

(32) Born in Massachusetts in 1830, Robert H. (Bob) Paul sailed around the world on a whaling voyage as a boy of fourteen. At nineteen he followed the Gold Rush to California, where he remained nearly thirty years. He was twice elected sheriff of Calaveras County. In 1872, he took employment with Wells, Fargo and Company, which transferred him to Arizona in 1878. Paul served as Pima County Sheriff, later worked as a detective for the Southern Pacific Railroad. From 1889 to 1893, he was United States Marshal for Arizona Territory.
    Breakenridge, p. 238.

AHS #22250

"The Lookout in Cochise Stronghold, Arizona." Original photo by Mollie Fly, wife of C.S. Fly.

(33) Apparently from Texas, Curly Bill Brocius may have been an alias for William ("Curly Bill") Graham. Or, as historian Paula Mitchell Marks suggests, the Curly Bills may have been separate individuals who overlap in an historical record most meager. By most accounts Brocius came to Arizona Territory in 1878, leading a herd of cattle to the San Carlos Apache Reservation. What we know as fact is that he was a rustler, was part of the Clanton faction, and on the night of October 27, 1880, he was arrested for the shooting of Tombstone City Marshal Fred White—a precursor to the OK Corral fray.

The following day, the *Tombstone Epitaph* had this to say:

"A lot of Texas cowboys, as they are called, began firing at the moon and stars on Allen Street, near Sixth. City Marshal White, who happened to be in the immediate neighborhood, interfered to prevent violation of city ordinance, and was ruthlessly shot by one of the number. Deputy sheriff [Wyatt] Earp, who is ever to the front when duty calls, arrived just in the nick of time. Seeing the Marshal fall, he promptly knocked his assailant down with a six-shooter, and as promptly locked him up, and with the assistance of his brothers, Virgil and Morgan, went in pursuit of the others. That he found them, an inventory of the roster of the City Prison this morning will testify."

White lingered several days before succumbing, during which time he told friends gathered about his bed that the shooting had been accidental. Nevertheless, Brocius stood trial for murder. He was acquitted.

On the night of December 28, 1881, some two months following the gunfight near the OK Corral, Virgil Earp was ambushed as he left the Oriental Saloon, leaving his left arm crippled for the remainder of his life. Diarist George Parsons wrote, "It is surmised that Ike Clanton, 'Curly Bill' and McLaury did the shooting." No one, however, was brought to trial for the deed.

It has been said by many writers that in late March, 1882, Brocius was shot dead by Wyatt Earp acting in an official capacity. But the truth may never be known. Earp, in old age, claimed to have shot him, but curiously, for some time after his alleged death, Brocius was sighted here and there by folks deemed reliable.

To add to the confusion, some writers of history suggest Brocius committed suicide.

Tombstone Epitaph, October 28, 1880.
Marks, pp. 103–06, 318, 356–360.
Breakenridge, pp. 185–86.
Burrows, pp. 34–35, 37–39, 61, 124.

swear in the voter, and under the direction of the boss who had brought him to the polls, that was easily handled.

At the first county election in Tombstone, I served as one of the tally clerks. A heavy vote was cast, as the sheriff's office was well worth striving for. Each candidate had runners out to bring in all available voters. They came into town by wagon loads, and it was rumored that all available men on both sides of the Mexican line cast votes that day.

We were all night counting the votes and it was far into the next day before some of the returns came in, as it was one hundred miles or more to some of the outlying polling places. The count for sheriff was running close, with the Democratic candidate about fifty votes behind his opponent, but there seemed to be an unaccountable confidence among the Democrats that they would win. They kept repeating, "Wait 'till the returns from San Simon get here."

It was just as day was breaking that the rapid hoofbeats of a horse were heard far up Allen Street. There soon appeared a jaded horse and rider, the latter waving a bundle of papers—the returns from far away San Simon, which was the headquarters of Curly Bill[33] and his rustlers. The lone rider was Curly Bill himself.

Thought to be Josephine Sarah Marcus Earp, Wyatt's common-law wife of nearly 50 years. Some historians question its authenticity.

(34) Looming east and stretching north of Tombstone are the Dragoon Mountains, ancestral home of the Chiricahua Apaches and named for a US Dragoon regiment that garrisoned many posts in Arizona Territory during 1857–58. Little known prior to 1876, when the Chiricahuas were forced onto the San Carlos Reservation, the Dragoons soon teamed with prospectors. From a rugged canyon—now called Cochise Stronghold—in the Dragoons, Cochise spent a dozen years leading raids on ranches and settlements. His enemies never succeeded in routing him.

Wilson, pp. 163–64.
Workers, *Arizona*, p. 440.
Barnes, p. 134.

(35) Stifled in his ambition for the presidency, explorer-turned-politician John Charles Fremont was appointed governor of Arizona Territory in 1878 by President Rutherford B. Hayes. Much of his time was spent outside the territory on personal business, giving his detractors—of which there were many—grounds for charges that he paid little heed to the needs of Arizonans. Fremont resigned on October 11, 1881. On October 25, the *New York Herald* opined that Hayes' successor, President Chester A. Arthur, had demanded the governor's resignation because Fremont ". . . seemed to regard the climate and society of New York as more agreeable and attractive than that of Arizona."

Woznicki, Robert. *History of Arizona*. Phoenix: Messenger Graphics, 1987, p. 169.
Faulk, Odie B. *Arizona: A Short History*. Norman: University of Oklahoma Press, 1970, pp. 125–26.
Phillips, Catherine Coffin. *Jessie Benton Fremont: A Woman Who Made History*. Lincoln: University of Nebraska Press, 1995, pp. 297–305.

(36) John Harris Behan was a most political man. During his lifetime, he served as sheriff of Yavapai and Cochise Counties; he was a member of the territorial legislature; he was superintendent of the territorial prison at Yuma; and he served as customs inspector. Born in Westport, Missouri in 1845, he came to Arizona Territory in 1863 as a civilian employee of the California Column during the Civil War. At Tombstone, where Behan was appointed Cochise County Sheriff, enmity developed between he and Wyatt Earp when his mistress, Josephine Sarah Marcus, traded his bed for Earp's, never mind that Earp was a married man. That did not sit well with Behan, and it did not sit well with Earp that Behan reneged on a promise to make him a deputy sheriff. Behan, who in has later years worked for the Southern Pacific Railroad, died in Tucson in 1912.

Marks, pp. 53–54, 59–60.
Boyer, Glenn, ed. *I Married Wyatt Earp: Recollections of Josephine Sarah Marcus Earp*. Tucson: University of Arizona Press, 1976, p. 15.
Breakenridge, p. 185.

With all due formality we opened the package and tallied the votes—one hundred straight Democratic votes for Shibell—which were counted in. There was one lone Republican ballot for Bob Paul to show, as Bill said, that the vote was on the square. This of course elected Shibell, and a right royal celebration was staged by the Shibell following. But in the final election count all this came to no avail, for Paul carried the election into court and the San Simon vote was thrown out. For what were probably very good reasons, Curly Bill and his outlaw gang failed to appear in court to answer the subpoenas, and as they constituted the entire voting strength of San Simon, their case was lost by default.

It was soon thereafter that the Territorial legislators met, and a bill passed dividing Pima County. The southern and eastern part became the county of Cochise, named after the old Apache chief, whose old stronghold in the Dragoons[34] lies just east and in plain view of Tombstone.

Tombstone became the county seat. The first county officers were appointed by the Territorial governor.[35] Johnny Behan was made sheriff[36] and M.E. Joyce was

William M. (Billy) Breakenridge,
Earp foe whom Gray admired.

chairman of the Board of Supervisors. These were the most important offices and eventually held control of county affairs.

Billy Breakenridge,[37] Johnny Behan's undersheriff, has vividly told much of the doings of that administration in his "Helldorado." Breck, as he was familiarly called, was the mainstay of the sheriff's office, and deserves credit where credit was due.

Johnny Behan was a good fellow, but it takes more than a good fellow to make a good sheriff. He loved to sit in a poker game with those old professionals, Dick Clark[38] and Napa Nick, and I guess they, in turn, liked to have him sit opposite them with his customary canvas sack full of gold and silver.

The sheriff's office in those days was easy money with its generous fee of ten percent of all tax collections to fall into the sheriff's hands. And as the Southern Pacific Railroad, with its many miles of rails across Cochise County, paid most of the county's taxes, the cost of collection was practically nothing.

(37) Born December 25, 1846 at Watertown, Wisconsin, William M. Breakenridge arrived in Tombstone during the final days of December, 1879. In January, 1881, Sheriff John Behan appointed Breakenridge deputy sheriff of Cochise County.

Few historians share Gray's enthusiasm for Billy Breakenridge, who much glamorized his role as law officer in his 1928 autobiography. In the main a valuable document, the book suffers from jumbled sequencing, incorrect dates, and an occasional flight of fancy.

Breakenridge, p. 185.

(38) Richard Brinsley Sheridan Clark was born at Cayuga, New York, April 15, 1838. He was just shy of twenty-one when he turned up in Colorado to ply his trade in the mining camps as a professional gambler. After four years as a Union soldier during the Civil War, Clark roamed the boom towns of the West and developed a reputation as a high roller. In 1880, he followed the boom to Tombstone where he opened the Alhambra Saloon and bought an interest in the gambling concession at the Oriental—which he later sold to Wyatt Earp. According to a Tombstone Saloon keeper, "Wherever skill of the mind or fingers could be employed to bring in the money, Dick Clark and his brethern used what gifts they had." Clark died at Albuquerque in 1893; his body was returned to Tombstone and buried in Boot Hill.

Sonnichsen, C.L. *Billy King's Tombstone.* Caldwell, ID: Caxton Printers, Ltd., 1942, pp. 117–41.

Marks, p. 84.

(39) By most accounts Fred White was an honest, dedicated lawman. Elected Tombstone's first town marshal in January, 1880, ten months later he was dead—victim of an indiscriminate shooting. William (Curly Bill) Brocius was tried and acquitted, White's death ruled accidental. Considered by many a prelude to the shootout near the OK Corral, the White killing continues to generate controversy—few historians in agreement about its particulars.

On October 28, 1880, the pro-Republican, pro-Earp *Tombstone Epitaph* reported the following: "About 12:30 last night a series of pistol shots startled the late goers on the streets, and visions of funerals, etc. flitted thru the brain of the *Epitaph* local [reporter], and the result proved that his surmises were correct. The result in a few words is as follows: A lot of Texas Cowboys, as they are called, began firing at the moon and stars on Allen Street near Sixth. City Marshal White, who happened to be in the immediate neighborhood, interfered to prevent violation of the city ordinance, and was ruthlessly shot by one of the number. Deputy Sheriff [Wyatt] Earp, who is ever to the front when duty calls, arrived just in the nick of time. Seeing the marshal fall, he promptly knocked his assailant down with a six-shooter, and as promptly locked him up; and with the assistance of his brothers, Virgil and Morgan, went in pursuit of the others. That he found them, an inventory of the roster of the city prison this morning will testify. Marshal White was shot in the left groin, the ball passing nearly thru, and being cut from the buttocks by Dr. Matthews. The wound is a serious though not fatal one. Too much praise cannot be given to the marshal for his gallant attempt to arrest the violators of the ordinance, nor to Deputy Sheriff Earp and his brothers for the energy displayed in bringing the murderers to arrest. At last account, 8:00 a.m., Marshal White was sleeping and strong hopes of his ultimate recovery were expected."
Tombstone Epitaph, October 28, 1880.

(40) As noted earlier, Michael Gray was Tombstone Justice of the Peace. Wrote the *Tombstone Epitaph:* "The party [Curly Bill Brocius] who shot Marshall White Tuesday night was brought before Judge Gray yesterday morning on a warrant charging him with assault to murder. The complaint was made by Deputy Sheriff [Wyatt] Earp."
Tombstone Epitaph. October 29, 1880.

(41) That John Peters Ringo was ". . . an heroic type of man . . . apparently of some education," as Gray writes, fits the mythical image of this enigmatic outlaw created by a plethora of writers, most notably Walter Nobel Burns in his most fanciful 1927 book, *Tombstone: An Iliad Of The Southwest.* In fact, nothing in the historical records substantiates such claims (a nephew stated that Ringo was a grammar school drop out and a drunk). Little of substance is known about Ringo. It is known, however, that he abandoned his San Jose, California home at nineteen and went to Texas where he involved himself with outlaw gangs. He came to Tombstone in 1879, and aligned himself with the Curly Bill Brocius gang. In July, 1882, Ringo was found sitting upright against a blackjack oak tree on the banks of Turkey Creek in the Sulphur Springs Valley. He was dead from a bullet wound in the right temple. In his latter years, Wyatt Earp took credit for the killing. Ringo's biographer, Jack Burrows, discounts Earp's claim, theorizing that Ringo committed suicide.
Burrows, pp. 7–9, 148–49, 188.

ONE OF THE PASTIMES of the would-be bad men, passing under the name of "Rustlers," was the practice of shooting up the town. This generally consisted of charging through the main street by a reckless bunch of horsemen who shot out all the lights. Only once do I remember an attempt of this kind being made in Tombstone, and that was by Curly Bill and some of his rustlers. But City Marshal White was on the job and, single-handed, interfered and checked the gunplay at once. Unfortunately, however, the marshal received a wound which proved fatal within a few days. Curly Bill surrendered himself and acknowledged having shot White, but claimed it was an accident.[39]

When brought before my father,[40] who was justice of the peace, on the following morning, Bill was held to answer before the district court at Tucson and was rushed immediately out of town on his way to the Tucson jail. As the feeling among the people of Tombstone was strong against Curly Bill's gang, they were glad to escape to safety.

When the trial came up at Tucson, Curly Bill put up a defense that his pistol would go off at half cock and that in handing over his pistol to Marshal White, at the latter's command, it was accidentally discharged without intent on Bill's part.

No doubt the truth of the matter was that Curly Bill, as was the custom among the rustler gang, had filed off the safety catch on his pistol so that by lifting the hammer with a slight touch of the thumb, it would drop back and explode the cartridge immediately. By this method the holder of the pistol could fan the six shots in rapid succession—and as being quick on the trigger was the mainstay of the gunman, to perfect himself in this was his pride. At all events, there were no witnesses to disprove Bill's defense, as Marshal White, the only witness against him, was dead. The case was dropped and Bill was again a free man, but I doubt that he ever came to Tombstone again.

Among the colorful characters of those days, John Ringo[41] stands out as much superior in calibre to the other rustlers, if there could be made such a distinction. Ringo was tall, dark, rather an heroic type of man, always quiet in his manner, and apparently of some education. No one knew much about him. He seemed to be Curly Bill's right hand man and was no doubt feared most by the Earps of all the rustlers. In fact, most everyone was expecting it to end in a gunfight. And their expectations were not far wrong, for a gunfight came dangerously near one day on Allen Street.

The Crystal Palace Saloon, 1880.

Ringo, on horseback, was riding out of town when he saw three of the Earps together in front of the Crystal Palace Saloon.[42] Ringo rode up and dismounted near them and called out to Wyatt that they had just as well have it out there and then. Ringo pulled from his neck his big red silk handkerchief, flipped it in the air towards Wyatt, told him to take the other end and say when.

Of course Wyatt Earp was too wise to be caught in such a trap, but to the few scattering onlookers, it seemed a critical moment. Both men were of undoubted courage but the Earps knew it would not do to take up the challenge at that time. And so Ringo rode on out of town and never came back. In fact, within a week he was found dead in a canyon of the Chiricahuas, sitting with his back against a tree and a bullet hole through his body.

(42) The most enduring, if not the most famous of Tombstone's saloons and gambling halls, the Crystal Palace was built on the northwest corner of Fifth and Allen Streets in 1879 as the Golden Eagle Brewery and was Tombstone's first two-story building. The name was changed to the Crystal Palace Saloon in 1881.

It was common for young boys to loiter outside the town's saloons and gambling dens where, for tips, they would care for the patron's horses. The boys so coveted the Crystal Palace—because tips from its patrons were much bigger than at the other establishments—that fistfights for territorial rights often broke out.

During the Great Depression, the second story—where Virgil Earp and legendary gunshot surgeon Dr. George Goodfellow had their offices—was removed to save money on taxes.

The Crystal Palace stands today impressively restored.

Interview with Wallace E. Clayton, Tucson, April 18, 1995, author's files.

Arizona Capital Times. June 23, 1995.

(43) No evidence exists to indicate involvement by Buckskin (called such because he habitually wore fringed buckskins) Frank Leslie in Ringo's death. He was, however, a killer. His first victim was Mike Killeen, who was shot June 22, 1880. Killeen lingered for more than two months, putting his signature to a death-bed statement printed in its entirety by the *Tombstone Epitaph:*

"At the ball I wanted to see my wife. I heard that she had gone home with Leslie, and when I was told she had gone home I went down to the [Commercial] hotel with the expectation of finding both of them in Leslie's room, but they were not there; meanwhile, I started towards the porch, having heard voices, and I thought it might be them; I got to the door of the porch and satisfied myself she and Leslie were sitting side by side, his arm around her waist; that settled it; I thought I would go off now; started back again: [George] Perine came along pistol in hand and knowing him to be a particular friend of Leslie I looked for trouble as in the early part of the evening he went into Tasker & Hoke's and bought a box of cartridges and filled all chambers of his pistol and deposited the remainder of the box with me; I started away from the porch when Perine came along and yelled out, 'Look out Frank, there is Mike,' with that Leslie rose from his chair in a half standing position, pulling his pistol; he fired the pistol at me and I fired one shot at him; I saw I was in for it and I made a jump and caught the pistol and beat him over the head with mine, which I had in my hand at the time; I happened to look and saw Perine standing in the door with his pistol levelled at me; he pulled the trigger, which he repeated twice, firing in all three shots; by this time I had used up Leslie pretty well; then turned and jumped and caught Perine's pistol, and did the same to him; by this time people commenced to congregate and I dropped this man, not thinking of my own wounds; all I knew was I was shot in the nose somewhere. I fired two shots myself intentionally, and every time I would strike the pistol went off accidentally; fired at Perine when he fired at me; one shot was at Perine and one at Leslie; fired at Leslie when he pulled his revolver first and stood in a half stooping position; this was right after he first fired at me."

Leslie stood trial for murder and was acquitted. He promptly married Killeen's widow, but they did not live happily ever after.

On November 14, 1882, near the Oriental Saloon, Leslie shot and killed Billy Claiborne, alias the "Kid." Four days later, a coroner's verdict stated that ". . . the shooting was done in self-defense, and, in the opinion of the jury was justifiable."

Leslie's third killing occurred July 10, 1889, when, after a day of drinking and quarreling, he shot to death his mistress, Mollie Williams.

This time the court was not kindly disposed, but sent him to the territorial prison at Yuma to live out his life.

The widow of his first victim, to whom he was married at the time of Mollie's killing, promptly divorced him.

Apparently from Texas, Leslie came to the San Carlos Apache Indian Reservation in 1877 as an army scout. Later he became a bartender in Tombstone and a partner in the Cosmopolitan Hotel.

Tombstone Epitaph. August 24, 1880.
Tombstone Epitaph. November 18, 1882.
Martin, Douglas D. *Tombstone's Epitaph: The Truth about 'The Town Too Tough to Die'.* Albuquerque: University of New Mexico Press, 1951, pp. 79, 81, 93–95.
Breakenridge, p. 197.

It was never divulged who did this or caused it to be done, but many of Ringo's friends felt they knew. Evidently, it was a cowardly murder, whatever the motive. Some believed that Frank Leslie[43] was the agent sent out by the Earps for this work, but I hardly think the charges justified, as Buckskin Frank had never shown any evidence during his career which would make one think he could be guilty of such a cowardly deed.

Wyatt Earp (seated) with Bat Masterson.

ONCE AT OUR ANIMAS VALLEY RANCH[44] in New Mexico, where Jim Crane[45] was an occasional visitor, Frank came out and reported his mission was to arrest Crane and take him to Tombstone on the charge of stage robbing. At that time, Jim was in the habit of riding to the ranch about noontime and eating lunch there. I told Frank that this was his custom and said also that I did not think he would be able to arrest Jim without killing him, and that I objected to any such method being sprung at our house. Both men would be our dinner guests and I expected that hospitality to be undisturbed by either party. However, my warning was not necessary.

Jim Crane rode up at his usual time on a fine saddle mule, unmistakably a refuge from some army post. And as dinner was ready, I asked both in to the meal. It happened we three were alone, except for our old cook, Moody. Jim Crane packed his carbine—a short, Sharpes rifle—into the cook tent and sat down on Leslie's right with the gun across his lap and the muzzle in Frank's direction.

I don't think any of us relished that meal much, and I know I should have preferred to be elsewhere. But, as might have been expected, when all of us were on edge, no sign of conflict appeared. Leslie did not even mention the purpose of his mission, but simply said that he must start for Tombstone at once. Immediately after lunch he mounted his horse, held out his hand to bid me goodbye, saying in a low voice so Jim wouldn't hear, "Tell Jim if they want him, someone else will have to serve the warrant."

When I repeated this to Jim, he simply smiled and said, "I guess so."

I heard later that Leslie had reported back to his office that he could not find his man. This same Buckskin Frank, as he liked to be called, had a more checkered career than most gunmen. He was a man of much intelligence with all his gun plays.

He would tell of years with Buffalo Bill, and when dressed up in his buckskin suit with his silver-mounted guns, he looked the part. He was an expert bartender and knew all that old-time trade's fancy stunts in mixing and pouring drinks, and was for a long time the chief attraction at the Oriental Saloon owned by Supervisor Joyce in Tombstone.

A few days after my arrival in Tombstone in 1880, Leslie shot and killed Mike Kileen on the second story porch of the Cosmopolitan Hotel. That affair had no witnesses except Kileen's wife and she sided with Leslie's

(44) Headquarters of the Gray Ranch was some thirty miles south of the town of Animas in the southwest corner of New Mexico. It is a working ranch today and still is called the Gray Ranch, but the Gray's tenure was short lived. After receiving a government patent on the land, Michael Gray sold the ranch on November 20, 1883.
    Hilliard, pp. 10, 15.

(45) Jim Crane was a known outlaw who, along with Bill Leonard, Harry Head, and Doc Holliday, was suspected of robbing the Benson stage late on the night of March 15, 1881—another precursor to the gunfight near the OK Corral. The *Tombstone Epitaph* broke the story the following day:
    "At about 11 o'clock last night, Marshall Williams [a Wells, Fargo and Company agent] received a telegram from Benson stating that Kinnear & Company's coach, carrying Wells Fargo & Co.'s treasure, had been stopped near Contention and 'Budd' Philpot, the driver, killed and one passenger mortally wounded. Almost immediately afterwards A.C. Cowan, Wells Fargo & Co.'s agent at Contention City, rode into this city bringing a portion of the details of the affair. In a few minutes after his arrival, Williams, the Earp brothers, and several other brave, determined men were in the saddle, well armed, enroute to the scene of the murderous affray. From telegrams received from Benson at the *Epitaph* office, the following particulars of the affair were gathered:
    "As the stage was going up a small incline about two hundred yards this side of Drew's Station and about a mile the other side of Contention City, a man stepped into the road from the east side and called out 'Hold.' At the same moment a number of men—believed to have been eight—made their appearance and a shot was fired from the same side of the road instantly followed by another. One of these shots struck 'Budd' Philpot, the driver, who fell heavily forward between the wheelers carrying the reins with him. The horses immediately spring into a dead run. Meanwhile Bob Paul, Wells Fargo & Co.'s messenger, one of the bravest and coolest men who ever sat on a box-seat, was ready with his gun and answered back shot for shot before the frightened horses had

Tombstone, looking south, 1881.

whirled the coach out of range. It was fully a mile before the team could be brought to a stand, where it was discovered that one of the shots had mortally wounded a passenger on the coach named Peter Roering. As soon as the coach could be stopped, Paul secured the reins and drove rapidly to Benson, and immediately started back for the scene of the murder. At Benson a telegram was sent to the *Epitaph* office stating that Roering could not possibly live. There were eight passengers on the coach and they all unite in praise of Mr. Paul's bravery and presence of mind.

"At Drew's Station the firing and rapid whirling of the coach sent men to the scene of the tragedy, where they found poor 'Budd' lying dead in the road, and by the bright moonlight saw the murderers fleeing rapidly from the place. A messenger was at once dispatched to inform agent Cowan of the circumstances, and within 20 minutes after the news arrived Mr. Cowan had dispatched nearly thirty well-armed volunteers after the scoundrels. He then rode rapidly into Tombstone, when the party mentioned above started out to aid in pursuit. This, with Mr. Paul's party, makes three bodies of determined men who are in hot chase and Mr. Cowan stated to an *Epitaph* reporter that it is almost impossible for the murderous gang to escape, as the pursuers are close at their heels and have the moonlight in their favor. Should the road agents be caught they will meet with the short shift which they deserve."

Morgan Earp apprehended Luther King, who admitted that during the attempted holdup he had held the outlaw's horses. King was turned over to Sheriff John Behan, but promptly escaped from jail by walking through an open door. It was thought the other suspects had fled to Mexico.

On June 22, 1881, Kate Elder, Doc Holliday's hard-drinking mistress, told Behan that Holliday was guilty of Philpot's murder. He was arrested, but released on $5,000 bond posted by Wyatt Earp and others. Evidence was not sufficient, however, to warrant a trial, and Holliday was released after a hearing before the justice of the peace.

Tombstone Epitaph. March 16, 1881.
Martin, pp. 172–74.
Breakenridge, pp. 211–13.

self-defense story. A short time later, after Frank had been acquitted, she became Mrs. Leslie.

A year or so later, Frank committed his second killing in Tombstone. Billy Claiborn, a young cowboy of about twenty years, after an all night's carousal in town, staggered into the Oriental Saloon in the early morning when Leslie was alone on duty behind the bar. Leslie claimed that he put the boy out of the place and that "the kid," as he termed him, went away but soon came back with a rifle in his hand. Seeing him approach, Leslie stepped out on the sidewalk and shot him down. No one was quicker on the draw than Buckskin Frank. He again was acquitted, as he was the only living witness.

A few years went by and Frank was in charge of a small cattle ranch about twenty miles from our Rucker place in the Chiricahuas, known as the Horseshoe Valley. A woman whom he called his wife was living with him at this ranch. Leslie's former wife had long since separated from him. One night Leslie chased this woman out of the house and shot her dead. It happened that a stranger was at the ranch—a mild-mannered fellow who had come afoot and was staying over the night.

This man became alarmed at Leslie's rage at the woman and had run out of the house as Leslie grabbed the gun, starting in pursuit of her. The stranger was some distance away when he heard the shooting and saw the woman fall. Naturally, he kept hurrying away in the dark to escape any trouble with Leslie.

Leslie soon realized his own danger with this witness alive, so he saddled up a horse and followed in pursuit. About two miles away was another small ranch house where my old cook, Moody, who had been with us so many years, was temporarily stopping as caretaker for the absent owner.

Moody said he was awakened by the wandering stranger calling to him. After telling Moody what had happened at the Leslie ranch, Moody took the stranger out and hid him in a corner of the chicken house, knowing Leslie might come soon and search the ranch house. It was but a brief time thereafter when Leslie rode up, called to Moody and told his story of a stranger grabbing a gun and killing his wife, saying he was now after him.

Luckily it was a dark night and though Leslie rode by the chicken house which had slat sides, he did not catch sight of the man hiding inside. If Leslie had seen him, he would have been a dead man.

Leslie evidently realized he was in a bad hole, and probably thought he had better get his story to the sheriff before this witness could be heard from. But the witness realized his own danger if Leslie should find him, and so he made all haste to reach Tombstone and place himself under the protection of the law.

He arrived at the sheriff's office after Leslie's surrender. The case was tried and Leslie pleaded guilty to manslaughter and received a sentence of seven years in the Yuma penitentiary. That ended Buckskin Frank's career in Tombstone. And only within the last year, I read of his death in Oakland, California. His was a rare case of a gunman reaching old age.

Nellie Cashman,
"Angel of the Mining Camps."

NO ONE SHOULD REFER TO THE EARLY DAYS of Tombstone without a good word for Nellie Cashman. If ever a tablet is erected in Arizona to commemorate that state's worthy pioneers, the name of Nellie Cashman should be among them.

(46) The daughter of Patrick Cashman and Fanny Cronin, Ellen (Nellie) Cashman was born in Midleton, County Cork, Ireland probably in 1845; she was baptized in Midleton on October 15, 1845. Another daughter, Francis—whom Nellie would care for most of her life—was born a few years later. Widowed, Fanny left Ireland with her two young daughters sometime around 1850, for the United States. The family settled in Boston where they remained until 1865 or 1866, then set sail for San Francisco. Sister Francis married in 1870 and two years later, Nellie and her mother moved to the mining camp of Pioche, Nevada where they opened a rooming house. It would be the first of many such stops for Nellie. By the end of 1873, boom days at Pioche were over and the Cashmans moved to the Cassiar District of British Columbia. By 1876, Nellie was back in San Francisco. Three years later, in June of 1879, she opened the Delmonico Restaurant in Tucson, advertising "The Best Meals in the City." But Tucson would be a short lived experience. Tombstone had burst onto the map and opportunity beckoned. Wrote the *Tombstone Nugget* of April 1, 1880, "Miss Nellie Cashman of the famous Delmonico restaurant, in Tucson, has opened a gent's furnishings goods store in Tombstone, on Allen street, adjoining Ward's market. She will keep a large supply of furnishing goods, both for the ladies and gentlemen, including boots and shoes, and as Nellie was never outdone in any business she has undertaken, her success in our midst is double sure." In addition to the Nevada Boot & Shoe Store, Nellie would open a grocery called the Tombstone Cash Store, and the Arcade Restaurant & Chop House. She immersed herself in charitable work and community activities, as evidenced by this item in the September 25, 1880 issue of the *Tombstone Epitaph*: "Nellie Cashman, the irrepressible, started out yesterday to raise funds for the building of a Catholic church. We don't know what success attended her first effort but will bet that there is a Catholic church in Tombstone before many days if Nellie has to build it herself."

Later, Nellie would operate the Russ House, a combination hotel and restaurant at the corner of Fifth and Tough Nut streets, and the Delmonico Lodging House. Other Arizona enterprises included a hotel in Bisbee and another in Nogales.

Addicted to the boom and often ravished by the bust, Nellie would win and lose fortunes as she moved from camp to camp—including stops in Mexico, Alaska, and Canada.

Nellie Cashman died in Victoria, British Columbia, January 4, 1925.

Chaput, Don. *Nellie Cashman and the North American Mining Frontier.* Tucson: Westernlore Press, 1995, pp. 2–3, 5–6, 12–14.

Tombstone Nugget. April 1, 1880.

Tombstone Epitaph. September 25, 1880.

Anderson, Mary W. "They Called Her the Angel: Plucky Woman Prospector Known for Good Deeds." *Tombstone Epitaph.* November, 1980.

I don't know that anyone knew much of Nellie's life story. She was a native of Wales, and had come to Tombstone among the first. She kept a lodging house for miners, was the friend of every miner in the camp, and controlled the miners' vote at every election.

But Nellie was far from being a political grafter. All her efforts seemed to be solely for the benefit of the miners, to help them when they were sick or in want, and to pass the hat around in aid of any suffering. How she managed to make a living when often her lodging house became a free hospital, was difficult to solve.

I have heard old miners tell of knowing Nellie up at the Stikeen in British Columbia, when she dressed in men's clothes and worked as a miner in all the severe cold and hardships suffered there. Afterward, she went to the wild camp of Bodie, and there was never even a hint of any scandal or wrong-doing in her life.

Nellie would not rank as a beauty and her voice was rather harsh—hardly distinguishable from a man's—but to see her go by in the evening helping Father Gallagher home, you would know she was not lacking in that forbearing spirit and kindliness of heart that only a true woman can have. Good old Father Gallagher at times would take a drop too much.

In later days when Allen Street was no longer a busy thoroughfare and only a few old-timers were holding forth on the shady side of the street discussing the paling days of the past, Nellie Cashman's name was always mentioned with much reverence.

It may not be orthodox to mention the lower strata of humanity which exists in all mining camps, as well as in the big cities and towns of our country, but the story of Tombstone is not complete without mention of the good deeds which often came from places many considered wholly bad.

I think it is only fair to say that no member of humanity is wholly bad. When misfortune came to Tombstone, either from some mining accident or unfortunate illness which called for the community's help, the women of the camp's "nether world"—the prostitutes—were the first to respond, and sometimes came close to bearing the whole load.

All old-timers will remember that Nellie Cashman always called for help from "Black Jack," known as the queen of the red light district, and Nellie said her greatest help came from the back street which had no name on the map.[46]

THERE CAME A DAY when the reign of the Earps received its hardest blow, and that was the passing of Morgan Earp. It was rumored that this was an act of revenge for the death of John Ringo, who had many friends among the rustlers.

The scene was a billiard room of an Allen Street saloon. The rear door had its lower panels in frosted glass and the upper panels in clear glass. Morgan Earp was playing billiards and as he moved around the table with his back to this door, only a few feet away, a shot rang out. Morgan fell, mortally wounded.

It was some minutes before the discovery was made that the shot had been fired from outside this rear door—the bullet passing through the frosted panel, which hid from sight the killer who had evidently watched his victim through the upper part of the door's glass. Thus the killer had ample time to get away.

For some reason the Earps accused Frank Stillwell, with whom they had evidently had trouble—and Stillwell was close to John Ringo and Curly Bill.

The following morning, Stillwell was located in Tucson. The night clerk at the Palace Hotel[47] had booked

Campbell & Hatch Saloon & Billiard Parlor, where Morgan Earp was assassinated.

(47) Located on Meyer Avenue, the Palace was the first building constructed in Tucson specifically as a hotel. Built of fired brick, Fred Maish and Thomas Driscoll opened the one-story hotel in the fall of 1877. It consisted of little more than a saloon in front with sleeping cots in the back room. Later, the north wing was enlarged and a second story added, increasing its capacity to some sixty rooms. The Palace was Tucson's first hotel to feature real bedsteads with mattresses and springs. Indoor plumbing and baths were early innovations. The dining room seated ninety people and offered a substantial menu. A billiard parlor adjoined the bar, and a modest stage hosted traveling vaudeville shows. When the railroad arrived in Tucson in 1880, the Palace was one of only two hotels in the city. For a brief time, Nellie Cashman operated her Delmonico Restaurant from the Palace Hotel. The building was razed in 1923.

Harte, pp. 54, 80.

Carmony, Neil, ed. *Whiskey, Six-Guns and Red-Light Ladies: George Hand's Saloon Diary, Tucson, 1875–1878.* Silver City, NM: High-Lonesome Books, 1994, pp. 19, 127–28.

Kimmelman, Alex Jay. "Strictly White and Always Sober—Tucson's Pioneer Hotels: A Photo Essay." *The Journal of Arizona History,* Vol. 35, No. 1 (Spring, 1994), pp. 67–68.

Arizona Daily Star. December 1, 1893.

(48) The *Tombstone Daily Nugget,* the pro-Democrat, anti-Earp newspaper, offered this account: "Tucson, March 21–This morning at daylight, the track man at the Southern Pacific Railroad depot found the body of Frank Stilwell about one hundred yards north of Porter's Hotel at the side of the track, riddled with bullets. The circumstances of the case, so far as learned, are as follows: Stilwell arrived here Sunday to appear before the grand jury on a charge of stage robbery near Bisbee, last November. He was under bonds for his appearance. Last night, when the west-bound passenger train arrived, it brought Virgil Earp and his wife, en route for Colton, California where the remains of his brother Morgan, killed at Tombstone Saturday night, had been forwarded by Sunday's train, accompanied by Wyatt Earp, Sherman McMasters, Doc Holliday, and a man known as Johnson, all heavily armed with shotguns and revolvers. A few moments before the train started, Stilwell and Abe [sic] Clanton (brother to William Clanton, who was killed in Tombstone by the Earps), went to the depot to meet a man by the name of McDowell, who was to have come in as a witness before the Grand Jury. On their arrival at the depot, they saw the Earp party walking on the platform. Stilwell advised Clanton to leave at once, saying they wanted to kill him. Clanton left a few moments later. Stilwell was seen walking down the track in the direction where his body was found. Four of the armed men who were on the platform soon followed. One was described as a slender, light-complexioned man, wearing a white hat. Just as the train was leaving, six shots were heard in the locality of the assassination, but attracted no particular attention, and nothing was known of the tragedy until this morning, when the body was discovered. Six shots went into his body: four rifle balls and two loads of buckshot. Both legs were shot through and a charge of buckshot in his left thigh and a charge through his breast, which must have been delivered close, as the coat was powder burnt, and six buckshot holes within a radius of three inches. Stilwell had a pistol on his person which was not discharged. He evidently was taken unawares as he was desperate in a fight and a quick shot. His watch was taken in the hurry of which a part of the chain was left. There is much excitement here concerning the assassination, and many speculations are rife. Some say that he was decoyed to the spot where he fell as he possessed

Tucson's first railroad depot, where it was alleged that Wyatt and Virgil Earp, and Doc Holliday murdered Frank Stillwell in retaliation for the murder of Morgan Earp.

strong evidence against certain stage robbers. Others think that he was trying to get away from the Earp party and was overtaken, while it is thought by some that he went down the track to shoot one or more of the Earp party as the train was moving out two of them being on board. The killing is thought to have been done by four of the party who accompanied the Earps here, as the four men who followed the deceased down the track. were not seen again. This morning at one o'clock, as the east-bound freight train approached Papago, nine miles east of here, it was flagged, and four armed men got on the train. They are strongly suspected. The deceased was twenty-seven years of age; was a native of Texas, is a brother to the famous scout, Jack Stilwell. He has been in Arizona four years, was a teamster at Signal for some time and lately has been keeping a livery stable near Charleston and Bisbee, and was an ex-Deputy Sheriff of Cochise County."

Tombstone Daily Nugget, March 22, 1882.

The *Tucson Weekly Citizen* offered quite a different appraisal of Stilwell: "Frank Stilwell has of late years been known as a desperate character and for awhile was commissioned as deputy sheriff under Sheriff Behan of Cochise County, but was removed because of a discrepency in the accounts regarding the amounts of certain license money which had by him been collected. He was afterwards involved in the brutal killing of old man Houton, whose brains were beaten out with rocks from some difficulty relating to the famous Brunckow Mine, lying south of Tombstone and which was, at the time of the old man's death subject to relocation. Houton and others, among them, Stilwell, were in the Brunckow area and intending to relocate it on the following morning. Houton, most unfortunately for himself, was the successful one to the chagrin of Stilwell and gang which determined upon his removal which they effected by first shooting and afterwards brained the old man with rocks. A number of arrests were made but, because of some technicalities in the law, the implicated ones were liberated. Stilwell next came into notoriety on the robbing of the Bisbee stage. He was accordingly arrested and underwent an examination in Tombstone but, again, the uncertainty stood his friend as on the elicited facts it was impossible to convict him, but he was held to appear before United States Commissioner T.L. Stiles to answer for robbing of the mails. The indictment against him was still pending but his death as stated settles all accounts. He was buried this afternoon, the coffin being conveyed to the grave in an express wagon, unfollowed by a single mourner."

Tucson Weekly Citizen, March 28, 1882.

Stillwell for a room at 5 a.m., and vouched for his presence at this hour. It was contended that it was impossible for a man to go from Tombstone to Tucson—a distance of seventy-five miles—between the hours of 11 p.m. and 5 a.m. by any method of transportation then extant.

The sheriff would not hold Stillwell in the face of this alibi. A long time afterward it came out that an old roan saddle horse could have told a different story had he the power of speech. But the sequel followed quickly.

Wyatt, Virg Earp, and Doc Holliday started with Morgan's remains to Colton, California for burial, and it was at Tucson, while the passenger train stopped for the supper hour, that they evidently heard of Stillwell's movements.

Stillwell must have gone to the neighborhood of the Tucson depot to watch the Earps. Anyway, in the railroad yards, between some side-tracked freight cars, Stillwell's body was found shot in several places.[48]

Nothing more seems to have been done about this, as a short time later the Earps and Holliday returned to Tombstone from their California trip, and at last the sheriff, Johnny Behan, seemed to realize it was time to act. At least it was intimated to the Earps that some action was contemplated, so they quietly and hurriedly mounted their horses and rode away, never to return again to Tombstone. There was no effort made to apprehend them or to call for an accounting. Tombstone simply drew a long breath of relief, and never again did it call on a gunman to take the helm.

AT THE HEIGHT OF ITS PROSPERITY, Tombstone had its big fire, which almost swept it off the map. Most of the business section, its two big hotels—the Grand and Cosmopolitan—and all but one saloon, went up in smoke. No water was available with which to fight the fire, for in those days all water was hauled into town in tank wagons from wells about three miles north of town. The only means of fighting a fire was to use giant powder to blow up buildings.[49]

Tombstone was surely a hot place that day, but men fought gallantly to salvage what they could. And long before all the smoke had cleared away, work was speeded up to rebuild, and probably Tombstone was a livelier town in the next few months than ever in its career.

The Oriental Saloon escaped the fire and, with its salvaged barrel of whisky, was reported to have made M.E. Joyce a small fortune.[50]

It was the fire that hurried along the formation of a

(49) Tombstone twice—June 22, 1881; May 25, 1882—was devastated by fire, leaving the town in ruins. Gray seems not to distinguish between the two conflagrations, but in his memoir combines them as one.

The 1881 fire began in a most unusual manner. The proprietors of the Arcade Saloon rolled a barrel of bad whiskey onto the sidewalk, preparing to send it back to its distributor. Attempting to measure its contents, one of the men dropped a gauge rod into the barrel. A bartender came forward with a wire to retrieve it. One story says that he lit a match, another that he held a lighted cigar in his mouth. Either way, the result was the same. The barrel exploded in flames, and in moments Tombstone was aflame.
Sherman, p. 153.
Marks, p. 157.

(50) Joyce had been hard hit during the fire of 1881. The Oriental escaped with but minor damage in the 1882 blaze (which started in a water closet at the rear of the Tivoli Saloon on Allen Street), and it is said that Joyce sold drinks at exorbitant prices. Wrote the *Tombstone Epitaph*, ". . . all the liquors he had on hand he distributed to the gallant defenders of the city. . . ."
Chaput, *Cashman*, pp. 51–52.
Tombstone Epitaph. May 27, 1882.

AHS #42002

Tombstone, Arizona. Allen Street after the fire of June 22, 1881.

good water system. Heretofore, all water had been hauled in. Some men made small fortunes at this business, delivering water for a dollar for a fifty gallon barrel. One double team and driver could easily make two trips a day, or about twenty dollars a day.

We kept at home a saddle mule, but when our water bill amounted to nineteen dollars in one month, Mr. Mule was hastily sent out to pasturage. To take a bath used up close to one dollar's worth of water. Anything short of that, in vulgar parlance, was termed a spit bath.

A few years later, this ended with the establishment of a good water system. A company was organized that brought in a good water supply from the Huachuca Mountains[51] with a twenty-eight mile pipe line. The time came when the pressure at the nozzle of a fire hose was sufficient to tear to pieces an ordinary miner's cabin. It took two strong men at the hose nozzle to keep it from running wild.

By that time, the long strings of mules and ore wagons had quit raising dust on Fremont Street, and had departed to Cripple Creek and other newer camps in Colorado. The few people left in Tombstone would not number more than ten percent of the population during its boom days.

No doubt the water company proved a bad investment. But even then, Tombstone held its head up and never became a ghost town. It remained the seat of Cochise County for many years, and the old courthouse in its setting of green lawn and fine umbrella trees could tell of many thrilling scenes.[52]

ONE OF THE MOST SPECTACULAR SCENES ever witnessed in Tombstone was the trial, conviction and subsequent hanging of the four hustlers who had held up and shot up Bisbee. The hanging took place in the prison yard, and on the date of the execution, Tombstone was so crowded with people it was as though a circus was in town.

But it was an earnest crowd of miners from Bisbee, and cattlemen from the range who came to uphold by their presence their sense of justice in the execution of these outlaws.

This scene was followed a short time later by a posse of five hundred Bisbee miners appearing at daybreak and demanding of the sheriff the fifth man of the Bisbee massacre, who had escaped with a twenty-five year prison sentence.

(51) Southwest of Tombstone and bordering Mexico is the range known as the Huachuca Mountains (Sierra de Huachuca). The name was taken from a rancheria which was settled south of the range as early as 1680.
Wilson, p. 9.

(52) After the boom ended, attempts were made to move the seat of Cochise County from Tombstone to the still-flourishing towns of Bisbee or Douglas, but residents resisted until 1929, when, at last, voters cast ballots in favor of Bisbee. Delays followed, however, and Bisbee did not become the county seat until 1931.

The old county courthouse at Tombstone—a Victorian edifice completed in 1882 at a cost of $50,000—was abandoned and stood vacant and neglected for fifteen years, its yard strewn with castoff furniture and debris. In 1946, a group of businessmen acquired the property intending to convert it to a hotel.

Many of the county records were still in the courthouse, papers from the past not considered important enough to be moved to the new county seat. In a tragedy of historic proportions, the new owners had all the papers loaded on a dump truck, hauled to a mine shaft and dumped. Barry Goldwater and historian Bert Fireman learned of the tragedy and flew to Tombstone to retrieve what they could. It was a futile effort, however. Water filled the shaft, and virtually everything was destroyed.

Fortunately, plans for the remodeling were abandoned. The property reverted to the county, and in 1955, the Tombstone Restoration Commission acquired it. In 1959, it was turned over to the State Parks system and since has served as a museum. Today, some 75,000 visitors meander through the historic structure each year.
Rogers, W. Lane. "Courtroom in Tombstone." *Arizona Capitol Times*. May 14, 1993.

The Tombstone lynching of John Heith.

The Bisbee people believed he was equally guilty and they came to demand this man and to execute him. All this was carried out quickly and without a show of resistance. A nearby telegraph pole crossarm was the gallows, and it was said that the prisoner was the coolest and the least nervous man in the crowd. He even offered to make—and did make—the hangman's knot when some miner fumbled at the job, and then said he was ready. At once, many hands seized the rope, pulled the body up to the crossarm and left it hanging there. By the time the citizens of Tombstone knew of what had taken place, the posse was well on its way back to Bisbee.[53]

(53) In December, 1883, five ne'er-do-wells held up a Bisbee store filled with shoppers. For reasons that remain obscure, three men stationed outside opened fire, killing five people, including a pregnant woman. A posse was quickly formed to track down the killers. Posse member John Heith so often led the men on false trails that he fell under suspicion. The five were arrested and so was Heith. He had not participated in the holdup, but was the admitted ringleader. The others were sentenced to hang, and did so legally. Heith was given twenty years in jail. That angered Bisbee residents who stormed the Tombstone jail, seized the prisoner and hanged him from a telegraph pole. Dr. George E. Goodfellow, heading up a coronors jury, wrote, "We the undersigned find that J. Heath [sic] came to his death from emphysema of the lungs—a disease common to high altitudes—which might have been caused by strangulation, self-inflicted or otherwise."

Given the town's propensity for violence, it is interesting to note that Heith was the only person lynched at Tombstone.

Faulk, p. 179.

Trimble, *Arizona*, p. 71.

Rogers, "Courthouse . . ."

Dr. George Goodfellow, who headed the coroner's jury after Heith's lynching.

(54) Estimates vary widely; some are as high as 15,000.

(55) Tombstone's elevation is 4,539 feet.

(56) A most respected man, Dave Neagle resigned as superintendent of a Mexican mine in 1880, and migrated to Tombstone where he became a deputy sheriff under John Behan. Later, he was elected Tombstone city marshal. Thought to have been born about 1847, Neagle left Tombstone in 1882. His life was lived out in California, principally in San Francisco. He died in 1926.
    Marks, pp. 122, 319–20.
    Breakenridge, p. 120.

AT THE HEIGHT OF ITS PROSPERITY, Tombstone's population was estimated at twelve thousand.[54] At that time, more transients passed through Tombstone than through many big cities. Many came just for curiosity to "look-see," as the Chinaman would say. But most came to make their fortunes in mining or at the gambling tables. Win or lose, both were fascinating games and there were no quitters.

You never heard a hard luck story in Tombstone. Everyone had great expectations. A man might not have a dollar in his pocket, but he had millions in sight. He could draw from his pockets a bunch of mining locations, each showing title to fifteen hundred by six hundred feet of untold wealth along some lead lode or vein that only needed a little development to become a second Comstock.

Meanwhile, one could eat on credit at most restaurants, especially the Chinese ones. And you might even, with a few glowing words, manage to exchange a location notice for a suit of clothes at a store, especially if the merchant were a late arrival, and hence more susceptible to taking chances in the mining game. And, too, if the merchant were a Jew, he was found to be the easiest victim for the prospector's story. It was the day of what we termed the "two-bit capitalist."

We were all "Colonel Sellers" with millions in sight.

Even the appearance of the great John L. Sullivan and William Muldoon, the great wrestler, did not attract much attention from our absorbing dreams of great wealth.

Tombstone could always rightly brag of its climate. Its five thousand feet elevation[55] gave it ideal summer temperatures, and its winters were always mild. In summer an occasional violent lightening, thunder, and a torrential rain storm was a welcome visitor if you were lucky enough to be under shelter. It was always a thrilling exhibition of the elements and was generally followed almost immediately by a clear sky and bright sunshine, leaving a well washed land and balmy pure air in its wake.

With the advent of a good water system, gardens appeared. It might seem strange to relate, but at more than one Territorial Fair at Phoenix, Tombstone gardens took first prize in peaches, and even for the mammoth pumpkin.

AFTER THE EARPS and Doc Holliday made their sudden exit from Tombstone, Nellie Cashman with the aid of her miner friends, backed one of their number for city marshal, and their choice, Dave Neagle,[56] won. He served Tombstone well as its peace officer. This was the same Dave Neagle who later became bodyguard for Judge Fields, and in this capacity encountered Judge David Terry at the Lathrop dining room bar, which resulted in Terry's death from Neagle's pistol shot. Thus more notoriety, if not fame, for another of Tombstone's products of he-men.

FOR ONE RAISED in sight of the heavily wooded and chaparral covered hills of northern California, it is a sudden shock, if not a disappointment, to come face to face with miles of dead level—the terrain of much of southeastern Arizona. What hills are on the far away horizon are mostly bare of vegetation, flat-topped as though nature had sliced off the useless tops—or resembling a cake spoiled in the cooking.

You will be sadly disappointed if you hope to find a longed-for drink of water there. In most places you must go down hill for water, dig your firewood with a pick, and cut hay with a hoe.

Go out on the treeless valley and look closely on the ground in the neighborhood of a sparse growth of mesquite bushes and you will soon discover long, black-looking roots uncovered in spots. Put your pick under these and pry them up, and it is surprising how soon you can load your wagon with the best stove wood of any land. It is hardwood, but brittle, and will hold the heat like coal.

So you dig your firewood in the valleys, and with a hoe cut the Gaieta grass which grows from one root into a big armful. In early times, Mexicans would pile a heavy bunch of this on their donkeys' backs and, in this way, deliver a load of hay to you.

You soon got into the habit of squinting your eyes, a habit so noticeable in old-timers when looking at the landscape; and, too, you acquire a patience you never knew before—a patience to look calmly at some spot on the horizon, maybe fifty or more miles away, the spot you hope to arrive at sometime in the future. And you resign yourself to the slow shuffle of your cow pony mount. This is his all-day gait and he will get you there, but force him to move faster and you will find yourself with a tired-out mount, stranded far from bed and board.

Once at the old Rucker Ranch we had as guests two Englishmen who were traveling over the Southwest. That night, while having supper, a message overtook them calling for their immediate return to England. We knew the next eastbound overland train passed through Willcox on the Southern Pacific line at midnight. It was then 4 p.m.

and Willcox was sixty miles away. In those days, the horse was the only way of getting anywhere, so I offered to drive them in our ranch buckboard to Willcox to catch the night's train. We hurriedly got away with two ranch ponies drawing the buckboard.

In less than an hour we were out of the hills and the long, level Sulphur Springs Valley stretched out before us. Our road lay down this valley in as straight a course as a country road ever got to be. It was summer and the usual summer rains were on; the accompanying lightening and thunder had my passengers continually worrying lest I miss the road in the darkness. To pacify their fears I told them to watch when the lightening flashed and they could see the wagon track plainly ahead in full view.

The team had struck that steady shuffle-like trot, making probably five or six miles an hour. My Englishmen passengers at first impatiently urged me to speed up, but this I refused to do as I knew we would easily make it, which we did—drawing into Willcox at 11:30 p.m., in plenty of time for supper before train time. And then my passengers felt so relieved at making the train they overwhelmed me with thanks and praise for that pair of horses that had jogged on hour after hour and never lost the road. They probably long remembered that long, dark ride—with no street lamps—only the horse sense of two tough Arizona ponies who knew the game.

THERE WERE BIG STRETCHES of wild country in Arizona in the 1880s, and one might ride horseback for days without meeting any human or habitation. Water was scarce and what few springs there were in the country were easily missed by the traveler, for cattle had not yet broken trails to watering places.

Going eastward from Tombstone you cross the Dragoon Mountains into the big Sulphur Springs Valley, thence through the Chiricahua Mountains into the San Simon Valley,[57] then through the Stein Peak Mountains into Animas Valley of New Mexico—and right there under the shadow of Animas Peak is a big green meadow of about one thousand acres which was, at that time, covered with red top clover and watered by numerous springs or eye holes, as they were called. These holes were deep and apparently part of an underground lake.

There was a story that a rider once came to one of these holes and took the bridle off his horse to allow him to drink. The horse stepped in, disappearing at once from

(57) Embracing the New Mexico border northwest of Willcox is the San Simon Valley. When members of the Mormon Battalion came through the area in 1847, they told of a valley carpeted with native grasses stirrup-high; some of the richest cattle grazing land in the West. Sonoran beaver were found in the San Simon River, and deer and antelope flourished in the valley.

Wilson, p. 17.

Trimble, *Roadside,* p. 34.

sight, leaving the rider standing there with the bridle in his hand, and nothing else to show that he ever had a horse.

This was the spot we had picked for a cattle ranch, and it seemed just right for the purpose. That green spot was surely a cheerful sight to one accustomed to the dry, dusty surroundings of Tombstone. It was virgin land, unsurveyed, with no neighbors. It seemed a cattleman's paradise.

We had hardly got started with our camp and commenced the making of the adobe sun-dried bricks for our ranch house when our troubles began.

A horseman appeared and presented a letter signed "George Washington Jones," which gave notice that the writer was owner of the tract of land we were on, and warned us to vacate within twenty-four hours or suffer the alternative of being shot off.

We had paid Curly Bill, the rustler, three hundred dollars for his squatter claim on the land and also had a written contract or guarantee from Bill that he would uphold our rights against all claimants. It being unsurveyed land, possession of course was the only title possible but we paid this sum to Curly Bill for the sake of peaceful possession of land in a country where law officers seldom, if ever, ventured, and self-preservation was really the only law to follow. So we told the messenger that we were there to stay, and kept on with our house building.

I think it was the next morning when I was out early with wagon and team to pick up a load of dry wood for camp use. About two miles west of the ranch, I met three horsemen. As soon as they came in sight I knew they must be the three hunted stage robbers who had tried to hold up the Tombstone stage a few months before—Billy Leonard, Harry Head, and Jim Crane. They were well armed, but their clothing was almost in tatters and they looked wild, wooly, and hungry.

After greeting them, I asked them to come to our camp and have dinner with us, explaining at the same time what we were doing in Animas Valley, and our purchase of the rights of Curly Bill, whom I felt they knew and were associated with.

After giving them a good dinner and fitting them out with what clothing we could spare, I showed them the letter from George Washington Jones. Jim Crane spoke up at once and said not to worry over it; that he knew the writer, though that was not his real name. He said he would make it a personal matter to see that he did not bother us. In other words, Curly Bill's guarantee to us was law to them.

We felt more at ease but still felt that G.W. Jones might

appear with an armed force of his followers, and that brother and I would be found alone to hold the ranch. Our few hired men at work on the house could not be expected to take a hand in our fight.

Things moved fast the next few days. One morning a rider appeared and asked if he could sell us a quarter of beef. He said he was camped at the Double Dobes, about eight miles away, and had killed a beef out of a herd they were holding there. This we were glad to do as we had been eating antelope steaks until we longed for a genuine beef steak again.

At that time, antelope were very plentiful. There was a willow thicket at a water hole about a quarter of a mile away, below our camp, and they came there to drink. Brother or myself would often go there early and lay for them in the willows, and we seldom failed in getting a good shot, for they would file in like a herd of sheep. But on this morning I drove a team over to the Double Dobes for the beef. On arriving there I was surely surprised, and a little alarmed when the place seemed to be alive with men.

Saddles and guns were lying about and men were asleep on the grass, as well as on the floor of the house. There must have been fifty men and I knew from their appearance that they were the rustler type.

Jim Crane stepped out as I drove up to the house and was smiling at my apparent confusion in the midst of this small army. He told me that I need worry no more about George Washington Jones for, as he put it, "he had fixed him good and plenty." I felt it wise not to ask for particulars, so with my quarter of beef I pulled out for the ranch. It was several days before I heard the complete story.

It seems the Wells, Fargo Express Company had printed circulars which offered a reward of $1,500 each for Leonard, Head, and Crane for the holdup of the Tombstone stage, the offer to hold good whether they were dead or alive.

This holdup had occurred in the early spring of 1881 and later Jim Crane told me the story of it which I give here in brief.

The stage left Tombstone in the evening and drove the twenty-five miles to Benson. About ten miles out of Tombstone was a deep draw crossing the roadway, out of which the stage horses could only go in a walk. It was at this point where the holdup was attempted.

Bob Paul was shotgun messenger that night but had traded places for the time with the driver, Bud Philpot, who has holding the shotgun. Paul, who was a veteran with Wells, Fargo, didn't intend to be held up, so when a voice from the roadside called, "Hands up," Paul plied the whip on the horses and they broke into a run up the steep roadway.

Either by luck or by Paul's good driving, they safely made a getaway. The hold-up men fired volleys at the stage, killed an inside passenger and Bud Philpot with the shotgun, but Paul drove into Benson with the strongbox safe and his dead men aboard.

Jim Crane said the whole thing had been planned by the Earps. Morgan Earp was to go out that night as messenger and he had given the tip that about twenty thousand dollars was in the Wells, Fargo strongbox.

The hold-up would have met with no resistance, and it looked like easy money. But Bob Paul stepped in as messenger. His was an iron nerve, and he was a man who had never failed to come through. Bob evidently had planned to hold the reins that night, and he did. He simply ran away from the robbers.

As officers of the law, the Earps made a big showing in apparent pursuit of Crane, Leonard, and Head, but had no intention of finding them. I urged Jim to give himself up and tell the whole story of the plot, thinking that he had a good chance for a light sentence, but circumstances or fate willed it otherwise. He met his fate tragically on his way to Tombstone.

At Hachita,[58] New Mexico lived two brothers by the name of Heslett, who planned on getting this Wells, Fargo reward, which was the tidy sum of $4,500 for the three robbers. They had heard of these men heading for Hachita and accordingly concealed themselves behind an old adobe wall which the road skirts just a mile or so from town. Somehow Jim Crane was not in the party that day and, as planned, Leonard and Head were shot down as they rode past the adobe wall. Then the Hesletts rode boldly into Hachita and told of their deed, treating everybody on the strength of the easy money they thought they had made that day.

Jim Crane soon heard of the killing. He got together a bunch of rustlers, and leaving them hiding close by, rode into Hachita alone. He found the Hesletts in the saloon getting pretty drunk. Jim played friendly and the three were soon seated at a game of cards. Suddenly rising from his chair opposite the two brothers, Crane shot them both before they could make a move, and thus avenged his comrades, Leonard and Head.

The shots were a signal to the outside bunch of rustlers who rode to the saloon door ready for any emergency. But no one dared to interfere, so Jim and his escorts rode leisurely out of town.

(58) Located thirty-seven miles southeast of Lordsburg on the Southern Pacific Railroad line, Hachita was given a post office in 1882. It was closed in 1898, reopened in 1902. Hachita is the trading center for the Hachita Valley.

Pearce, T.M., ed. *New Mexico Place Names: A Geographical Dictionary.* Albuquerque: University of New Mexico Press, 1965, p. 68.

With the passing of the Hesletts came the end of the G.W. Jones of my letter. I never heard of any attempt of peace officers to follow this up, and the reward offered by the Wells, Fargo was never claimed. And this was the bunch of rustlers I found at the Double Dobes, or Flying Cloud, as the rustlers had more romantically named their mountain retreat.

Who built the two adjoining adobe houses there was a mystery, but in those days the place was never occupied except as a rustler rendezvous, probably because it was high in the foothills of the Animas Mountains. You could see for miles over the valley, noting any approaching danger, such as a wandering sheriff or other officers.

A few months after my meeting with this small army, I happened in at the Double Dobes on my way to the ranch, returning from a trip for supplies to Lordsburg,[59] and I ran into a couple of fellows camped there. They told me they were freighters and were going to El Paso to get work for their mules. I saw quite a number of big mules on the *cienega* below the house. With them was a white mare packing a bell. At the time, I believed their story and thought no more about it, but that evening when I arrived at the ranch and told my brother about this outfit, he remarked that the bunch of mules and the white mare were probably Charley Gough's big team of twenty mules which hauled wood for the Tombstone mines.

It just happened that I had to make a trip to Tombstone soon, so I concluded that I would start the following day. On my arrival there I hunted up Charley Gough, who I found had lost his stock and had been riding for days in a vain search for them. He took the next train to El Paso with warrants in his pocket for these two unknown men, and on arriving went to the one big feed corral in El Paso at that time, in search for his stock. He camped there, thinking it was the most likely place for the men with his stock to come. Securing the aid of El Paso authorities, he took up his watch, sleeping near the gate of the feed lot.

I think on his second night there he was awakened by the familiar tinkle of the old bell mare's coming, and he was there at the gate to meet his lost herd. He had no trouble arresting the two horsemen as they dismounted, who, of course, thought they were safe.

The two men were taken back to Tombstone, tried for grand larceny, and sentenced to twenty-five years each in Yuma Penitentiary. Gough later told me these men tried to find out how he knew they were going to El Paso with the mules, but he would not expose my part in the game.

(59) Located some twenty miles from the Arizona border, Lordsburg is the seat of Hidalgo County, New Mexico. The town took its name from a construction engineer on the Southern Pacific Railroad.

Workers of the Writers' Program of the Work Projects Administration. *New Mexico: A Guide to the Colorful State.* NY: Hastings House, 1940, p. 375.

However, they surely had not forgotten my meeting them at the Dobes.

Their telling me of their destination shows the simple nature of many of the rustlers' band, and that most of the so-called criminal element were of a low order of intelligence.

The big bunch of rustlers with Jim Crane at the Double Dobes was the largest gathering of the tribe I ever heard of, although about a month later we had sixty come to dinner in one day at the ranch. I know I pitched in to help old Moody, our cook, and a fifty pound sack of flour went into biscuits before the last man was fed. As a consequence, the following morning I had to pull out for Lordsburg to get a load of grub. I was a tenderfoot in those days and I paid dearly on this trip for a little experience.

I HAD A GOOD FOUR-HORSE TEAM and a barrel of water aboard the wagon to drop off at midway point, as the road to Lordsburg was seventy-five miles without a habitation—and without a water hole the entire distance. Coming out with a load would mean slow going, and the need of water for the team. This was in June before the summer rains were due and the days were hot. When I dropped off the fifty-gallon barrel of water, it never occurred to me to remove the stopper in order to let air into the water, although I knew from my school chemistry that water would spoil without contact with air.

On my return trip a few days later with a heavy load of provisions, lumber and fixtures for the ranch house, about twenty-five miles out of Lordsburg a front wheel collapsed under the heavy load and I was stranded. I decided my only course would be to pull out for the ranch with my horses to get our other wagon, for I doubted if repairs could have been made in the small town of Lordsburg.

So I started riding one horse bareback, stringing the others ahead. In after years that ride would have been easy for me, but at that time I was very new to the game. When after what seemed almost unbearable discomfort from the heat, thirst and the chafing of my legs from riding bareback, we arrived at the water barrel. I found, to my utter dismay, upon removing the wooden plug and tipping the barrel, that the water would not run. It had become thick and ropy and smelled vile. Here I was, forty miles from the next water and my horses were pawing the ground in their eagerness for me to give them a drink.

I felt as if I was almost done for, but I knew it was my own fault for leaving the stopper in the barrel in that hot weather. The only thing left to do was to pull out for the nearest water, which was at the ranch. I took Dolly—the only pacer in the bunch—for my mount, as my legs were raw from the long, hot, bareback ride, and I could not have stood much more of a trotting horse.

I had quite a little trouble getting my loose horses to leave the barrel, as they could smell the water in it. I have often since felt for a horse when I had to overtax his powers by a hard ride, but I never felt more conscience-stricken than I did over this barrel incident. All things, however, come to an end and so did that long road home.

It was more endurable when the sun set. I was never so glad of the cool shade of night. When along about midnight I heard the lead horse splash into water, I simply rolled off into that wet spot and absorbed all the water, inside and out, that I could hold.

It seemed almost worth that hard day's torture just to feel the delightful sensation of a good drink, and having the satisfaction of having made the trip. I was too sore from that bareback ride to move out of camp for several days, but my brother went back for the load with fresh horses and a good wagon. He said he found the water in the barrel good and sweet again. My having left out the stopper let the air in contact with it, and purification had taken place.

A SHORT TIME LATER I had to make a trip to Tombstone. I rode horseback and on my return I crossed the Stein Peak Mountains through Skeleton Canyon,[60] where there was only a horseback trail. When riding into the canyon from the west, I noticed buzzards circling over a spot about half a mile off the trail. Riding there to investigate, I saw a dead mule—pack saddle equipment still in place on his back.

For years, that old *apparaho,* made of rawhide and stuffed with straw, lay out in all kinds of weather. It became a landmark of a sort at the entrance of Skeleton Canyon. Nothing was left of the mule carcass but a few bleached bones, but the *apparaho* held intact until one day a prospector happened along. Out of curiosity he stopped and cut it open. Hidden in the now much-rotted straw he found one hundred and fifty Mexican silver dollars, or Dobe dollars, as commonly termed. Not a fortune, but a good grub stake for a prospector. Probably one hundred riders had passed that way before this little horde was found.

I knew at once that this must be part of a Mexican smuggling train, as this was a route they often took. And

(60) Skeleton Canyon winds through the most rugged part of the Peloncillo Mountains (which straddle the Arizona/New Mexico border northeast of Douglas) from the Animas Valley in New Mexico to the San Bernardino Valley in Arizona. Here it is alleged that, in 1882, Curly Bill Brocius and Old Man Clanton massacred a band of Mexican smugglers, killing about fifteen and leaving their bodies to be picked over by coyotes and buzzards. For many years, skeleton fragments remained scattered about, giving the canyon its macabre name.

Four years later, on September 4, 1886, Geronimo surrendered to General Nelson Miles at Skeleton Canyon.

Workers, *Arizona,* p. 376–77.
Trimble, *Roadside,* p. 83.
Wilson, p. 17.

because the mule had been shot, I guessed at once that it was the work of the rustlers.

About a mile further up the canyon was a dead horse by the trail, and this had a Mexican riding saddle on, easily distinguished by its big flat pommel. That told the tale of a running fight between rustlers and smugglers, the rustlers evidently having won.

I hurried on to the ranch. My brother had heard nothing of this and it made us quite uneasy, for we knew that if any Mexicans had escaped, they would get back across the line and would return in force to revenge the outrage.

And so it turned out. But little did we think that revenge would strike us and not the guilty rustlers who were probably well out of the way by this time.

I had planned to return to Tombstone to resume my work at the post office after a short lay-off, which had been given me so that I might help get our ranch started. My brother, however, begged me to remain at the ranch another week, as he wished to go to Tombstone and would return in that time. I consented and he rode off—to his death.

Often a trifling incident or change of plan leads to success or disaster. The day before brother Dick was to start, we heard that Lang's ranch, about ten miles southeast of us, was starting a hundred head of beef cattle for the Tombstone market and would camp in Guadalupe Canyon[61] the following night. It occurred to us that it would be best for Dick to go that route and camp that night with Lang's outfit, as they would have five or six men which was a big enough force, it seemed, to scare off any bunch of Mexicans who might be out to avenge the smuggler train disaster. If this had not come up, Dick would have gone the more direct route I had followed through Skeleton. But fate ruled otherwise, and Dick rode into a trap without a chance in the world to escape alive.

I saw him ride gaily off on a Friday, and on the following Sunday, August 12, 1881, I next saw his dead body in Guadalupe Canyon with a bullet hole over his heart. Our first news of the tragedy came to the ranch on Saturday evening. A man by the name of Harry Earnshaw staggered into our camp in an exhausted condition, and it was some little time before he could tell the story.

He said he was with Lang's outfit, had come out from Tombstone with the object of buying some milk cows, but not finding what he wanted, was returning with Lang's beef herd to Tombstone. They had driven the herd of one hundred steers into Guadalupe Canyon on Friday, the day before, and made camp in the first clear spot they found,

(61) Located in the extreme southeast corner of Arizona, and embracing a part of New Mexico and Mexico as well, Guadalupe Canyon was a favorite hideout of both Mexican and American cattle rustlers, smugglers, and other assorted outlaws during the 1870s and 1880s.

Barnes, p. 193.

which was near the rock–built monument that marks the four corners of Arizona, New Mexico, Sonora, and Chihuahua. It seems that during the night the herd stampeded and ran back up the canyon, and in rounding up the scattered herd some of the cowboys ran across my brother Dick, who had evidently been detained and had made camp alone.

On learning of the trouble with the herd, Dick had saddled up and helped them drive the beeves [sic] back to camp. It seemed that a chain of circumstances was leading him blindly on to his fate. Just before daylight, Charley Snow, a cowboy who was on herd, rode into camp and Earnshaw heard him tell the cook, old man Clanton, who was starting breakfast, that he felt sure a bear had frightened the cattle and he was going to circle around in the brush in the hope of getting a shot at it. This move of Snow's evidently started the trouble.

The Mexicans must have been concealed in the surrounding brush, and Snow probably rode right into them, for almost at once a volley of shots rang out, coming from all sides. Earnshaw had no gun and like most any tenderfoot in that position would have done, he just got up and ran. He did not know the direction he took, but just kept going with his boots in his hand. He did not see what happened to the others, except old man Clanton whom he saw fall face forward into the fire he had started for breakfast.

Our ranch was about fifteen miles from the place, and when Earnshaw staggered in about dusk, he must have gone many miles out of his way, as he said he had never paused in his flight except to stop a minute to pull on his boots. How he happened to find us must have been pure luck for he had never been there before.

There were only two of us at the ranch, as the house had been finished and the builders had returned some time before to Tombstone. So our only recourse for help was to go to a new mining camp on the east slope of the Animas Mountains called Gillespie,[62] twenty miles away.

I rode horseback there that night, finding twenty-five miners at the camp. They, to the last man, nobly responded to my appeal for help. All had horses or mules to ride, and in scarcely no time all were mounted and on the way back with me. We stopped at the ranch to get a wagon and team, loaded on the needed supplies, and pulled out for Guadalupe Canyon.

This was the rainy season and the ground was muddy in places, therefore it was just at sunrise when we got there. I will always remember what a quiet spot it seemed.

(62) Named after an early day settler, Gillespie is situated on Stockton Creek on the east side of the Peloncillo Mountains in Graham County, not far from the Clanton ranch.
Barnes, p. 178.

It was a clear, bright morning that dawned on that little valley in the hills of Guadalupe, but we knew at once that death was ruler there. The ghoulish-looking buzzards were in the tops of every tree with their wings outspread, probably to feel the warmth of the morning sun, and waiting for that sun to prepare their feast. Since then I never see a buzzard but that scene is recalled: such a fiendish-looking bird, depressing—but probably has the keenest eye of any—one that can discover death's victim almost immediately, and a bird that is the world's most vigilant undertaker.

Out of a clear sky a black speck appears and soon other black specks, coming nearer and nearer. Soon they are high overhead beginning to circle slowly, all following the same course in their circling round and round—and you know that somewhere within that circle on the earth below lies a corpse, be it man or animal. It cannot escape this detective.

And in that grassy glade, now so still and peaceful-looking, lay four human bodies, probably just at the spots they had been sleeping when the first fire of the attacking Mexicans had caught them. All were perfectly nude, having evidently been stripped of their clothing by the Mexicans. The only thing left of the camp outfit was the buckboard standing near the ashes of the campfire. It was probably left because it would have been almost impossible to take it over the mountain trail which the Mexicans had to travel in order to reach their homes.

The dead lying there were Billy Lang,[63] cattle rancher; Jim Crane, the outlaw (Crane being on his way in to surrender to the sheriff as we had talked him into doing); old man Clanton, the cook mentioned before; and my brother Dick, just turned nineteen.

There were still two of Lang's outfit missing and we spread out in search of them. We found the dead body of Charley Snow, the man who had told the cook he was going to look for the supposed bear. Evidently he had made a gallant fight as his body was riddled. He lay about a half mile from the camp.

The other cowboy, Billy Byers, we found alive some five miles away. He was shot through the front of the abdomen and the ball had gone clear through his body, but evidently not deep enough to penetrate an vital part, as he was walking along in a dazed condition, completely out of his head.

His wound was in a frightful condition from the heat and the flies, but some of our miner friends knew what to do, and they cleaned and dressed the wound. Billy soon

(63) Billy Lang remains an elusive figure. It is known, however, that he and his father, Will, operated a ranch that was used as a base of operations for cattle rustlers and horse thieves raiding in Mexico. It is not known if the Langs were a party to such activity.
Hilliard, p. 26.

revived enough to tell us something of what had happened. He said the first shots woke him up from a sound sleep and he raised up in his bed to see what was up, just then realizing he had been shot and fell back in a daze. He then remembered a dark man on horseback who was almost over him, and saw that this man was firing down at him with a pistol. How the man missed him Billy felt was a miracle, but evidently the sight of Billy's bloody clothes was convincing proof to the man that he was already dead, and too, it was perhaps that blood-stained clothing which kept the Mexicans from stripping his body—this latter fact keeping them from discovering that he was still alive.

With this wounded boy, all were present or accounted for. We had to bury Charley Snow where we found his body, as it was too far gone to be moved. The other four bodies and the wounded boy were placed in the wagon.

That quiet gathering of the dead cast a feeling of sadness over the bunch of hardy miners. They were accustomed to seeing many tragedies suffered in the lives of pioneers, but this seemed such an unjustifiable sacrifice. It was undoubtedly the work of escaped smugglers from the Skeleton Canyon fight taking revenge on the first Americans they found, and this, after all, was but one of the many tragedies that have occurred on the Mexican border.

We took our dead back to the ranch and in coffins constructed of lumber for which we tore up flooring, with the aid of our miner friends we buried the four bodies in a little square plot on the top of a nearby knoll, rendering an equal and honorable reverence to all. Jim Crane, the outlaw, had gone before a higher court and we were no more his judges.

This little *Campo Santo* on the lonely hilltop marked the end of our hopes for the Animas Valley ranch prospect. My father and I felt conditions were too hard at that time to fight against. We knew the valley would be a place exposed to Mexican raids and felt that it would be impossible to protect ourselves against them. We had the place surveyed, filed preemption claims on the land, and abandoned it for a time to the antelope, the coyote, and to those weird spirits supposed to be the cause for the name Animas given to that valley by the Mexicans.

Lang's cattle had been driven away and sold to close up his estate, and for the following year, I made a trip out from Tombstone every month to sleep one night at the ranch in order to comply with the preemption law. Even the rustlers kept out of the valley for fear of meeting the Mexicans.

ON ONE OF OUR TRIPS into the Animas Valley we saw a horseman at a distance, and with field glasses recognized him to be a rustler known as Russian Bill.[64] To see what he would do, we put our horses to a fast gallop to overtake him, and when in hailing distance, called out, "Mexicans are coming, Bill!" Bill didn't stop for further news but hastily cut loose a sack tied behind his saddle, put spurs to his horse and soon disappeared from our view in a cloud of dust. We rode on and picked up his sack which held quite a chunk of fresh beef. Bill had evidently found a stray animal lost from the Lang herd when moving out of the valley—and it served us for supper. We never saw Russian Bill again.

He claimed to have come to the United States as an attache of the Russian Legation at Washington, but if he had ever been anybody of importance he had long since degenerated into a trifling way of living. Even the other rustlers avoided him as being mean and cowardly, so Russian Bill had become a lone wanderer. He did not last long.

Only a short time after that he rode into the little mining camp of Shakespeare,[65] a few miles from Lordsburg. Tying his horse in front, he went into the general store and asked the clerk to lay out his entire stock of silk handkerchiefs. Bill picked out several of the louder colors, and seeing that the smooth-faced boy clerk was alone in the store, he pulled out his big Colt pistol and told the clerk to "charge it to Russian Bill."

But the tenderfoot clerk, probably knowing the ways of the rustler tribe, had a small pistol handy under the counter, and reaching underneath, he pulled this pistol out, quickly raised it to Bill's face and pulled the trigger. Poor Russian Bill dropped to the floor like a log.

Some miners, hearing the shot, rushed in from the outside to find Bill only creased in the neck, and they tied his hands and feet before he recovered consciousness. Calling together the few men in camp they held court over Russian Bill. The morning revealed all that was left of Bill, hanging by the neck from the limb of a nearby tree.[66]

EARLY IN THE SPRING OF 1882, father and I were returning from a trip to the Animas ranch with a team and buckboard, which meant that we had had to go around to the north of the Chiricahuas through Apache Pass[67] and Fort Bowie,[68] as that was the only wagon road. At Fort Bowie we were warned that the Indians were out. Loco[69] and his

(64) Russian Bill remains an enigmatic character. His claim to have been a Russian count and former officer of the Imperial Army have never been authenticated. That he was a rustler, however, appears a certainty.
    Myers, p. 86.

(65) Two-and-a-half miles south of Lordsburg, Shakespeare was known in the 1850s as Mexican Springs. In 1858, the Butterfield Overland Stage built a station here, and another was built in 1867 by the National Mail and Transportation Company, which changed the name to Grant. Later, the name was changed to Ralston, still later to Shakespeare. A post office was established in 1879, abandoned in 1885. Today, Shakespeare is a ghost town.
    Pearce, p. 154.

(66) Of the tales told about the demise of Russian Bill, Gray's is as plausible as any. Another version is that Bill, in the company of one Sandy King, stole some horses in or about Shakespeare, New Mexico. Caught, the men were lynched from the rafters of an eating establishment and left hanging while the executioners finished their meal.
    Myers, p. 226.

(67) Apache Pass was perhaps the most dangerous point on the immigrant trail to California. Separating the Dos Cabezas and Chiricahua mountains, it is a rugged, twisting defile, six miles in length that connects the Sulphur Springs and San Simon valleys. In July, 1858, the Butterfield Overland Mail Company opened a stage station in the pass. Attacks by Apaches were not uncommon and between 1861 and 1864, when Cochise ran unchecked, drivers were offered triple pay to make the run through the pass.
    Workers, *Arizona*, p. 436.
    Trimble, *Roadside*, p. 134.

(68) Named in honor of Colonel George Washington Bowie of the California Volunteers, Fort Bowie was established July 28, 1862, at the eastern entrance to Apache Pass. At nearby Bowie Peak (elevation 6,110 feet) was Arizona's busiest heliograph station. The fort's mission was to protect water supples, control access to Apache Pass (fourteen miles south), to provide escorts for couriers and supply trains, and to attack Apaches whenever the opportunity arose. Because of limited space, a new fort was constructed a half mile east in 1868. By the 1880s, Fort Bowie had become one of the most important military posts in the Southwest, as the army determined to subdue the Apaches. The fort was decommissioned on October 17, 1894, and fell to ruin. Its few remains have been designated a National Historic Site.
    Wilson, p. 95.
    Workers, *Arizona*, p. 437.
    Trimble, *Roadside*, p. 141.

(69) Born in the early 1820s, Loco—who lost an eye to a grizzly as a young man—was considered a peaceful man respected by both whites and Indians. He headed a group of Chihenne Apaches, as did his more militant contemporary, Victorio. Loco was a prominent figure of the 1870s and 1880s, and died in captivity at Fort Sill, Oklahoma in 1905.
    Sweeney, Edwin R. *Cochise: Chiricahua Apache Chief.* Norman: University of Oklahoma Press, 1995, p. 448.
    Thrapp, Dan L. *Conquest of Apacheria.* Norman: University of Oklahoma Press, 1967, p. 231–50.

(70) In 1871, as part of its "Apache policy," Congress appropriated seventy thousand dollars "to collect the Apache Indians of Arizona and New Mexico upon reservations . . . and to promote peace and civilization among them." The San Carlos Reservation was formally established west of Globe by executive order on December 14, 1872. Peace, however, was not readily gotten. During the next fourteen years, various bands of Apaches slipped on and off of the reservation on deadly raiding parties throughout southern Arizona and northern Mexico. Although reduced in acreage, San Carlos remains a reservation today.

Debo, Angie. *A History of the Indians of the United States.* Norman: University of Oklahoma Press, 1970, p. 270.

Debo, Angie. *Geronimo: The Man, His Time, His Place.* Norman: University of Oklahoma Press, 1976, p. 85.

(71) Born at Hinsdale, New Hampshire, January 10, 1828, Henry Clay Hooker followed the gold rush to California, arriving there in 1853 or 1854. For the next dozen years he operated a successful hardware business at Placerville. Uninsured, he lost everything when it burned to the ground shortly after the Civil War. In an effort to recover his financial losses, he purchased some 500 turkeys at $1.50 each and drove them overland to Carson City, Nevada where he sold them at $5.00 a head. He came to Arizona in 1866, as a government beef contractor, supplying army posts throughout the territory. In 1872, he established the Sierra Bonita Ranch, located some thirty miles north of Willcox in the Sulphur Springs Valley. By the mid 1870s, Hooker was running 11,000 cattle on his range. He became known throughout the territory for his purebred cattle, and his palatial ranch home became a gathering place for important visitors. He got on well with the Apaches and was seldom bothered by raiding parties. Hooker died in Los Angeles, December 5, 1907.

Sheridan, Thomas E. *Arizona: A History.* Tucson: University of Arizona Press, 1995, p. 130.

Trimble, *Arizona,* p. 161.

Clayton, Wallace E. "Arizona Cattle Empire: 300,000-Acre Sierra Bonita Ranch." *Tombstone Epitaph.* June, 1986.

Hooker, Mrs. Harry. "Five Generations of Hookers on the Sierra Bonita Ranch." *Arizona Cattlelog.* December, 1949, pp. 32–36.

Hill, Gertrude. "Henry Clay Hooker: King of the Sierra Bonita." *Arizoniana,* Vol. 2, No. 4 (Winter, 1961), pp. 12–15.

(72) Camp Grant (originally designated Fort Breakenridge) was established in 1859 on the San Pedro River at its junction with Arivaipa Creek, south of present-day Winkelman. Abandoned in 1861, it was re-established as Fort Standford in 1862 by the California Column. Renamed Camp Grant in 1866, in honor of General Ulysses S. Grant, the post was abandoned in October of that year due to unhealthy conditions. A new post was established December 19, 1872, at the foot of Mount Graham, some fifteen miles north of Willcox, and was commissioned a fort.

In his 1891 book, *On The Border With Crook,* John G. Bourke wrote from first hand knowledge that Fort Grant was "recognized from the tide-waters of the Hudson to those of the Columbia as the most thoroughly Godforsaken post of all those supposed to be included in the annual Congressional appropriations."

Its garrison was withdrawn in 1898 to participate in the Spanish-American War, and Fort Grant was abandoned in 1905. In 1912, the government gave the buildings to the state and a boys' reform school took up the site.

Barnes, p. 188.

Sheridan, p. 79.

Workers, *Arizona,* p. 436.

band had left San Carlos[70] and headed for Mexico. They had raided the Colonel Hooker[71] ranch near Camp Grant,[72] taken two hundred horses, and were then in the Dragoon Mountains.

Troops were in pursuit and, in fact, all the cavalry had left Bowie except a few men to guard the post. We were advised not to try crossing the Dragoons to Tombstone, but we were anxious to get home, as this was the first big outbreak in years and wild reports were afloat that the Indians might sack Tombstone.

Of course this was a wild exaggeration, but nobody seemed to know how many Apaches were out on the trail, except that their stealing two hundred horses from the Hooker ranch meant that they were in strong force.

AHS #44224

Henry Clay Hooker, legendary Arizona cattle baron.

We arrived near the south pass of the Dragoons a little before sundown. There was a cattle ranch here where a family had lived, and as soon as we caught sight of the ranch houses we hoped to see some of the children at play about the place, as had been their habit on our previous passings. But there was not a soul in sight. Just below the house were a couple of horses with their heads down but not grazing, and we could see they had been hurt. One was a white Indian pony with a pack on his back of what appeared to be a squaw's outfit. The other animal was a sleek sorrel cavalry horse. Both animals seemed to have a foreleg shot, as blood had clotted on them and their legs were hanging limp.

It was pitiful to see their apparent suffering. I was walking ahead of our team with rifle in hand for protection, and I surely felt shaky about advancing. Just then I would have given anything to see a ranch youngster running out to greet us. But not even a chicken or a dog was about the place, where previously there had always been so much life.

We knew though from the wounded horses that it must have been some hours since the Indians had been there, and that they must have gone on. So we pulled up the road through the pass that led to Tombstone. About a half mile up the canyon we passed the trail the Indians had

Fort Bowie, 1886. Headquarters for generals Crook and Miles.

AHS #25614

AHS #19484

Camp Grant, 1871.

taken. The ground was soft from the late rains, and they had made a trail that was pressed down nearly a foot below ground level, and in Indian style, they had evidently gone in single file to make such a deep trail.

There were all kinds of rumors afloat in Tombstone. Many were alarmed and had organized an armed force to keep out the Apaches.[73] But we knew from the direction of the trail in the pass that the Indians were hurrying to get away into the Sierra Madres. The troops never checked them, although they had quite a skirmish with them at South Pass, where the wounded horses were that morning.

This was but the beginning of those Indian raids from San Carlos which wrecked many a southern Arizona home and left a trail of many dead men's bones for ten long years or more afterward.

One had a chance with the rustlers, or even the border Mexicans, for their ways were very much in the open where you had an even break. But against the Apache you hadn't the ghost of a chance. Of all the American tribes, the Apache was undoubtedly the most difficult foe that our army ever encountered. You could never see him, unless possibly he was seen by his victims at the instant of a fatal shot striking them. He seemed uncanny in the way he could ambush his victims and then apparently fade away into the night, or into the landscape even in the daytime.

IN DECEMBER OF 1882, we ventured again into cattle raising. In going back and forth into the Animas Valley from Tombstone, we often crossed the Chiricahua Mountains by way of Camp Rucker,[74] then a United States Army post. On

(73) Never was there an Apache raid on Tombstone.

(74) Located in White River Canyon on the western side of the Chiricahua Mountains, Camp Rucker was established as Camp Supply, April 28, 1878, and for a brief time was called Camp Powers. The following July, the camp was devastated by raging flood waters, taking the life of Second Lieutenant John A. "Tony" Rucker, who drowned while attempting to rescue a fellow officer. The post was redesignated Camp John A. Rucker, December 9, 1878.

In 1880, an adobe hospital, commissary, and other buildings were erected, but Camp Rucker was largely a tent camp throughout its short existence. The camp was abandoned on November 22, 1880.

Wilson, pp. 114–20.
Barnes, p. 370.

one of our trips we learned the order had come from Washington to abandon the fort. That meant all the improvements would then be open to location of the first comer. So we were ready to take possession as soon as the troops left. This place was well equipped with several well-built adobe houses and a large barn. By purchasing from Norton and Stewart their sutler store building for one hundred and fifty dollars, our title was complete for the whole place.

When we started our ranch prospect at old Camp Rucker, the country thereabout was thickly covered with oak brush and all kinds of wild vines, which suggested an extreme fire hazard. Our father soon put a remedy into action, and that was our little herd of Angora goats.

Camp John A. Rucker, prior to its abandonment by the army.

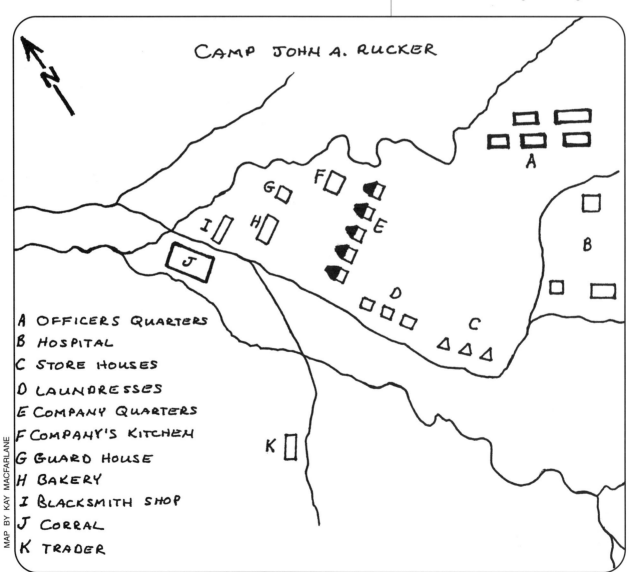

CAMP JOHN A. RUCKER

A OFFICERS QUARTERS
B HOSPITAL
C STORE HOUSES
D LAUNDRESSES
E COMPANY QUARTERS
F COMPANY'S KITCHEN
G GUARD HOUSE
H BAKERY
I BLACKSMITH SHOP
J CORRAL
K TRADER

MAP BY KAY MACFARLANE

We bought almost a dozen nanny goats of the common short-hair breed, and imported from a California breeder a thoroughbred Angora male goat, and this started our "fire warden" force. For years we kept our goat herd at about two hundred and fifty head and had about as fine a bunch of silky mohair as could be seen anywhere.

Training a few to come home to their stockade corral a night, we seldom had any trouble with the herd. We never had any loss by any wild animal raids, and all we had to do was shut the corral gates at night and open them the first thing in the morning. The goats always kept fat browsing within reach of the ranch. They grazed only on brush and willow bark, and were not grass eaters, so they were not a menace to the cattle in that respect.

There is quite a profit in the Angora goat business if they are properly cared for. The mohair sells generally for a much higher price than wool, and a young goat is as fine a piece of meat as one could wish to eat. Even when range for cattle became short and cattle were thin, our goats kept as fat as butter. Their forage was always plentiful. In the spring of the year the willow thickets along creek beds were their diet, and they would eat the bark and leave other feed. At any time of the year one could get a five gallon tin of purest tallow in butchering a six months old kid.

I'm sure one can't find any kind of domestic animal more adapted to the brushy country, nor one more self-sustaining and profitable than the Angora goat. Of course the mountain lion will play havoc with them, but I don't remember our ever losing a goat by a lion. The goats seemed to know their danger and kept up the habit of coming home at night to be locked up in their stockade pen. In the daytime they seemed able to stand off any enemy attack.

Hogs were also quite an asset, as they soon learned to forage in the neighboring woods. It was surprising how they flourished. Acorns, the wild black walnut which grew abundantly in the Arizona hills, and manzanite berries were a few of the native products which a hog hunted out for his dish. There was also the juniper berry, which often lay inches deep under a juniper tree. Even our horses grazed on juniper berries and I don't know of a feed more fattening, as these berries contained much sugar and starchy ingredients. In the spring when a juniper tree is in bloom, often on riding through the mountains we would suddenly see a puff of smoky air go up from some tree. It resembled very much the smoke signal used by the Apache which he makes to send word to his fellows. The puff was the escaped pollen from juniper blooms.

Of late years we read much about the disappearance of the wild pigeon which once filled our woods with vast flocks in the acorn season. In our early years at Rucker, these pigeons would come every fall. It seems hardly believable that they are seen no more. They are undoubtedly the same bird known as the passenger pigeon.

John Chisum, from whom the Grays purchased cattle.

MY FATHER BOUGHT us a start in cattle and my first cowboy initiation was driving this herd to the new ranch in December of 1882.

We purchased 334 head of mixed stock cattle from the historic old cattle king of Lincoln County, New Mexico, and it was probably almost his last transaction in cattle. He had staked one of his old-time cowboys to this herd to run on shares, and the death of this man—McKensie—had brought old John Chisum[75] out to Arizona to close out the ranch.

John was then a very old man; I think close to eighty, but was as straight as an Indian and seemed as keen of mind as in his younger days when he built up his vast herds on the Pecos River. But he had lost much of his property through the absconding of a trusted man.

I remember him on the day I met him when I went to receive our little herd of cows. The cowboys strung the cattle out across the field and the old man and I took stands on horseback where the herd would file along in between us. I noticed his method of counting. He placed a handful of pebbles in one coat pocket, and on each twenty head passing by he would transfer a pebble to the other pocket. It was simple. I doubt if old John would have been able to carry bigger numbers in his head, but it was said of him that he had never been known to make a mistake by his method, even when the count ran into the thousands.

Our tally that day was 334 head. I mention this to show how small an investment in those days was needed to make a start in business as compared with present times. That herd was bought for $20 per head, or a total of $6,680. That sum of money today would not buy any business of any consequence.

We moved out to the Rucker Ranch with the herd, and not only made our living from them, but at the end of three years we had more than seven hundred cattle carrying our brand, and were not a dollar in debt. This was accom-

(75) John S. Chisum—no relation to Jesse Chisholm for whom the trail was named—was perhaps the largest single cattle owner in the West. Born in Tennessee, Chisum (1824–1884) had scant education, but possessed an uncanny memory for numbers and prices. At age thirteen, his family moved to Texas. Thirty years later, with 10,000 head of cattle, he moved to New Mexico Territory. By 1873, an estimated 60,000 to 100,000 cattle carried his brand. Chisum played a role in the Lincoln County War and later helped elect as sheriff Pat Garrett, who killed Billy the Kid.

Monaghan, Jay, ed. *The Book of the American West.* NY: Bonanza Books, 1963, pp. 374–75.

plished with, at all times, at least eight people, not including a couple of hired men, to feed, besides the hospitality always extended to passing travelers.

Conditions in that part of Arizona in the early Eighties were ideal for good seasons of grass and water. When we turned the cattle loose on December 23, 1882, in Rucker Pass, snow almost four inches deep lay everywhere and it looked bad for the cattle, as they were thin in flesh and we had no hay to feed them. But there was plenty of brush and dry grass under the snow, and very few died that winter. And the next spring was among the best I ever knew in Arizona.

Over the divide in the east at the head of the San Simon Valley, is where most of the stock drifted. By the following May it was covered with wild flowers and green feed, with springs bubbling up in many places. The cattle thrived beyond all expectations in those early years of the Eighties, and market conditions were good. The main redeeming feature was the light overhead. In the years of good grass and water, a couple of men to a thousand head of range cattle was an ample labor force.

The southern Arizona cattle business commenced to grow by leaps and bounds. Everybody, it seemed, was flocking in with herds of cattle from Texas, from Mexico, and elsewhere, and the country finally got much overstocked. Then, along in the early Nineties, a succession of dry years came on and cattle perished by the thousands. Water disappeared where there was still some grass and grass disappeared in reach of the remaining water holes. Then the bottom dropped out of the cow business altogether.

Before the collapse, vast herds of feeder steers were shipped from Arizona every spring. I remember one spring the cattlemen of the San Simon Valley gathered and shipped in one herd, ten thousand steers that were loaded at San Simon station on twenty trains for Montana, all purchased by one buyer. As high as forty thousand head were shipped in one year at the Willcox station of the Southern Pacific.

Railroad Avenue, Willcox, 1880s.

It was unfortunate that big cattle companies invaded the country with their vast herds. They not only ruined the small cattle man, but in the end, ruined themselves. It was a nice business while the grass and water were plentiful, but when the drought came and nothing could be done to save the starving herds, it became a heart-breaking existence.

But even in good grass years it was not always a round of pleasure. There was always the Apache to think of. Many times we would hear that Indians were off the San Carlos reservation, and maybe the following week would come word of another Apache killing of some rancher or lonely prospector. I don't know why our ranch always escaped Apache raids, but I guess it was much a matter of luck. Once we had a close call but did not know our danger until afterward.

WE HAD AN OUTLYING cow camp in the head of the San Simon Valley about twelve miles east of Camp Rucker Ranch. One fall a fellow cowboy and myself had been putting up a stack of wild hay for winter horse feed, and on our last day of hauling in the hay we had brought a load to camp. Being late, we were tired and so we left the load on the wagon until the next morning. In moving camp from our hay ground we had put our camp outfit, as well as our guns, on the bottom of the wagon and loaded hay on top—a foolish, or rather thoughtless thing to do—but no Indian news for some time made us heedless to danger.

Early the next morning we saw a line of cavalry troops away off to the south, coming rapidly at a gallop towards our camp. Captain Lawton[76] was in command. As he rode up he seemed quite excited and said at once that he was very glad to find us alive, for they were following a fresh Indian trail that was heading for our camp. As he was telling us this, we noticed his Indian scouts had all gathered at a water hole about a hundred yards from our house, and they called to Captain Lawton. We walked over there and could plainly see signs on the wet bank made by the Apaches in kneeling down to drink.

Captain Lawton said that at least twenty renegades were in the bunch. He said it was probably our dog who had saved our lives. The dog barked a great deal, but we supposed he was barking at the coyotes, and anyhow, our guns were under the hay load. Lucky for us they were inaccessible or we would have gone gunning for a coyote and probably have been killed by an Indian.

Lawton hurried away on the Indian trail, saying he

Captain Henry W. Lawton, who later became a major general.

(76) Born March 7, 1843, near Toledo, Ohio, Henry Ware Lawton was a student at Methodist College in Fort Wayne, Indiana when he enlisted in the army April 18, 1861. He rose through the ranks from sergeant to first lieutenant., and was mustered out of the Civil War as a brevet lieutenant colonel. He re-entered the regular army July 28, 1866 and was promoted to captain, March 20, 1879.

Lawton arrived at Fort Huachuca June 21, 1884, and participated in the expedition from May through September, 1886, which culminated in the surrender of Geronimo. Lawton's command escorted Geronimo to Skeleton Canyon to meet General Nelson Miles.

As a major general of volunteers, Lawton was killed in the battle of San Mateo in the Philippines, December 19, 1899.

Altshuler, Constance Wynn. *Cavalry Yellow & Infantry Blue: Army Officers in Arizona Between 1851 and 1886.* Tucson: Arizona Historical Society, 1991, pp. 198–99.

(77) Born June 4, 1860, at Brownsville, Texas, Britton Davis was the son Edward J. Davis, Union brigadier general during the Civil War and later governor of Texas. A West Point graduate of 1881, Davis was assigned to Arizona Territory in the spring of 1882. After a few months at Fort Thomas, he was reassigned to the San Carlos Reservation where he lived among the Apaches. He and Lieutenant Emmet Crawford, acting Indian agent, wanted to teach stock raising to the Apaches, but the Indian Bureau wanted to make farmers of them—a notion at which the Apaches bridled. He was largely responsible for keeping the Indians on the reservation until the spring of 1885.

Davis resigned his commission, June 1, 1886. He persued mining and cattle interests in Mexico until the stirrings of revolution in 1911, then moved to New York state. In 1924 he settled in San Diego where he wrote *The Truth About Geronimo*, a book critical of General Nelson Miles. He died there January 23, 1930.

Altshuler, pp. 94–95.

(78) Nana, Loco, and Bonito were the first Apache leaders to start back to the San Carlos Reservation. They crossed the Mexican border with 49 men and 273 women and children. Other bands, including Geronimo's—which was comprised of fifteen or sixteen men, about seventy women and children, and some 350 head of cattle—came in later, and Davis was dispatched to the border to escort them.

Debo, *Geronimo*, pp. 188–89.
Debo, *History*, p. 277.

hoped to be in time to head off any killing, but he was only in time to bury a prospector found at a water hole ten miles down the valley. Then the Indian scouts lost the trail, a condition that often seemed to happen when a trail was rather hot. The captain warned us to be on the lookout for ourselves, as these renegade Indians were upon a raid for horses and would soon be headed back for the Sierra Madres.

And so it proved. They left their course marked by the dead men murdered en route. Lawton was no doubt an able officer and he realized the inability of the soldiers to run down the Apache; that there was no doubt of there often being collusion between the scouts and the hostile Indians.

After Geronimo's first flight from San Carlos, during which time he made his headquarters across the border in the high Sierra Madres, and from which numerous raids on American ranches and lives were made, he notified the authorities of his willingness to surrender if allowed to go back to the reservation and resume his old status there. A Lieutenant Davis[77] was sent to escort Geronimo in,[78] and our

This remarkable photo was taken by Camillus S. Fly, famed Tombstone photographer, when the Apaches were still at war with the United States. Nana sits on horse, Geronimo is just in front.

AHS #19749

first news was from Davis, notifying all the ranchers that Geronimo would pass through the country on his way back, and that he would have with him a herd of cattle and horses which no doubt were the result of his raids in Mexico and elsewhere.

Geronimo had agreed, according to Davis, to take his tribe back to San Carlos providing he was given immunity from punishment, and could keep all the livestock he and his bunch had accumulated. To this, Davis had agreed. Davis' troop was to travel a day's march ahead of the Indians to notify all ranchers and request that they not molest the Indians in any way. The bunch of Indians were on our ranch for about four days, first camped about a mile from our San Simon camp, and then moving on to Rucker Pass for a few days. We saw much of Geronimo and his warriors. He had about forty Indians with him, probably twenty-five warriors, and the balance squaws and children.

There was one curly-headed boy who looked strange among all the straight-haired boys. He undoubtedly was a captive child, but strange to say, he was more unapproachable than any of the other children. He would run off and hide whenever we went to their camp.

Geronimo was bringing in a good size herd of stock, about one hundred and fifty cattle and one hundred horses and mules. He was riding a fine saddle mule which we

US Indian Agency. San Carlos Apache Reservation, Arizona, date unknown.

AHS #44755

AHS #22247

Geronimo (right) at the time of his surrender in September, 1886. Taken by Tombstone photographer C.S. Fly.

(79) Monte is a game in which two cards are chosen from four laid out faceup. A player bets that one of the two will be matched in suit by the dealer before the other one.

(80) George Crook was born September 23, 1829, near Dayton Ohio, and graduated from West Point in 1852. He served in California, Oregon, and Washington state until the outbreak of the Civil War. He commanded the cavalry of the Army of the Potomac late in the war and was present at Lee's surrender at Appomattox. He returned west late in 1866, and built an enviable reputation as an Indian fighter. On June 2, 1871, he was named commander of the Department of Arizona. Historian Dan Thrapp calls Crook the "finest choice" that could have been made for this most difficult assignment.

Thrapp, Dan L. *Al Sieber: Chief of Scouts.* Norman: University of Oklahoma Press, 1964, p. 87.

tried to trade for or buy from him, but he would not part with it. I did buy, for a dollar a head, about twenty cattle that were fagged out. That was Geronimo's price mark.

At their camp, the Indians were inveterate gamblers, playing a Mexican card game called Monte,[79] and they used Mexican card decks. One of our cowboys tried to get in the game and, though the Indians were betting cows, he was allowed to put up one dollar against a cow. But he found the Indians too clever at that game and he lost several dollars before he was convinced.

In a couple of days the Indians moved over to Rucker, about twelve miles over the Chiricahua Mountains, and most of the time I rode alongside Geronimo on his mule. He would talk Mexican and apparently knew a few words in English. Geronimo was then probably about sixty years old and looked much like a stocky-built Mexican. He had with him some young Indian warriors who were as trim and fine specimens of the American Indian as it is possible to find.

Their cattle and horses of course had been stolen. Most of the cattle bore a brand of a big ranch in the Mexican state of Chihuahua, of which we knew. Later, I sent word of this to the ranch and they tried to get some compensation for their loss, but did not succeed. They were prohibited from seeing Geronimo's herd at San Carlos for fear of starting the Indians off the reservation again.

But it was not long until Geronimo was off again on the warpath, and he terrorized southern Arizona and northern Mexico for many months. General Crook[80] was then in command of the forces on his trail, and I was down on the line when he was camped at Silver Creek.[81] Geronimo was then with his band only a few miles distant, across the line in Sonora at the head of the Yaqui River.[82]

Geronimo had sent word to General Crook that he would surrender again on the usual terms of resuming his life as before at San Carlos with no penalty attached for his misdeeds. This was apparently all arranged satisfactorily, but trouble arose to break it all off. General Crook blamed it on a man who had taken whiskey to the border to sell to the large detail of Crook's own soldiers. The general claimed this man—one of the Tribolets[83] from Tombstone—had taken whiskey to Geronimo's camp.

The outcome was that Geronimo disappeared back into the Sierra Madres and General Crook was left holding the sack. This, they said, broke the general's heart and he asked to be relieved. Always before, his policy of dealing with the hostile Indians had been successful, but he had failed to reckon with the interference of John Barleycorn.

AHS #25624

General George Crook astride his mule "Apache."

AHS #34-19604

General Nelson A. Miles cuts a dashing image in full dress uniform.

(81) Silver Creek is a small stream flowing southeast from Arizona into Mexico. Here, on June 15, 1883, General Crook camped with some 300 Apaches in his charge. Writes Will Barnes, "This was doubtless after Crook's capture of Geronimo's band while enroute with them to San Carlos." According to Angie Debo, there were 325 captives in Crook's party, 52 men and 273 women and children. She, however, puts the date at June 10.
    Barnes, p. 407.
    Debo, *Geronimo*, pp. 189–91.

(82) The Yaqui meets the Rio de Bavisque in the Sierra Madre about 125 miles due south of present-day Douglas, Arizona in Sonora, Mexico. Geronimo had requested and been granted by Crook more time to gather his people together for their return to San Carlos.
    Debo, *Geronimo*, p. 188.

(83) Not only had Tribolet instituted a drunken debauch among the Apaches, he convinced Geronimo that plans had been made to hang him should he cross the border into Arizona Territory.
    Debo, *Geronimo*, p. 264.

Apache prisoner of war train en route to Florida, photographed at San Antonio, Texas. Naiche is in high boots front center, Geronimo sitting on his left.

AHS #19796

(84) Nelson Appleton Miles was born August 6, 1839 at Westminster, Massachusetts. Appointed a first lieutenant in the 22nd Massachusetts Infantry, September 9, 1861, he enjoyed a distinguished Civil War record and was mustered out a major general of volunteers, September 1, 1866. Almost simultaneously, he was appointed a colonel in the regular army. He married Mary Hoyt Sherman, niece of General William T. Sherman, June 30, 1868. Miles served largely in the West, and was credited with the capture of Chief Joseph of the Nez Perce in 1877. On December 15, 1880, he was promoted to brigadier general. He commanded the departments of the Columbia and the Missouri, and on April 12, 1886, assumed command of the Department of Arizona. The following September, Geronimo surrendered to Miles, effectively ending Arizona's Indian wars.

On September 29, 1895, Miles became Commander-in-Chief of the Army, a capacity in which he served until his retirement on August 8, 1903. He died in Washington, DC, May 15, 1925.

Wooster, Robert. *Nelson A. Miles & the Twilight of the Frontier Army.* Lincoln: Bison Books, 1996, pp. 1–5.

Altshuler, pp. 230–31.

(85) Variously spelled Natchez, Nachez, Naiche; the latter is most used by historians. Born about 1856, Naiche was the son of Cochise and his first principal wife (Cochise was a polygamist who had three wives), Dos-teh-seh. Like his father, whom he resembled, Naiche was a tall man—5' 11"—whose quiet reserve commanded respect. After the death of Cochise and his oldest son, Taza, Naiche became leader of the Chiricahua Apaches.

Thrapp, *Sieber,* p. 222.
Sweeney, pp. 142–43.
Debo, *Geronimo,* pp. 91, 101–02.

(86) Gray expedites relocation to Fort Sill by some eight years. Thinking they were to be returned to their ancestral lands, the vanquished Apaches were forced aboard trains and transported by a circuitous route to Fort Marion, Florida. Later, they were transferred to Fort Pickens, Florida; still later to Mount Vernon Barracks, Alabama. Not until October 10, 1894—almost a decade following surrender—was the much diminished band of Indians shipped to Fort Sill, Oklahoma.

Debo, *Geronimo,* pp. 296, 321, 334–34, 364.

There was some talk of prosecuting Tribolet, but nothing was ever done about it. And Geronimo's tribe raided the country as they willed until General Miles[84] finally induced him to surrender. Geronimo, Chief Natchez,[85] and his whole tribe were moved bodily to Fort Sill,[86] Oklahoma, so far from their home they did not know the way back.

When General Miles was given the Geronimo case to solve, he immediately started a vigorous campaign. Our Rucker ranch became a sort of headquarters. Just back of the ranch on a high peak was placed a heliograph station from which sun heliograph messages could be sent to all Arizona posts. The troops no longer had a lazy camp life but were kept busy, and messengers were coming and going at all hours. When the order to send daily riders on various errands came, it was amusing to us cowboys.

Cavalry horses had always traveled in company file and most all those old horses simply refused to leave the company. Soldiers would start off and ride but a short distance when their mounts would whinny and dash back to camp. In those days they did not train a cavalry soldier as they do now, and some had never ridden a horse out of company ranks, where one simply fell in behind another. It sometimes took a lot of effort to get a horse out of camp. Often a soldier would ask a cowboy for help, and the latter would have to use all his skill to break this unruly habit.

AHS #19818

However, General Miles had given the order and it was executed. The horses did not all stay as sleek and round as they had been before.

General Miles did not kill any Indians in his campaign, to speak of, but his energy in the field worried Geronimo, as he had to keep constantly moving, dodging the troops. He sent word that he was willing to surrender, and I believe Lieutenant Gatewood,[87] who could speak the Apache tongue, volunteered to go into Mexico and arrange a meeting with the Indians.

Anyhow, it was all fixed up and Skeleton Canyon, where it opens into the San Simon Valley, was the spot agreed upon to meet with General Miles. The evening before this treaty meeting, Miles came to the Rucker Ranch. The following day he rode in a four mule ambulance to Skeleton Canyon.

He asked at our ranch for a guide for the trip, and Bob Beale, who was stopping at the ranch, volunteered his services. The general's orders were to take a beeline, and this was regardless of the roughness of the country. So Bob followed these instructions strictly and he said he gave the general a ride he would remember. He ventured to say it was as rough a road as any government ambulance ever traveled. There was a sort of road across the San Simon Valley on which better time could have been made, but General Miles had said to follow a straight line and his orders were obeyed to the letter. But with all the rough jolting the general must have endured, he was game and he kept his mule team in a gallop much of the way.

Geronimo (left) and Naiche, at Fort Bowie following their surrender.

Naiche, son of Cochise, and his wife, Nah-de-yole.

(87) Born at Woodstock, Virginia, April 6, 1853, Charles Bare Gatewood graduated from West Point in 1877. As a second lieutenant, he came to Camp Apache, February 5, 1878. He spent much time in the field, and during Crooks campaign in the Sierra Madre, routed a group of hostile Apaches. Promoted to first lieutenant, January 3, 1885, serendipity brought Gatewood and Geronimo face to face in an encounter that resulted in Geronimo's final surrender. From October 10, 1886, to September 14, 1890, Gatewood served as an aide to General Nelson A. Miles. He died of cancer, May 20, 1896, at Fort Monroe, Virginia.
Altshuler, pp. 138–39.

Geronimo (left) surrenders to General Crook (right, in sun helmet). He would be on the warpath again soon.

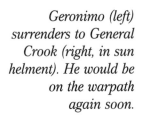

(88) Little of certainty is known about the Apache Kid. Historian Dan Williamson contends he was born in Aravaipa Canyon around 1860, was named Oska-ben-nan-telz, "terrible tempered," and was a member of Chiquito's band. Jess G. Hayes, claims he was born in a wickiup near present-day Globe in 1868, was named Haskay-bay-nay-ntayl, "the tall brave man destined to come to a mysterious end," and was the oldest of seven children. William Sparks says his name was Ski-be-nan-ted; C.L. Sonnichsen writes that it was Zenogolache, "the crazy one." To add even more confusion, on a well known photograph of Apache scouts, the Kid's name is given as Es-ki-bi-nadel.

What is known is that the Kid enlisted as an army scout, rose to the rank of sergeant, and held the trust of legendary scout Al Sieber. Then things went wrong. The Kid was accused of murdering a fellow Apache. While awaiting trial, he and other Apaches escaped from the guard house, and Al Sieber—caught in the middle of the mele—was shot and wounded. This did not sit well with Sieber. Captured, the Kid was tried for the orginal crime, convicted of murder and sentenced to be executed by firing squad. The sentence was reduced, however, and he was sent to Alcatraz. Later, it was ruled that civil courts had no jurisdiction in such matters, and the Kid was returned to the San Carlos Reservation where he was charged with assault with intent to commit murder in the shooting of Sieber. Convicted, the Kid was sentenced to serve seven years in the Yuma Territorial Prison. He did not, for he escaped en route. Never was he recaptured. Over the years a plethora of crimes were laid at his feet.

Williamson, Dan R. "Al Sieber, Famous Scout of the Southwest." *Arizona Historical Review*, Vol. 3, No. 4 (January, 1931), pp. 60–76.

Hayes, Jess G. *Apache Vengeance*. Albuquerque: University of New Mexico Press, 1954, pp. 1–5.

Sparks, William. *The Apache Kid, A Bear Fight and Other True Stories of the Old West*. Los Angeles: Skeleton Publishing Company, 1926, p. 10.

Sonnichsen, C.L. "The Apache Kid." *Around Here, The Southwest in Picture and Story*, Vol. 10, No. 1 (1952), pp. 61–62.

Thrapp, *Sieber*, pp. 320–41.

They arrived at the appointed meeting place long before mid-day. Geronimo and his chief, Natchez, were on hand and in a few minutes terms were agreed upon. Soon these two Indians were sitting in the ambulance with the general. A fresh team was attached and off they went at a fast gait down the San Simon Valley to the railroad, a ride of about fifty miles. I think the Indians assumed they were going back to San Carlos, but immediately upon their arrival at the railroad station they were put on a train awaiting them, and banished forever from their old haunts of pillage and destruction.

We all breathed a sigh of relief then, hoping this would end the Indian menace, but it proved a very short respite as the notorious "Kid" Apache[88] appeared and raised merry hell, as cowmen termed it, for another spell.

Lt. Charles Gatewood, who induced Geronimo to surrender.

The Apache Kid (center), with two other scouts.

AT THE OUTBREAK of the Kid, I was one day at a cattle roundup near the railroad at San Simon Station,[89] when the station agent there hunted me up and informed me that he had just overheard a message going over the wires to the Associated Press that a Mr. Hardy of Toronto, Canada had been killed by Indians near the Rucker Ranch in the Chiricahua Mountains. No further particulars were given and I could not understand it, as I knew of no man of that name being at the ranch.

Being much worried over this news and, because of the distance, having no quick way of investigating, I dropped everything and started for home. It was about a sixty mile trip, but I made it on horseback that night. Here is the rather strange sequence of circumstances which I learned:

It seems that my mother had received a letter sometime previously from a Doctor Haynes of Los Angeles, in which he had inquired if she could accommodate himself and a Mr. Hardy, an invalid lawyer of Toronto, for a short time. He hoped the dry, high air at Rucker would improve the health of Mr. Hardy, then threatened with lung trouble. To this my mother had given her consent, and they came to the ranch just two days before the killing. My mother said they had rested at the ranch house their first two days and on the third morning rode off up the canyon on a couple of gentle ranch ponies, taking one rifle along in case they saw deer or other game.

Now for the balance of the story as told by Dr. Haynes: They followed an old road for several miles that led to

(89) Located on the San Simon River some thirteen miles west of the New Mexico border, a post office was established here March 16, 1881.
Barnes, p. 386.

an abandoned sawmill. Finding nothing to shoot at in the way of game, they ate a lunch put up for them by Mother. Then they turned homeward and had reached a point about two miles from the ranch. Mr. Hardy was riding in front and had the rifle tied on top of his coat, just behind the saddle—which seemed to me to be the most fatal thing to do in case of any trouble.

Just where the old mill road approached the rather steep bank of the creek, a shot rang out and Dr. Haynes saw his friend topple out of the saddle. He jumped off his horse and started toward the fallen man, at the same time calling out, "You have made a mistake," evidently thinking the shot came from someone who had mistaken Hardy for a deer.

Just then the Indians jumped out from behind the creek bank and Dr. Haynes, suddenly realizing the situation, broke for the brush on foot. As he ran, he looked back and saw some of the Indians following him. Why he wasn't killed is a mystery, but in his running he found that his field glasses, hung by a strap over his shoulders, were checking his flight, so he threw them off. This probably saved his life, as the Apache values the field glass very highly.

Soon Dr. Haynes overtook his saddle horse, which was headed back for the ranch, where he arrived much exhausted. That was about the whole story. Mr. Hardy's body was recovered. The horse he had ridden was lying dead close by. Hardy's gold chain and watch were missing, and the former in time solved the puzzle.

The killing of Hardy almost became an international incident. His sister in Canada brought the matter up with her government, and our government at Washington detailed an army officer to investigate. Mr. Hardy's sister raised the point that our family, according to testimony, had lived at Rucker Ranch over ten years, and in all that time Indians had not raided or killed any of us, while on the other hand, her brother was there but two days when he met his death.

No doubt the Indians had been watching Dr. Haynes and Mr. Hardy, and knew from their movements and the way the rifle was safely tied behind the saddle where it could not quickly be used, that these two men would not be able to make any defense. Whereas they knew that we cowboys always had our guns ready for any emergency. Also, in answer to the query from Mr. Hardy's sister as to why we ranchers had always escaped Apache raids, I think an incident that happened long before the "Kid's rampage" might be an explanation.[90]

(90) The name is variously spelled Harding, Hardie, Hardy. The killing of Robert Hardy, which occurred in May, 1890, was but one of many depredations linked to the Apache Kid. Say-es, who escaped with the Kid en route to the Yuma Territorial Prison, is thought to have been the killer. It is written, however, that the Tombstone doctor who examined the body reported that Hardy was not killed by Indians—a conclusion drawn on the fact that the body had not been mutilated.

Wilson, p. 128.

De La Garza, Phyllis. *The Apache Kid.* Tucson: Westernlore Press, 1995, p. 111.

EVEN WITH ALL THE CRUELTIES of the Apache in his long war against the white man, I still believe he has an inborn sense of justice and does not forget a kindness ever done him. In the early campaigns against Geronimo, the army had among its scouts a half-breed Indian who went by the name of Mickey Free.[91] Evidently, the first name disclosed his Irish paternity. Mickey Free spoke broken English and was nominally leader of his scout troop.

He came to our ranch a number of times with his troop, and I remember that my mother always had some little treat to give Mickey for his scouts—such as a batch of doughnuts or cookies, or even jerky, the sun-dried meat of which Apaches were fond.

Anyhow, Mickey Free told mother she need never worry, that the Apaches would never raid our ranch—trying to tell her in this way, probably, that he appreciated her kindness. The story of Mickey Free, I believe, later revealed

(91) Not unlike the Apache Kid, the body of folklore enveloping Mickey Free makes difficult the task of separating fact from fancy. Apparently half-Irish, half-Mexican, Free disappeared from a ranch west of the Chiricahua Mountains when he was about twelve-years-old, and given to the White Mountain Apaches. In late January, 1861, Second Lieutenant George N. Bascom left Fort Buchanan with fifty-four men en route to Apache Pass where it was thought the boy was held. Unaware, Cochise, his wife and son, brother, and two nephews parlayed with Bascom inside an army tent. The brash lieutenant demanded the boy. Cochise truthfully denied any knowledge of the affair, and promised to find him if possible. Bascom thought the chief was lying and said he would hold him hostage until the boy was returned. Cochise drew his knife, slashed the wall of the tent, and escaped. Bascom made prisoners of the other Indians.

This most unfortunate affair concluded when Cochise killed three hostages taken from a nearby stage station; Bascom hanged Cochise's brother and two nephews. His wife and son were taken to Fort Buchanan and released.

Some years later the captive was inadvertantly freed—and thus the name, Free—when soldiers attacked a hostile Apache camp. The name Mickey was probably given him for his red hair and Irish countenance. Fluent in Apache, he spoke Spanish and knew enough English to sign on as an interpreter at the San Carlos Reservation, December 4, 1874. His salary was $125 a month.

For many years, Free worked for the army as interpreter and scout.

Thrapp, *Sieber*, p. 185.
Debo, *History*, p. 164.
Debo, *Geronimo*, pp. 62–63.

AHS #34-19581

(92) Born September 6, 1844 in Philadelphia, Emmet Crawford enlisted in the 71st Pennsylvania Infantry May 28, 1861, serving as a lieutenant in both the 13th and the 37th US Colored Infantry. Mustered out May 19, 1867, he became a second lieutenant in the regular army, January 22, 1867, and was promoted to first lieutenant June 5, 1868. He first saw duty in Arizona Territory at Camp Verde, where he arrived February 15, 1871. The following December, however, his regiment was reassigned to the Department of the Platt, where it saw action against the Sioux in the Big Horn and Yellowstone campaigns.

Promoted to captain March 20, 1879, Crawford returned to Arizona in 1882, and was stationed at Fort Thomas. In 1883, he followed Crook into the Sierra Madre, then served as the military superintendent of the San Carlos Reservation. In late 1885, Crawford was back in the Sierra Madre. By January he and his Apache scouts had found Geronimo, who promised to surrender the following day. But Crawford's days were numbered. On January 11, 1886, his command was fired upon by Mexican irregulars. Mortally wounded, Crawford died January 18.

Altshuler, p. 84.

Captain Emmet Crawford, who figured prominently in the Apache campaigns.

that he was implicated in the killing of Captain Crawford[92] by one of his scouts and that he had deserted to join the hostile Indians. At all events, I believe Mickey Free kept his word with us. And I think that we were the only ranchers ever to have an Apache come in to surrender.

Early one morning at the old Rucker Ranch we caught sight of a white rag "flag" moving back and forth on the end of a long pole, maybe a half-mile away. Wondering what it might mean, we hurriedly waved a similar white signal in answer. Soon we could see a string of horsemen coming toward us. It proved to be a couple of Apache squaws, several children, and an old, gray-haired Indian man on their ponies.

They all held up their hands and the squaws called out, "Biskit, biskit." Evidently they were hungry and mother brought out a good supply of cooked meat and bread. The Indians got off their ponies and sat on the ground, apparently enjoying the meal. All we managed to make out was that they were Apache and wanted to go to San Carlos. Keeping up with Geronimo was evidently too much for them and he had probably sent them back to the reservation, hunger then bringing them to our place. They seemed much pleased that we did not intend to detain them, but on the other hand, loaded them up with cooked bread and meat for the balance of their trip. We learned afterward that no other ranchers had had a call from them, nor did any of the other ranchers see them, and we learned that this little bunch had surrendered at San Carlos.

The mystery of the Hardy killing was soon cleared up. One of the companions of the Kid returned to San Carlos, and he was carrying Hardy's gold watch chain. That was conclusive proof of the Kid's party doing the killing. The watch was never recovered.

The story of the Kid's life might well fit into the old dime novel thrillers. He and several other Apaches had been sentenced by the court to the Yuma Penitentiary, and Sheriff Reynolds[93] had started with a deputy to escort them there. As the story goes, they had to make a stage ride to reach the railroad and at one point was a long hill to go up. At the driver's request they were walking behind the stage, as it was enough for the horses to do to pull the empty stage up the steep incline.

According to the word of the driver, who escaped, though wounded, the Indians were handcuffed in bunches of twos, the deputy in front and Sheriff Reynolds at the end of the line. Evidently the Indians, at a prearranged moment, knocked down the two officers, probably using the handcuffs as weapons, took their guns and killed both, and then, fired at the driver, who managed to get away. That was the start of the Kid's outing on the warpath. And no doubt the killing of Hardy was their work on their way to the Sierra Madres in Mexico where the hostile Indians always made for in their breaks.

A few months later, we lost a couple of saddle horses from our horse camp in the San Simon in a mysterious way, and the solution of this came out months afterward.

A troop of cavalry came into Rucker one evening and a few Indian scouts were along, also an Indian squaw riding a pretty yellow horse—what Mexicans term a palomino. As they filed by our front gate I recognized the palomino as one of our lost horses and told the commanding officer of this. He seemed to doubt my claim at first, but when I showed him my brand on the horse's left thigh, he acknowledged my just claim. He explained that this squaw had been a companion of the Kid, had escaped from him and had gotten back to San Carlos. He was bringing her back over the Kid's route in hopes she could lead them to the renegade's present whereabouts.

I got my horse back, but the poor squaw almost had a fit about it. Indians are always partial to a yellow horse, and she was, no doubt, quite attached to this one. The other horse was never recovered.

From the squaw we found out that she was with the Kid and they had caught the horses by hiding behind a water trough to which the horses had come to drink.

The Kid must have died unknown, as time went on and, at last, the death toll from the Apache stopped for good. But he had left his death mark far and wide.

(93) As sheriff of Gila County, Glenn Reynolds was charged with transporting the prisoners from the county jail at Globe to Casa Grande, where the following day they would catch the 4:00 p.m. train for Yuma. Al Sieber had offered him an escort of Apache scouts, but Reynolds turned it down in favor of a lone deputy, W.A. "Hunkydory" Holmes. The third man in the party was stagecoach driver Gene Middleton. Thrapp, *Sieber*, pp. 337–38.

COMING HOME with our stray herd from a roundup down the San Simon, we two cowboys had planned to camp that night at the San Simon Company horse ranch. About a week before, Jud White, whom we called Comanche as he hailed from that named county in Texas—had been sent to look after the horse ranch, and we figured on having supper with him. But we found poor Comanche shot to death a short distance from the camp. Evidently he had walked to the spot probably early in the morning to get his stake horse, and the Indians were laying in wait for him.

We turned our stray herd loose and rode hastily back to the roundup wagon. All hands came back with us to bury poor Comanche where he had fallen. He was a thoroughly good lad and brave as they make them, but he had had no chance to defend himself. We missed him deeply.

Often I have heard it commented on by strangers to those times, that a little handful of Indians so terrorized the country that they killed first and last many times their own numbers, but were themselves seldom or ever minus one of their number after the fray.

To me it seems a sufficient answer to this to state that General Miles had over two thousand trained troops in the field for many months before Geronimo's surrender to him; his surrender being probably because the Indians had become worn out from being kept on the move, and also because Geronimo was quite an old man.

In many years on the Arizona range I can truthfully say that I never saw an Indian while on the warpath. I have been close enough to find fresh killed beeves [sic] still warm that Indians had shot down—beeves with just a small chunk of meat cut out. And I have run onto their abandoned horses still wet with sweat and trembling from a hard ride—but the Indian was nowhere to be seen.

The Indian had developed the knack of hiding to a higher proficiency than probably any other human being, and the Apache was better at it than any other tribe of Indians. This art, you might call it, was their chief asset, for the Apache is not a good horseman. When in a hurry he will always go afoot, and there is no doubt whatever that renegade Apaches have left the San Carlos reservation and crossed the Mexican line the same day—and that is one hundred miles as straight as you can go.

In going any place, a straight line was what they followed, even if a mountain happened to be in the line. Probably, too, they sought high points to give them a good view. In this way they could get ahead of, and ambush the lonely rider. That was perhaps what was done in the instance of the Hardy killing, for we found evidence of the Indians having crouched down behind the creek bed just below where the trail passed.

It was always wise, if one had to cross a mountain or brushy country alone, to avoid the trails. In doing so, the Indian cannot anticipate your whereabouts and so cannot lay for you in advance. And, too, it was always safer to go by night as the Apache never attacked after dark. His favorite time was just at dusk or at break of day. He feared a conflict as much an anyone and he aimed always to have the drop on the victim. Knowing his nature, we always observed these precautions, and we had a good dog generally at camp or on our trips.

MANY A LIFE IS INDEBTED to the dogs of Arizona in the Indian days, for Indians were not only afraid of the dog's attack, but they could not creep up on their victims without arousing the dog, who would bark.

A cowboy also depends on his horse as a lookout. A horse's keen scent and hearing will always detect the near presence of an animal or man. I think that if either Mr. Hardy or Dr. Haynes had been as familiar with horses as we had learned to be, they would have been warned of the presence of the Indians in time to escape. Their horses must have shown, by the pricking up of their ears or some movement of the head, that something unusual was nearby.

One of my first experiences in our Animas Valley venture showed the value of a good dog. Sometime before, in Tombstone, I had been given a so-called bloodhound which had followed a horseman across the Arizona desert all the way from Bodie, California. This hound was only about a year old but weighed fully eighty pounds. Having no home for him, the owner had turned him over to me to keep for him, but at the same time said he would probably never come back for him. At all events, I kept him about the post office where I worked, and whenever I rode to the New Mexico ranch I would let him follow. I always felt safe with old Pard lying on the foot of my blankets at night.

Early in our house-building, I rode into the mountains at the south end of Animas Valley one day in search of some cedar suitable for make *vigas,* the Spanish name for house rafters. As our roof was to be made according to the Mexican style—a layer of dry grass on willow twigs, topped with a layer of mud, and that covered with small gravel—it would require substantial poles for rafters to hold up such weight, and they had to be long enough to extend from wall to opposite wall of the house and hang over several feet on each side.

I was riding down an old trail into Bonita Canyon in the Sierra Madres. It was quite a charming place—so fresh-looking in its greenery, with a clear little creek. The dog, Pard, always kept just ahead of my horse. I noticed that he seemed uneasy. His hair was bristled up on his back and he gave out an occasional low growl. I pulled up my horse and looked high and low to see if I could discover the cause of Pard's actions. Suddenly my horse raised his head, and his ears bent forward. I caught sight then of a string of horse-men away off on my left on the side of the mountain, but so far away I could not make out if they were Indian, Mexican, or white.

Anyway, it was suspicious enough for me, and I spoke to Pard, saying, "Let's go home, Pard." A dog may not understand much, but old Pard was surely pleased. He wagged his tail and showed his pleasure in every manner that we were turning back—and we didn't let any grass grow under our feet, either.

Why, I never knew, but our dogs always hated the Apaches. Often when a troop arrived with scouts at our ranch or outside our camps, we would have to tie up the dogs or they would attack the Indian scouts. Possibly the reservation Indian may have had dogs, but the Apaches when on the warpath were never known to have any, and if they did run into dogs on their raids they always tried to kill them.

Apache Scouts.

AHS #19765

Once we left our dog, Don, a good-sized black shepherd, at our horse camp on the San Simon while a couple of us went off on a short cow hunt. A delay of some sort happened to us on the way back. Anyhow, I came alone and rode up to the camp a little uneasy, fearing poor Don was almost starved. There was always water there for the horse herd, but it had been almost a week since we had ridden off leaving some food out for the dog. After alighting from my horse at the cabin and seeing nothing of Don, who would ordinarily have been barking a welcome, I whistled some time for him and had about given up, when I saw him slowly dragging himself from the back of the house. He looked so used up—pieces of skin seemed torn off, and his eyes were bloodshot.

At first, I feared he had gone mad and I kept backing away as he came toward me, until I got to an old wagon we had left in front of the camp. I jumped up into the wagon bed so I would be safe. But reaching over and talking to old Don, now wagging his tail, I knew he wouldn't harm me.

I heated some water and washed off his head, finding that he had a fearful wound. Evidently a gunshot had torn off part of his jaw and all the teeth on one side. Luckily his tongue was all right. I found a pan of sour milk which he lapped up. We never expected we could save his life and would have ended it for him, but none of us had the heart to shoot the poor dog. He got well and lived several years, but we always had to make his meals of milk or chopped meat as the teeth that were left were all on the lower jaw.

We knew this must have been the work of Indians. When I recovered my palomino horse from the Kid's squaw, she told me the dog jumped at them as they were stealing the horses and that the Kid shot him through the head. So Don became our hero; the only survivor I ever knew of an Indian fight in our part of Arizona.

IN THE EARLY YEARS of our ranch life, deer were plentiful in the mountains, as were antelope in the valleys. And during our first winter, 1882–83, at Rucker, we depended altogether for meat on the wild game, as the cattle were too thin for butchering. It was no trick at all to get a deer when one was needed.

We had no game laws to observe in those days, but whenever a choice was open we would shoot the buck instead of the doe. Hunting was always our main sport and whenever conditions were too bad for outdoor work or riding after cattle, it was seldom too stormy for a deer hunt. Even when the snow was pretty heavy, as it got at times in the mountains, we would wrap gunnysacks about our feet for a substitute snowshoe, and strike out. It was always easier to stalk a deer track if it was fresh in the snow.

Often I have been asked if it were not a lonesome life on a cattle ranch. I never found it so. In the first place, it was always a busy life if one would do half the work in sight, for there were always chances for improvement to be seen requiring work. I don't remember ever finding time hanging heavily on my hands. For recreation, there were always the horses and the guns.

IN THE SPRING AND FALL came roundup times, which were always interesting occasions. Thirty or forty cowboys with six or seven horses apiece, a good wagon and good cook—that is a combination that can do more hard work and get along better together than any like assembly you could find. It was more like an outing than labor, but it was of that coordinate nature when all worked in harmony to produce a specific result.

A sample of the opposite kind of operation is the story of how a railroad contractor tried to operate a cow ranch. I think his name was Hanson, and he had invested in an Arizona cow ranch, already stocked.

It seems Hanson had to suspend his railroad work for a time. In order to keep his crew with him, he took them out to his ranch to round up and brand his calves. He had hired a cowboy to go along and help. At the ranch he gave them all mounts and they started out. As they came to a cow or a calf, he would detail a man to take it to the corral. In a short time all were in pursuit of separate cows and calves—that is, all except the cowboy, who was asked by Hanson why he didn't work, as he was hired for that purpose. The cowboy said he would have to quit, as he didn't know that way of handling cattle.

Everywhere you looked you could see men chasing a cow, but none could succeed in putting them in the corral, so Hanson came back to the cowboy, who was watching the proceeding, and asked him to take hold and boss the operation. This the cowboy did, soon having all the cows and calves in one herd. Then all hands easily drove them together into the corral where they were branded without further trouble.

The horse was the mainstay of the cattle business. We always took more pride in our saddle horse herd than even in improving the grade of our cattle. But with many

Montana buyers coming in for feeders, and their almost universal preference for white faces, nearly all the southern Arizona cattlemen bought graded Hereford sires for their herds. Rather strange, too, that as soon as cattle began to range about every water hole, the old-time rustler fortunately began to disappear.

This was a belated answer to President Arthur's proclamation, which at one time was tacked up at every post office in the Southwest. To the good citizens of Arizona it was a rather amusing document, as it stated a condition referring to a "lawless element wandering over the country in large bands," commanding them to "immediately disperse and go their respective ways to peaceful occupations."[94]

In the first place, it is hardly possible that the total number of rustlers ever exceed one hundred in southern Arizona and New Mexico. That could hardly be termed much of a menace to the peace of a country.

The rustlers were not wholly a bad set. They were mostly young men and boys hardly out of their teens, who fell into this life in search of adventure. In the early days they would be frequent callers at our ranch, mainly, I suppose, to get a square meal. I never knew them to steal from us except on one occasion.

About a dozen rustlers once rode up about midday. I asked them to dismount, saying we would soon have dinner for them. I was helping our cook to throw a meal together and could not very well keep an eye on them. But the old cook happened to glance their way and reported to me that one fellow was taking the cartridges from my belt, which I had left on my saddle lying on the ground.

At once, I walked out unarmed, and to Billy Leonard, who was called the captain, I reported the cook's story, adding that I could not stand for that—that they were welcome to all the food we had, but I must have the cartridges back. Leonard asked me who the man was and I pointed him out. He at once ordered the return of every cartridge, and told his men he would not stand for any such raids on our camp. I give them credit for never, at any time, repeating this attempt. Probably, if I had picked up a gun and demanded the return of the cartridges, I would have provoked a gunfight and neither old Moody or myself would have been left alive to tell the tale.

"That's the fellow who feeds all the rustlers," was a remark I overheard on a trip to Lordsburg for supplies. It was a suggestion, if nothing else, that we might be profiting by such a process. But there were no two ways about it. Either we had to be hospitable to all travelers alike or

(94) See Appendix G.

they would soon give a ranch the bad name of turning the hungry wayfarer away from its door. And that would be but the beginning of the end.

In a settled and law-abiding community you might get by with a so-called lofty stand of virtue, and declare your house was your castle, turning a deaf ear to any undesirable and ask him to move on. But on our southern Arizona frontier in those pioneer times, if you hoped to survive you had to be a good neighbor to all. Otherwise your only salvation would be to make a getaway, and be quick about it.

Your livestock, and in fact, all your possessions were at the mercy of any enemy, and your one and probably only sure protection was your reputation for fair dealing with your fellow man, and your willingness to play the good neighbor role. In short, in no land is a good reputation so bullet proof as it was on the frontier in our pioneer days. Rarely, if ever, did the good neighbor role lead to disaster.

Among the rustlers were undoubtedly some pretty tough characters—men who knew crime as a business. Being sought in other states, they had drifted to the Southwest frontier as their last refuge. But such men most always had a strain of honor in their heart, which placed them several notches ahead of our present day criminals. For one thing, they would not kill an unarmed person, as so often occurs in our so-called civilized world of today. Nor would they rob the hand that fed them. In short, the rustler was much of a gentleman even when playing the role of a Robin Hood.

And because of these facts, we found it always a wise policy never to carry firearms when at the home ranch, and to always request visitors to leave their pistols or rifles with their saddles.

Gradually, the rustler disappeared. Some met untimely ends, but most of them left for other parts or went to work and behaved themselves. A few hunted trouble, and finding it, met their death with their boots on, as they deserved. One of these was "Shoot-'em-up" Dick.

In Pinery Canyon on the west slope of the Chiricahuas, lived old Major Downing, then past seventy. One morning he missed his pair of work mules out of his barn. The old major was alone at the time, but getting his rifle he struck out afoot to trail them up. He found the trail leading up into the canyon and the high mountains, also a horse-track— evidence that they were being led off by a horse thief. The old major, a tall figure of military bearing, modestly and briefly told his story the next day to the sheriff in Tombstone. Here it is as he stated it:

He followed the trail for several miles and at last caught up to his mules tied to a tree. Nearby lay "Shoot-'em-up" Dick, sound asleep. The major first took possession of Dick's guns, awakened him, then meted out swift sentence to his prisoner.

The sheriff followed Major Downing back to the scene of the execution of his sentence, and found as he had represented, the corpse hanging to a limb of a tree. The sheriff's posse buried Dick on the spot. The major was generally commended for ridding the country of an objectionable character, and no arrest was ever made by the authorities.

Curly Bill, the most noted of the rustlers, disappeared just before the Earps quit Tombstone and his end is still a mystery. A prominent early day cattleman had offered a reward of one thousand dollars for Curly Bill—dead—and it was supposed someone, either the Earp party or another enemy, earned this reward.

The following is a passage quoted from a late book about Arizona:

"In 1863 Arizona was admitted to the territorial government, and from that time until about 1886 followed one of the worst periods of American border history, filled with prolonged Indian wars and the outrages of the heterogeneous elements—cattle thieves, Sonoran cowboys, miners and adventurers which then made up most of its population. It was during that period that the famous Apache chief Geronimo made his last stand."

That is the wrong view to hold against the people of Arizona and is apt to leave a wrong impression. As a rule, the pioneer miners and cattle ranchers of southern Arizona were men of good character and much courage, or they would not have survived the many hardships of this God-forsaken country—as many have termed it, and on the other hand, their lives were far from always being a struggle. With good grass years when water was plentiful, a cattle rancher had an almost ideal life. The stock took care of themselves, and to ride the range seeing contented, sleek cattle and horses bearing your brand, with the calf-life coming in the spring like government coupons, nothing seemed wanting to make a perfect day.

However, there came another day: a time of drought when starving cattle walked the range in vain search for food or water, and at last lay down to die at the few water holes left.

THE WINTER OF 1891–92, was very dry and cold. Early in '92, the water in the San Simon failed completely in the many little *cienagas* that had formerly watered the stock, so we had to start early in the season to drive cattle into the mountain canyons for water. I think it was in May of that year that we drove about five hundred head of our strongest cattle far up White Water Canyon,[95] where the creek was still running. Every morning a couple of us would ride out to turn back any stock that had tried to drift back to the old range, for it is a persistent trait of an old range cow to drift back to her old haunts even if dry and bare. She will leave good grass and water to do so, if not headed back by the cowboy.

It was on one of these mornings when two of us had turned the cattle well up White Water Canyon, that we had dismounted and sat down on the creek bank for a short rest. The day was quite hot and the air seemed very still. It must have been about noontime. I was startled by a strange noise which seemed to come from away up the canyon to our north, just like the fluttering noise that is made by a flock of birds in the air.

At once, we looked up the canyon but could see no birds to make such a noise, so it struck me that it might mean an earthquake. Then, almost instantly, the noise became deafening. First, it looked as though the top of a mountain peak away to the north had fallen off, then a great cloud of dust and smoke appeared there. Almost immediately, the nearer peaks acted the same and rocks were rolling off the hills on all sides. We tried to get on our horses but the ground rocked so we couldn't stand up and the frightened horses jerked away, disappearing into the black fog of smoky dust that now surrounded us, making it as dark as pitch.

It was an alarming experience to be suddenly enveloped by darkness. The rocks, in falling off the peaks, had set many fires, and mingling with the dust raised as a natural consequence of the falling debris, all was as dark as night.

We had left my mother at the ranch house that morning and our first thought was of her danger. We struck out as fast as we could foot it in the dark for our ranch, and it was surely a relief when we found everything all right there. The house had stood up under the quake, only a small crack appearing in one wall. My mother said she was out in the yard at the time, and safe. We found our saddle horses at the barn door awaiting us to be let inside.

It was about the third day thereafter that the air cleared up enough to allow one to find his way about as

(95) Located on the western side of the Chiricahua Mountains some twenty miles from Tombstone and variously called White River Canyon, the site was used as a camping place by soldiers in the early 1880s. General Crook headquartered here for a time.
Wilson, p. 116.
Barnes, p. 485.

usual. Then, on going back to the San Simon side of the mountains to see what damage had been done, we were agreeably surprised to find what the quake had done for us. At the mouth of the canyon we found a good stream of water in the creek bed where before it had been as dry as a bone. There were many cattle in sight, looking contented. This water kept running almost all year and no doubt saved us from a heavy loss of cattle.

That earthquake seemed to follow the mountain range into Mexico, for later in the year we went on a cow hunt to recover cattle which had drifted into Sonora. Going down the Yaqui River on the old trail we had followed in previous years, we came to a fifteen foot bluff cutting off the trail. This was evidence of the severity of the earthquake there. Had it occurred in a settled community, it no doubt would have caused immense disaster.[96]

ABOUT 1884, there commenced quite a move of Texas cattle to Arizona ranges. The San Simon Cattle Company[97] was one of the biggest outfits, and this company shipped in about twenty-five thousand head of cattle which they ranged over about fifty miles of the San Simon Valley, extending from our range near the Mexican line north to the Southern Pacific Railroad. The Sulphur Springs Valley was rapidly filling up with herds, both large and small, and the next few years saw the cattle business of southern Arizona grow to big proportions.

WILD GAME WAS ABUNDANT in those early days. We had deer, antelope, turkey, wild duck or quail at all seasons when we could find them. The once-noted Indian scout leader, Tom Horn,[98] came to the Rucker Ranch with his company of about forty Indian scouts. On their following day's travel across the Chiricahua range to our new cow camp in the San Simon, the Indians were permitted to hunt on the way, and that evening Tom told me they had killed twenty deer. Of course they spread out and made a drive over a wide section and probably shot nearly every deer that jumped up, but it shows how numerous deer were at that time. Of course does and bucks fall alike to the Indian hunter.

In the upper San Simon, antelope were quite plentiful. Once I captured two baby antelope. I had seen them at a distance with the mother antelope. Riding up hastily upon them, the little fellows dropped in the grass and they were so near the color of the grass I had to search some time for them

(96) Hardest hit in the earthquake of May 3, 1887—not 1891 or 92, as Gray wrote—was not southeastern Arizona, but northern Sonora, Mexico. Tombstone gunshot surgeon Dr. George Goodfellow volunteered his services and later was awarded a medal and given a horse by Mexican President Porfirio Diaz.
    Trimble, *Roadside*, p. 64.

(97) Large scale cattle ranching began in the San Simon Valley in 1883–84. By 1885, production exceeded demand for the first time in Arizona Territory.
    Wilson, p. 189.

(98) Tom Horn's activities in Arizona—particularly Tombstone, if ever he was there—remain elusive and controversial. Paula Mitchell Marks suggests he may have migrated from Fort Grant in 1880 with Frank Leslie and Frank Stillwell. In Horn's autobiography—a dubious account at best—he asserts that he was in Tombstone twice, once in 1883 when employed as an army scout. The time frame lends credence to Gray's claim that Horn visited the Rucker Ranch. Horn makes no mention of Gray, but tells the tale of what John Myers Myers calls a "heroic bender in Tombstone" with legendary scout, Al Sieber. Dan L. Thrapp, Sieber's biographer, makes no mention of such an incident.
    Marks, p. 62.
    Myers, p. 67.

before I was successful. They did not attempt to move when I picked them up. I took them to the Rucker Ranch and I raised them with an improvised milk bottle and diluted cow's milk, as plain cow's milk was too rich, as we soon found out. They became such slaves to the bottle that even when full grown, if you pointed any kind of bottle at them they would come running to you. I also had picked up a white tail deer fawn about that time and the three grew up together.

With these pets we decided a controversial question often argued by hunters, and that is, which is the speedier, antelope or deer? I have read stories which stated that the antelope is the fastest animal on four legs, but I dispute this statement.

Near the Rucker Ranch was a clear, level space that had been used as a target ground when this was an army post. Often, on this level space, which was about a quarter of a mile long, we would stage races with the antelope and deer. One person would hold all three by their little leather collars at the starting point, and another at the other end of the track would hold an attractive bottle in sight. At a given signal, the three were freed and would jump off together. The deer, in a couple of jumps, would take the lead and the antelope, running neck and neck, would be beaten by about one hundred feet in the quarter mile run.

It is possible that some specie of deer are not so fast as the little white-tail of Arizona, but I feel safe in placing the white-tail as the fastest of our wild animals. I have seen crack greyhounds fail to overtake antelope, so I judge the deer is more fleet than the greyhound. Our little pet deer would bound easily fifteen feet in one jump on the level, whereas the antelope would probably take four jumps to cover the same space, and that seems to me to account for the difference in speed.

There was other wildlife that was far from being an asset to the rancher. The mountain lion was our worst enemy and he levied a heavy toll, especially on our calf crop. Even our milk calves, kept in a corral close to the house, would sometimes fall prey to the lion.

One moonlit night I had a chance to see the lion's method. I heard a sudden commotion among the calves and, grabbing a double-barreled shotgun loaded with buckshot, I rushed out to the calf corral. There, lying on his back was a lion holding a big calf by his forepaws and scratching the life out of the poor calf with his hind feet. I took quick aim and fired both barrels at the lion. He let go of the calf and disappeared over the fence, but the poor calf lay dying from the great gash which the lion's claws had torn into its abdomen.

I was disappointed when the lion disappeared, but the next morning I found him lying dead only a short distance from the fence. Another time I was sitting about midday on our front porch at Rucker and had noticed a cow go by with a big yearling steer, still unweaned, following her. They were on their way down to the creek. Probably a half hour later I heard a cow bellowing as if in distress. I hastily jumped on my horse and rode in that direction. I soon found the same cow that passed me with her big steer calf. The cow's horn was red with blood and the yearling was lying dead close to a tree trunk. The cow was fighting mad and ran at my horse at every attempt I made to ride near the dead calf, but finally, getting her at a distance, I examined the yearling to find out what had killed it.

There was no sign of blood on the hide, or any wound, but on close examination I found that one side of the calf's head was badly shattered as if struck by a club. It was the work of a mountain lion, which had either jumped at the calf from behind a tree, or from some limb, and had evidently struck the calf with a blow from its jaw, just as a cat does with a mouse. Several months later, a hunter bagged a lion that had a fresh tear in its flank. No doubt, the old cow had rammed him with her horn in defense of her calf.

Once, during the night, our two dogs at Rucker barked furiously. Going to the door, I met the old dog, Banjo, coming onto the porch whining pitifully. I knew then that a lion must be about, for that was the only thing Banjo would not tackle. He would not hesitate to fight with a wildcat, but he drew the line at lions.

The other dog had given a short yelp but now all was silent. The next morning we found where the lion must have struck down the dog, just as the calf was floored by a sudden leap and a slap. There was the trail of the dog being dragged away, making a mark on the ground like dragging a board would make.

Another fellow and myself started to follow the trail, and though this dog weighed about sixty pounds, we followed the drag at least a mile up a steep mountainside where it disappeared into a cave under a big shelving rock. We hesitated a moment about proceeding into the cave, when out jumped a big lion, passing us by only a few feet. It disappeared so quickly we had failed to be ready to shoot before he was gone.

We then entered the cave, which was only about twenty feet deep, and found the dead dog. The lion had not yet commenced his eating so we put several doses of strychnine in the carcass, hoping the beast would return. It is difficult to get a lion by poison, as they generally eat as they kill and will not touch bait set for them no matter how tempting. But this lion came back, for the following day we found him dead on the creek bank at the foot of the hill where the dog had been dragged. Evidently he ate of the dog and had then gone to the nearest water, as all animals will do when poisoned by strychnine.

Our fight against the lions was never over until we invested in some good hounds. One summer, father and mother took a trip to his old home in Huntsville, Texas, and there he bought four bloodhounds at the state prison. I remember we rather made fun of his investment of one hundred dollars for four homely, sad-looking dogs with their long, droopy ears.

They were sold as trained trailers, however, and we soon found they knew their business in that line. When on a trail they made the woods ring with their baying, and all kinds of wildlife had to get up and travel. Sometimes they would get beyond our control and then it might be days before we would see any of these dogs, and then they would appear so worn out and famished that you could count their ribs. We would shut them in a pen and had to kill a beef to half satisfy their hunger.

We soon found these hounds, as the saying goes, a white elephant on our hands. It was about that time that the notorious train robbers, Evans and Sontag,[99] were at large and being hunted by sheriff and railroad posses in the Sierras of southern California. It occurred to us to lend a hand in the hunt by offering to the Wells, Fargo Express Company a couple of our hounds for trailing the wanted men, who were leading all the officers and men on a fruitless chase. So I took two of the dogs and delivered them to the Wells, Fargo agent at Tombstone. He at once shipped them to Visalia, California. It was some months before we heard of them again.

Both dogs had fallen in the front line of battle. They were put on the outlaws' trail and had followed it faithfully into a clearing in the mountains where stood a cabin. If the officers had been as brave as the dogs, Evans and Sontag would have been captured in that cabin. But for some unexplained reason, the dogs were not backed up properly. When the posse finally approached the cabin, they found the two dogs shot to death. The criminals had fled.

We were satisfied that our dogs had not been found wanting in the line of duty, and that Evans and Sontag knew a bullet was the only thing that could stop them.

(99) The Sontag brothers, George and John, and Chris Evans had an intense dislike for the Southern Pacific Railroad—John had been badly injured in a work-related accident. They expressed their dislike by commiting armed robberies of Southern Pacific express cars, beginning in January, 1889 and concluding in August, 1892. Eventually, each went to prison. John committed suicide in the Fresno jail. Evans, following a brief dash to freedom, was recaptured and lived out his life in prison. George was pardoned in 1908, took a job at a San Francisco gambling house, and wrote his memoirs.
Nash, Jay Robert. *Encyclopedia of Western Lawmen & Outlaws.* NY: Paragon House, 1992, pp. 288–99.

Between 1883 and 1886, the old Rucker Ranch saw many troops of cavalry and many young army officers camped there who afterward rose to high rank in the Spanish American and World Wars.

General Leonard Wood,[100] then an army doctor with the rank of lieutenant, made his home with us for several months at a time. At their urgent request, my mother boarded Lieutenant Wood and several other young officers at Rucker Ranch. Dr. Wood was a contract doctor, a slim, well-appearing and very likeable young officer.

Dr. Wood, as all know, rose to high rank in both civil and military life. We who knew him in those Apache days, without exception, gloried in the honors he so justly won.

Tom Horn and his company of Indian scouts often stopped over for a few days at a time. All the army men thought much of Tom Horn, a big athletic fellow who could out-rival the Indians at any of their feats of speed or endurance, and who talked Apache like a native. In those days, Tom Horn was an ideal frontiersman and a dead shot, a rider who would mount anything that wore a hide. He was a general favorite, especially with the scouts. Why he fell so far from that standard in later days was a mystery, as well as a deep regret to his many friends in Arizona.

AHS #19608

Lt. Leonard Wood, who later became Army Chief of Staff.

A word for the Texas cowboy:

I was thrown in contact with many of the Texas cowboys and gladly acknowledge the debt I owned them for what they taught me of the cow business. They were undoubtedly the best cowmen of our country and most faithful to their employers. I have told of the boy, Comanche, who was asked to go back to the horse camp and stay alone. He did not hesitate. His was but one sample of that loyalty which I generally found among them.

I once started out to drive a herd about two hundred and fifty miles to ship at Deming,[101] New Mexico. We had eight men in our crew and eleven hundred cattle. After our first day on the trail we ran into a sandstorm that lasted for

(100) Born October 9, 1860 at Winchester, New Hampshire, Leonard Wood graduated from Harvard Medical School in 1884. Soon after, he joined the Army Medical Corps and arrived at Fort Huachuca, January 5, 1886, serving as assistant surgeon. He received the Medal of Honor for his participation in the Geronimo campaign. Later, he became a close friend of Theodore Roosevelt, and during the Spanish-American War, helped organize the Rough Riders. Wood became Army Chief of Staff, July 16, 1910. He retired shortly after the United States entered World War I. In 1920 he unsuccessfully sought the Republican nomination for president, and later was appointed governor general of the Philippines, a post he held until his death, August 7, 1927. Fort Leonard Wood, Missouri is named in his honor.
Altshuler, pp. 376–77.

(101) Deming was settled about 1880 and named for Mary Ann Deming, who married Charles Crocker, a kingpin of the Southern Pacific Railroad.
Pearce, p. 46.

four straight days and nights. So severe was the wind that if we had been traveling against it we would have had to quit, but going with it we pushed on. It was a most trying time for all hands. We could not hold the cattle but had to let them drift with the storm. We followed, often walking and leading our horses which were nearly played out. So strong was the wind that it would blow the water from a tin cup before you could raise it to your mouth, and it was impossible to build a fire to cook by.

With all this hardship, not a man ever whimpered or said quit. When we arrived at last at the stock pens at Deming, we found the sand had piled up to the top of the gate.

The cowboy would never leave his boss in a tight place. He worked for a small wage, and that at times meant a twenty-four hour shift, when a stampede would catch him on herd. Then he would stay with the cattle or what part of them he could manage to check in their flight until help came the following day. Or he would manage to drive them back to camp.

I know of no other following that can show the loyalty of the old-time cowboy under every condition of endurance or hardship. Many of them were almost illiterate, yet they had a knowledge of nature which stood them in hand. They could tell time by the stars almost to the half hour, if not closer. When it happened that no one had a watch, they would stand guard and change guards by the position of certain stars which they knew by their own familiar names. On the darkest night I have followed them to camp when I had lost all sense of direction, but they could almost always locate the camp wagon, even when all landmarks were blotted out in stormy weather. Somehow, all people who live close to nature seem to have an inherited, as well as an acquired and developed, sense that the city boy rarely knows.

General Miles asked an old-time Arizona hunter if he was a good trailer. His answer was, "General, I can trail a jaybird across a rock." That may be a bit too much for belief, but with him it was almost as instinctive as it was with the Apache.

There is a case on record of a fellow holding up a stage that ran from Tucson to Altar, Mexico. A few miles out of Tucson the stage had to pass a rocky point. At that spot a fellow stepped out and held up the driver and passengers. On the next trip out from Tucson, the driver approached the point as he was telling his passengers about the holdup. At that moment, a man stepped out and said, "Here I am again," and held them up a second time.

AHS #2144

*Juan Elias,
who tracked
Bill Brazelton,
later became
mayor of
Tucson.*

AHS #78140

*Outlaw Bill Brazelton, propped up
against a Tucson building and
photographed in death.*

Every effort was made by the sheriff to locate and catch this highwayman, but to no avail. About a week passed before the sheriff put a noted Mexican trailer on the job. The Mexican went to the point of the holdup, and although many horses had passed over that road since the holdup, and tracks were quickly blotted out on that dry, dusty, wind-blown road, the Mexican picked up the trail of the robber's horse. He followed it painstakingly to the outskirts of Tucson where he found a deserted adobe shack where the rider had changed the horse's shoes, reversing them so that their tracks would seem to be going in an opposite direction. It appeared as though all tracks were going into the shack and none coming out.

The trail led us to a stable in Tucson and the location of the horse in a stall there, but the shoes had been changed back to their normal position. It was then an easy matter for the sheriff to catch his man. His name was Brazelton.

The conviction of this man quickly followed. The sheriff got the credit, but it was that unexplainable instinct—you might term it—of the Mexican trailer who could follow that horse track and detect it from all others, hundreds of them, by some slight difference that the trailer himself could not explain. The dog can trail by his nose but the native trails by that keen eye which is his inheritance from his ancestors, and can not be acquired by us in such perfection, no matter how hard we try.[102]

(102) In the main, Gray's version of this oft embellished tale follows traditional tellings. The Mexican tracker, Juan Elias, served as mayor of Tucson and held the dubious distinction of being a leader of the Camp Grant Massacre. William Whitney "Bill" Brazelton, who worked at Leatherwood's stable in Tucson, was not, as Gray asserts, convicted. He was shot to death—some say at the behest of his informant, a ne'er-do-well named David Nimitz—by a posse. In his August 19, 1878 entry, diarist George Hand wrote, "They laid him on a table in the courthouse. Hundreds went to see him as he was displayed with his guns and accouterments on." Later, Brazelton's body was propped against a wall and photographed for posterity.

Gray's use of the word "us" in reference to the posse is either accidental or the result of a memory lapse, for the incident occurred nearly two years before his arrival in Arizona Territory.

Sonnichsen, *Tucson,* p. 124.

Carmony, p. 194.

Herding cattle on the Arizona range.

(103) Situated on the west side of the Chiricahua Mountains, Turkey Creek takes its name from wild turkeys once plentiful in the region. Philip Morse began a sawmill operation in Turkey Canyon about 1872.

Barnes, p. 458.

(104) Named after Pennsylvania oil man and mining entrepreneur, John H. Galey, Galeyville was established in 1880 as a smelter town for the Tombstone mines. A refuge for outlaws said to be headed by Curly Bill Brocius, in its heyday the town boasted eleven saloons, two restaurants, two hotels, six mercantile establishments, a Wells, Fargo office, and a variety of other businesses. Galeyville's population peaked at about 400, but its heyday was short-lived. In 1882, the smelter was moved to Bisbee and many of the town's wooden buildings were dismantled and rebuilt in the neighboring town of Paradise. The post office closed May 31, 1882. Nothing remains today but a slag heap.

Barnes, p. 172.
Sherman, p. 58.

EARLY ONE SPRING, the cattlemen of the San Simon Valley were gathering at Turkey Creek[103] for the spring roundup. It was our first night out and, as grazing was poor at this point, we had hobbled our horses rather than put them under herd to give them a better chance to scatter out in search of what little feed there was. The next morning, the horse hunters did not find any of them, but did find a trail of many horses leading off to the east. We knew at once the Indians had raided us.

We had felt safe, as a company of U.S. Cavalry was camping at the old abandoned mining camp of Galeyville,[104] hardly three miles from our camp, and we did not expect the Apaches would dare venture so close to an armed force.

We got word to this troop at once, and soon the company was in saddle and all of the cowboys—about twenty strong—who could rustle mounts joined them, and we all hastened off on the trail of the stolen horses. It was easy to follow, as at least one hundred horses had been stolen. We followed the trail all day across the San Simon Valley and over the Stein Peak Mountains. From the summit of this range we could easily see a column of dust to the southeast which was evidently made by the fleeing Apaches and our stolen horses.

We still had a couple of hours of daylight, so we urged the captain of the cavalry to make haste that we might have a chance to overtake the Indians and recover at least a part of our stock. To our great disappointment, the captain told us he could take his troop no further. He claimed they had made a long march and that his horses were badly fagged, also he had brought along no pack train and was not prepared for further pursuit. He then left us and started with his troop back for Galeyville.

It was the old, old story so often put up by so many army men. When an Indian trail got hot some excuse was made for turning back. True, there were exceptions, especially among young officers, but the old, grizzled line captains had become a byword with Arizona ranchers for failures in fighting the Apache. The Apache knew about this weakness and acted accordingly.

We cowboys were left without support to follow the trail. It was a hard blow and it must be admitted, some harsh words were handed to the U.S. captain. I think many of the captain's men felt as we did and would have gladly followed us to the limit.

We kept on the trail a few miles further, but realized the futility of it. Even if we could overtake the Indians, we felt sure we were outnumbered, so we reluctantly turned back.

This was not the first time that a troop of cavalry had quit a hot trail. It was only one of many such episodes in those days, and you will not wonder that the pioneer ranchers of the borderland were bitter against our government for the poor showing of protection made against raiding Apaches.

Nothing remains of Galeyville but this sign.

GALEYVILLE

ESTABLISHED 1881   POPULATION 400

JOHN H. GALEY OPENED THE TEXAS MINE AND SMELTER IN 1881. MINING BOOMED AND DIED AND THE TOWN BECAME A HAVEN FOR LAWLESS MEN LIKE CURLY BILL AND JOHN RINGO WHO USED NEARBY GULCHES TO HOLD STOLEN CATTLE WHILE BRANDS WERE ALTERED. IN 1888 THE SAN SIMON CATTLE COMPANY FORCED OUT SQUATTERS AND THE REMAINS OF GALEYVILLE WERE CARRIED AWAY TO CONSTRUCT HOUSES IN NEARBY PARADISE.........

Either the red tape at Washington, which seemed at times to hold army officers from doing anything, or else the officers themselves who had waxed fat and lazy about the army posts, caused them not to care to make the necessary effort. In either case it is hard to restrain words of bitter comment on conditions which permitted a handful of Apaches to raid the country at will, ruthlessly killing and stealing, and terrorizing the whole southwest country—not only for days but for years—until General Miles was placed in command to end this outrageous condition.

That same year, the massacre of the soldiers in Guadalupe Canyon occurred. This unfortunate occurrence was brought about by the inefficiency of the army and some of the officers in the field, which was entirely uncalled for. I mention this unfortunate occurrence because I happen to know some of the proceeding events.

I had a cow camp at the head of the San Simon Valley where, generally, our old cook, Moody, held out. During the height of the Indian raids, a couple of cowboys and myself made this point our headquarters in order to keep a watch on our saddle stock.

At this time, Captain Hatfield[105] was camping with us with a cavalry troop. There was also another cavalry troop at the mouth of Skeleton Canyon, about ten miles east of us. These two troops were endeavoring to keep men patrolling to the east and to the west, morning and evening, to discover any new horse trails going either north or south. They knew the hostile Apaches had been on a raiding expedition into Arizona from their stronghold in Mexico, and they knew, too, that the return trip to Mexico would occur soon, as they would be taking back their booty. So they hoped to intercept them.

Unfortunately, a soldier knows little of the cowboy knack of trailing, or seeing signs of horse trails. The upshot was that a soldier patrol rode one morning across a south-bound trail of a bunch of horses, failing to observe tracks, and so reported to Captain Hatfield. Along about midday a cowboy, coming over the same ground, noticed the trail of horses going south, evidently having been made the previous night. Captain Hatfield was astounded at this news, and severely reprimanded his soldier patrol.

That night, a courier brought word of the Guadalupe massacre—the very misfortune the army had carefully planned to prevent.

In Guadalupe Canyon, a headquarters camp had been made and a large amount of ammunition and supplies were kept in some army wagons at that point. Anticipating the

(105) Born December 9, 1850 at Eutaw, Alabama, Charles Albert Phelps Hatfield graduated from West Point in 1872. In July, 1884, Hatfield was assigned to Camp McDowell, and the following November was transferred to Fort Huachuca where he participated in the Geronimo campaign. A career officer who served both in Cuba and the Phillipines, Hatfield retired a colonel in 1914. He died in Washington, DC, February 23, 1935.

Altshuler, p. 160.

return of raiding Apaches from northern points, one troop had come to our ranch as stated, one had located at the mouth of Skeleton Canyon, and another at Cloverdale Ranch in the Animas Valley. It was hoped to capture the returning Apaches, but the oversight of Hatfield's sign-riders had ruined the chance.

A small squad of men had been left with the wagon train in Guadalupe, and special instructions given the sergeant in command to have armed pickets out day and night. In fact, it was said the officer in command who had gone to Cloverdale, had sent a special courier over to Guadalupe camp that very day to emphasize the order for vigilance. This vigilance was evidently neglected, for while the soldiers were eating their noon meal they were attacked by the Apaches with such force they were nearly all killed or wounded at the first fire, and few shots were fired in defense.

The Apaches were evidently in desperate straits for ammunition, to have made the attack in broad daylight, for this was an unusual method with them. What they did not take, they set fire to. The man who had come over from Cloverdale that day with strict orders for the sergeant at Guadalupe, and another soldier, were the only ones left able to get back to Cloverdale and report the massacre. I think it was seven men of the defending troop who fell, and probably no Indian was injured.

This was one of the worst fiascoes of the whole Apache campaign. Had Hatfield discovered the trail in the early morning, as he should have done, he could easily have crowded the fleeing Apaches. If he had not overtaken them, he would have at least prevented the attack at Guadalupe. Such a miscue as this whole affair was, made us have little respect for the army maneuvers on the border. The bunch of attacking Indians at Guadalupe were no doubt the same bunch which had been raiding Arizona ranches for horses, and on their way back had found the small guard at Guadalupe Canyon.

Also, sad to relate, the sergeant at Guadalupe and some of his men were pretty drunk. This was not divulged at the time, but I know it for a fact, as some cowboys had passed the soldier camp the day before and found it in a demoralizing condition. This massacre has been described by writers in rather vivid terms which lauded the defending soldiers. But we knew at the time that a bunch of drunken men were helpless in the face of the Apaches who would take no chances. They had evidently discovered the soldiers' condition before attacking.

An Apache brave poses for the camera.

FROM EXPERIENCE of those years of overstocked range by the constant inroads of new cattle ranchers, and the natural increase of the herds to a point where a bad grass year led to incredible losses of cattle, one cannot help the thought that our land laws are not as they should be in regard to the vast acreage of our Western states, which are too dry for farming. One need only look at the big, fenced-in cattle ranches of Texas to find the answer.

In Texas, the rancher can regulate his herds to the capacity of his range and thereby prevent the total annihilation of the good forage grasses. In contrast with this, view the destruction which has taken place over many miles of Arizona and New Mexico.

In the early days of New Mexico and Arizona, the plains were covered with a good growth of mesquite, gramma and gaietta grasses, all being of the best stock feed. One could cut wild hay wherever a spot level enough for a mowing machine could be found. No doubt this condition could be brought back again if we had land laws permitting the leasing of large tracts, and allowing for the fencing of these tracts for cattle range purposes—thus enabling the cattlemen to regulate the size of their herds within reason.

As things are now in many sections, neither farming nor cattle raising can succeed. The passing of our grass lands in the West is the tragedy of this once fair land, and seems wholly inexcusable.

A watering hole on the range near Bisbee.

Cowboys pose for the camera.

WE PARTICIPATED in the biggest roundup of cattle ever attempted in southern Arizona. It was probably never surpassed anywhere for the size of the herd gathered for shipment.

We started at the south end of the San Simon Valley where it joins Mexico at the head waters of the Yaqui River at the old San Bernardino Ranch.[106] Our outfit consisted of forty cowboys, a chuck wagon, a horse herd of about two hundred head of cow ponies, and last but not least, Old Dry, our roundup boss—probably one of the best cowmen of the Southwest. Old Dry was a Texan, tall, slim and wiry; probably then past fifty years. He was a man of few words whose whole life had been spent on the cattle trails out of Texas into the northland.

It was probably on the old Chisum Trail[107] that he acquired the habit of speaking only when he had something to say, and that occasion was so rare that the boys began calling him, Old Dry. But even with his reserve, Old Dry was probably the best roundup boss and leader of men on the southern frontier.

Then there was old Billy, the cook. Small in stature, curly-haired, dark and close-mouthed, we all figured he was an old cow puncher as he seemed to know the business in all its phases. In those days out on the frontier, it

(106) After Mexico won its independence from Spain in 1821, significant land grants were made in return for military service. Lieutenant Ignacio Perez was given title to the San Bernardino which totaled more than 73,000 acres of prime range land in present-day southeastern Arizona and northern Sonora. This did not sit well with the Apaches, who set upon a course of systematic destruction of ranches and ranchers alike. By the 1840s, most of the grants had been abandoned. When Lieutenant Colonel Philip St. George Cooke and the Mormon Battalion marched over the San Bernardino in 1846, deserted cattle ran wild. Some forty years would pass before the Apaches were subjugated and forced onto reservations making it possible for large scale ranching to resume.

In 1884, John Horton Slaughter purchased the San Bernardino. In time, his ranch supported some 50,000 head of cattle and as many as 500 employees. Slaughter became a wealthy land baron and a most influential man in Arizona affairs, serving as sheriff of Cochise County and as a territorial legislator. He died in 1922 at the age of eighty-one.

Sheridan, pp. 48–49.

Wilson, p. 185.

Faulk, *Arizona*, p. 157.

Ibarra, Ignacio. "Frontier Sheriff Fought Crime in County." *Seasons*, January 27, 1989, pp. 20–23.

De La Garza, Phyllis. "John Slaughter Brought His Own Brand of Law and Order to Area." *Seasons*, April 30, 1990, pp. 10–14.

(107) He probably is referring to the Chisholm Trail.

was not considered politic to question a man's past. Seldom a general roundup happened in the San Simon without Billy to run the chuck wagon. Bareheaded and barefooted, he was in his element as camp cook, and his supreme qualification in the opinion of the punchers was that he could make a perfect sourdough biscuit. Hot, fresh biscuits were a feature of every meal—or else the punchers would rebel. It made no difference to Billy whether he had ten men or forty to cook for. He was always ready with his "chuck away" call long before daylight.

The cowboy was almost as quick to respond, for he had simply to pull on his boots with the spurs always attached, and he was fully dressed for the day. Rarely did he wear a coat while at work.

The night horse herder would have his herd in close to camp by the time breakfast was over, and breakfast was always a hearty meal. The cowpuncher on a roundup had to prepare for a long, hard day and no dainty appetite could withstand the strain. One can learn to stroke away a lot of bread, meat, beans and such when he knows it may be far into the night before he can eat again.

The grub invoice is figured out for forty men and runs about as follows:

> 500 pounds flour;
> 2 sides of fat bacon (for grease);
> Sack of potatoes;
> 100 pound sack of green coffee (always a hand coffee grinder is found secured to the outside of the grub box);
> 100 pound sack of sugar (but if it is a Texas outfit, the sugar is generally omitted, as Tex replies, "I never use it"); and
> 100 pounds of red beans.

That is about all required for forty men for one month. The meat is killed from the range, and that is always the best fat yearling heifer that can be found.

We see fat yearling steer beef in our markets, but the cowboy knows that a yearling heifer still following the mother cow, is far ahead and always the most tender beef on the range.

One may think this a very limited menu, but a camp cook can make out of this list of groceries a breakfast, dinner, and supper fit for any hard working, hungry man.

The old iron Dutch oven plays an important part. In it the cook puts a bunch of thick steaks—all bones cut out—an abundance of sliced potatoes and onions, and ample chunks of kidney fat, as well as a handful of salt and pep-

Arizona cattle baron John Horton Slaughter, who operated the San Bernardino Ranch and served as Cochise County Sheriff after the Earps' departure.

per. Then he puts on the oven lid and places a shovelful of hot oak coals on top and underneath. This is generally done by the cook a couple of hours before breakfast time when he first gets up.

Hot biscuits are being rapidly cooked in another Dutch oven. A cowboy demands hot bread at every meal. A big pot of red Mexican beans has been boiling the best part of the night. All this with a five gallon pot of strong coffee (no milk or sugar—these being used by an exceptional few), and there you have it—take it or leave it.

It might be interesting in this day of high beef prices to know what we were getting at the railroad shipping point for these cattle. They were contracted for by Montana buyers, and were termed feeders, to be turned loose on the northern range and when matured and fattened would be shipped to market at the Chicago stock yards. Here are the figures we would get F.O.B. at San Simon Station on the Southern Pacific railroad:

For 1-year-old steers: $8 each;
For 2-year-old steers: $12 each; and for those
3 years old and up: $15 each.

All during the Eighties and Nineties, we sold our steers at about these same prices.

Cowboys gathered around a campfire.

The man who says he cannot eat just after getting up in the morning has never gone through an Arizona roundup, where the cowboy says he must learn to eat with the appetite of a dog and work like a horse.

Each fellow would eat his hearty breakfast, grab up his *reata* or lasso rope, and hurry out to the horse herd to catch his mount for the day. A cowboy's mounts generally numbered about seven rugged little horses; rugged because they had to live on grass alone, and often scarce pickings at that. The cowpuncher must be able to catch, saddle and ride his own horse, moving fast with it all, for Old Dry was in the saddle and off before you could hardly turn around. He expected all to follow him. No "wait for me" call would be heeded.

When the sun appeared over the Stein Peak Mountains, we would be ten miles from camp and ready to start on the great circle—as the cowboys called it. That is, a circle outside the possible range of cattle with probably a ten mile radius.

Here and there a few men were dropped out to drive the section toward the central point until the boss and a few fellows completed the circuit of all the cattle, and they were headed for one common roundup ground. The old cattle had been rounded up so many times they knew where to go and stopped when they reached their customary roundup ground. It required but a sharp yell or two at the outside cattle to start a general migration towards the roundup. It is this habit to which range cattle are trained that makes possible the handling of large herds by comparatively few cowboys.

We were gathering steers from yearlings on this trip, and it was our first experience in shipping one-year-olds. Montana, however, was calling for the youngsters. This was probably the beginning of the reign of the "baby beef" of today.

The time was early February, and we cut out steers down to ten months—many suckling calves—as we figured they would be close to one year old by the time they reached the Montana buyer. It proved a lively job to handle those little fellows, most of them still following the mother cows. Our first day's roundup cut was about one thousand steers, and probably about half were yearlings. We always made a practice of night-herding steer gatherings, as there was always danger of injuring them in corrals by crowding or stampeding.

That first night out, four men to a watch were detailed to guard the herd. With the first guard out, the balance of us tied up our night horses and turned into our blankets. We got but little sleep that night. Along about ten o'clock one of the night-herders dashed into our camp and told Old Dry they needed help badly; that every yearling was bawling for his "ma" and trying desperately to get away. All of us rode hurriedly out to the herd and found it a bedlam of bawling, crazy calves. For awhile it took every man of the forty riders to hold the bunch.

We managed to hold most of the herd until they quieted down from exhaustion along about daybreak, so that most of us could go to camp for fresh day horses and breakfast, postponing all thought of sleep till some other night.

That day's roundup continued in the same manner down the valley, and Billy moved his cook camp about ten miles north. The yearlings we gathered that day, and afterwards, we kept in a separate herd and put each bunch in corrals for a period of two days and nights without water or feed. When released from this imprisonment they were so hungry and dry, they paid strict attention to grass and water and never seemed to bother anymore about their "ma's." This method might seem cruel today, but to us it seemed virtually the only way to handle these calves and break them to herd. When finally conquered, they proved the easiest of all the cattle to handle.

It required nearly two weeks of this kind of work of rounding up, cutting out the steers, and moving camp daily a few miles down the valley to finally reach the railroad shipping point at San Simon Station. By that time, our herd probably numbered fifteen thousand head, as it was impossible to keep many range cattle from drifting in at night. The herd covered so much ground when bedded down at night that the night-herders had to ride stations instead of the usual custom of the circling the herd, and it required fourteen men at a time to hold the vast herd.

It took ten days more of the hardest kind of work to cut out, class, and load twenty trains with the ten thousand steers contracted for. About five hundred head constituted a train load, and our program was to ship out one train in a day and another at night. And that was work.

The cattle had to be grazed and watered early in the morning, then cut out and classed as to age, brand, and in quality to meet the buyers' acceptance. Then came the loading into cars. The night loading was especially hard work and often dangerous. The men must still find time to eat at the chuck wagon, change horses, night herd, and if there is any time left, catch a few winks of sleep.

The matter of sleep, however, was secondary, for nearly every night we had a stampede. The cattle were hungry from the necessarily short grazing time, and hence were uneasy, running at the least alarm. Often the striking of a match to light a cigarette would start a run that kept the men on guard the balance of the night.

A stampede of the old-time longhorns was rather an appalling sight. The worst stampede generally occurred when all the herd was lying down and apparently asleep. An occasional long breath from some old steer would be the only sound heard. Then some alarm, often unnoticed by the herders—and every animal would be on its feet running pell mell in one direction, and in such a close flying wedge that their horns clashed against one another like the beating of a vast drum corps. Woe be it to the horseman caught in front of this charging mass of hooves and horns. He had to urge his mount to mighty effort to keep from being run down and trampled to death.

Cowboys always endeavored to get to one side of the leaders and gradually force the lead cattle over to change their course. By constantly crowding them he could make the leaders turn in a circle and turn into the tail end of the stampede. The whole herd would thus become a kind of merry-go-round, and this milling was the winning play of the cowboys, for soon the cattle would tire down from a run to a walk, and the stampede was over.

For a time, you would not give much for your chance of stopping this wild, running bunch of cattle, frightened as they were. Old trail hands tell of this being a nightly occurrence, sometimes with the herd going up the trail. It became a habit with some herds, persisting until the end of the journey. Maybe that is a part of the "romance" in the cowpuncher's life. He anticipates it with a kind of feeling of charm. He works that charm off with weariness of body and long hours without sleep, but when it is all over and the last car is loaded—the last car door closed and sealed—it is with a feeling of regret that he turns his horse's head back toward the ranch and home.

On the other hand, if he is lucky and is picked to go in charge of a trainload of cattle, there is joy in his mind, anticipating new sights, going places and seeing things, which is a dream we all have. This is the trip that he has probably looked forward to during long, hard months on the range.

Probably it will end in a few days spent in Kansas City or Chicago. Then surfeited with "the great white way" and with sadly depleted pockets, he boards the west-bound passenger train with little else than his transportation pass back to the range—to dream about it all over again. He will be happy with adventures to relate of the great "inside," as we called the busy life among the white-collared folk of "civilized" parts.

Those years were the golden era for the Western range cattlemen. Prior to 1893, grass and water were plentiful over the Southwest ranges. Taxes were not much of a consideration in those days. The tax collector had to take a cattlemen's word for their tally of cattle. The only way the cowmen could estimate a herd was by the calf tally at branding, and of course that tally was not for publication. One cowboy to about one thousand cattle was all the manpower needed to handle the cattle, except at roundup times when a roundup cook and a few extra riders would be needed.

It was all open country and cattle were free to wander at will except at general roundup time when each ranch would cut out and take home its strays, which had wandered away since the last roundup. In fact, we had to be neighbors, for if we fudged a little and put our brand on another fellow's calf, it would be discovered at the general roundup. It was a self-evident fact that your calf would not by rights suckle another fellow's cow. By unwritten law, payment in kind must be made. Probably a fairer justice reigned among the range cowmen than even in the so-called centers of civilization.

*Branding calves
on the Arizona range.*

No business had so small an overhead as cattle ranching in its palmy days of the open range, and the low prices I have mentioned left a nice return for the year's work.

Once I asked a Montana man what our cattle would finally bring him on the Chicago market. He replied that a fair average price for our steers when fattened on Montana grass and put in the stock yards at Chicago, would be around sixty dollars; but he added that his net, after paying railroad freight, keep of the cattle until maturity, and allowing for natural losses on the range, would not much exceed our sale price, if any. But the over stocking of big cattle companies and a succession of drought years brought about near annhiliation to the once prosperous range cattle business.

Our old ranch in the Animas Valley of southwest New Mexico became part of the Kern County Land Company[108] of California. At one time, it was claimed to be stocked with over forty thousand cattle. Fully half this number perished in the drought years, and the sad part is that the grass never came back to its old stand. Somehow it seems that nature has a way of defense when we destroy her resources. When the rain came again, a new kind of crop covered the land; grasses of poorer forage quality, noxious weeds, and the cockle burr, which no animal will touch for food, but which will cling to the poor horses' and cows' tails and make their lives a misery.

Throughout most of Western fed-out and worn-out ranges, we have now such grasses as the foxtail with its abominable bearded seeds, which will penetrate a sheep's skin and ultimately cause its death. This may bear out Darwin's theory of the survival of the fittest, but from a utility point of view it is a decided step backwards. What to do about it is one of our hardest problems.

Possibly Texas with its own public domain has come nearest to a solution by allowing its big, fenced-in pastures where the owners could control grazing, and by proper management, preserve the good forage grasses before they were tramped out and eaten out beyond recovery. It is hoped that our agricultural department at Washington will make an effort to bring about the reclamation of our Western cattle ranges.

Another grievance of the cattlemen was the order that came out from Washington that all fences on government land must be removed. Of course cattlemen knew that such a practice was not quite lawful, but if Uncle Sam permitted us to run our stock on the wild lands, we could see no harm in fencing in a few acres for horse pastures. It rather aggra-

(108) In the late 1870s, James Haggin and Lloyd Tevis acquired two ranches and other land holdings in the San Joaquin Valley in Kern County, California. In later years, ranches, including the Gray Ranch in the Animas Valley, were acquired in New Mexico. In 1890, the entire operation was incorporated as the Kern County Land & Cattle Company.
Hilliard, p. 69.

vated the bad feeling over the matter when Lieutenant Flipper[109] arrived to enforce this order.

Lieutenant Flipper was a colored man who had graduated into the army by way of West Point, but had resigned, it was said, on account of the white army officers' social isolation policy toward him. However, Flipper got this fence commission and he did not get a very cordial reception from the cowmen. I venture to say, every rancher was hospitable to Flipper, showing him all due respect, but the Westerner draws the line at mealtime, and Lieutenant Flipper always ate alone. This custom, as a heritage from slavery days, will probably die out gradually, and no doubt it should, as the law draws no color line.

In those trying days when we had to make daily drives of famished cattle into the mountains for water, we would search the neighborhood of the old water holes, which had become entirely dry, and at which many cattle would still persist in hunting for water. It was at one of these dried-out water holes that we found a cow lying down. We could not induce her to get to her feet so that we might drive her to water. She had evidently given up the fight, and though we packed water to her and stuck her nose in the bucket, she refused to drink. She would try desperately to hook us with her horns, and as we could not waste much time on the animal, we had to leave her lie there.

Day after day she lived on in this position under the hot summer sun. We marked off eighteen days before the end came to her. Eighteen days without a drop of water or anything to eat. It is a record hard to believe, but we saw her daily for that time and she was game to the last in fighting all our efforts of aid. I doubt if a human being could have lasted for twenty-four hours under the same conditions.

The years following the drought brought forth a new vocation, which the cowboys looked upon with much disgust, almost akin to grave robbing. That was the business of the sun-bleached bones of the drought victims. Near almost every railroad station there were accumulated great stacks of bones hauled in from cattle ranges. Men appeared with wagons and started to gather up bones and horns of the dead cows, and soon it was a common sight to see piles of white bones growing daily in size at every shipping point. It was probably a trade started in the old buffalo slaughter days.

"It is an ill wind that blows nobody good." So the bone man came and shipped off our dead herds leaving us no

(109) Lieutenant Henry Ossian Flipper, born March 31, 1856 in slave quarters at Thomasville, Georgia, was the first black man to graduate from West Point; the first black man commissioned an officer in the regular army. In the summer of 1881, while serving as post quartermaster at Fort Davis, Texas, Flipper was court-martialed for embezzlement when shortages were discovered in his account books. The court found him innocent of the embezzlement charge, but guilty of conduct unbecoming an officer. Punishment was dismissal from the army, June 30, 1882. Flipper became a land and mine surveyor and, fluent in Spanish, for a time maintained an office in Nogales, Arizona.
Altshuler, p. 298.
Warner, Ezra J. "A Black Man in the Long Gray Line." *American History Illustrated*, January, 1970, pp. 30–38.

C.O.D.s for the shipment. There was something about this bone business that seemed abnormal to the cowboy. These old dead cows had struggled hard for existence, and the cowboys had worked hard and unavailingly to keep them in food and drink. And now to see some stranger come along and disturb eternal sleep for a few paltry dollars, seemed the limit of greed and like robbing the grave.

Quite a few cattle would work their way back into places in the mountains that could not be reached in roundup times, and not being handled, many would become almost as wild as the deer. It was always a kind of sport that we looked forward to when other work was not pressing, to hunt out these wild specimens and try to move them down into some pasture among gentle stock.

Occasionally we would catch a glimpse of some among them that had become mavericks—that is, they had no brands on them and were as frightened at the sight of man as a deer would be. I remember a three-year-old bull maverick that proved quite a problem. He ran like a wild thing when we saw him. Two of us followed him through all kinds of rough and brushy places before we were able to chase him into an open spot and cast a rope over his horns. Then he turned to fight, but we managed to get a second rope over his horns, and then by one of us leading and the other following, we could hold him a prisoner between us. In this way we got the bull down out of the mountains to a corral.

After getting the animal into the corral we dehorned him, and in the company of some gentle stock, moved him to a pasture. The dehorning was necessary or the bull, never having been fenced in, would have run through a wire fence as though it were a clump of brush. And the dehorning made his head sore, tending to make him want to keep away from anything that might hurt him.

Our main effort was to round up all stock in the spring and fall and thus keep them used to the habit. Cattle soon learn to head for the accustomed roundup grounds when started in that direction, and often old cows become so well trained that they will stop at the spot used for roundup and patiently await further orders of the cowboy.

The range cowman has learned that good habits are about the best asset known. A well trained herd of cattle used to frequent roundups, reduces much of the cost of running a ranch. And such a well trained herd of cattle means a well managed ranch which attracts the buyer. Buyers avoid calling on a brand which has the reputation of being an outlaw bunch, that term meaning when the cattle had become wild, with many being what we termed "moss heads"—old runaway steers.

During the winter storms, many cattle would drift south into Mexico. This was a natural movement in search of a milder climate, and was probably an inherited trait of all Texas stock. Most of our cattle were of Texas origin. And so in the spring our biggest job would be for ranchers along the border to join forces and send an expedition into Mexico to hunt and drive home these strays. Generally, it would take a force of twenty or more cowboys the best part of a month to do this job properly.

Drift cattle generally followed the course of the Yaqui River south, and so our method was to go down this stream fifty or more miles and then work back to the line, gathering stock on the way. This is rough and brushy country, and we came back almost always with badly torn clothes and numerous scratches from mesquite and catclaw thorns. Most of the cattle we found on these trips would belong north of the line or to the big San Bernardino Ranch just south of the line, so it simply resolved itself into driving everything north as we advanced.

With our big force, we felt protected against any trouble with Mexican patrols, for we had learned from previous experience that a small bunch of two or three travellers into Mexico would almost invariably get into bad mix-ups. Once one of our cowboys took a notion to wander into Fronteras from our camp, and it was several months before we saw him again. To get him back we had to raise a purse of $250 and send it with a man who knew the ways of Mexican justice. He simply paid the proper officials to free our cowboy, who had about starved for months in a Mexican calaboose.

On arriving at the line with our strays thus gathered—and they often numbered as high as two thousand head—we would spend a day or two branding calves. Some of the U.S. Customs Patrol would generally appear, and they often introduced the subject of our paying duty before crossing the border on our homeward journey. But this did not seem fair to us as these cattle had strayed from home, and it was unreasonable to compel us to pay duty, which at times was as high as ten dollars on grown cattle. So we used a little strategy. When we had finished our branding, we made a pretense of turning our herd loose, but we did so with a start to the north. Later on in the night, after the customs officers had disappeared, we would make our getaway and soon have our big herd moving north and homeward.

Many would have already crossed the line. In fact, the line monuments were so far apart we really did not know

*Gray much admired the
hard working cowboy.*

the exact location of the "imaginary line" marking the boundary. We were never called down by our government for following the above method in recovering our stray cattle, although the order was that all going into Mexico must pass through Customs and bond their saddle stock. But that method would have caused us great inconvenience as the nearest Customs station was nearly one hundred miles west of our ranch.

We simply took the most direct method and avoided all unnecessary red tape. We rightfully owned all the stock we took out of Mexico, so nobody's rights were infringed upon. We simply followed the slogan, "There's no law west of the Rio Grande."

At best, it was a trying trip for both men and horses, and we lived on pretty slim fare. We traveled light as everything had to be packed in on our pack horses. Generally our food supply would get pretty low before we could get our cattle on the home range.

The border section of Mexico was then inhabited by a sparse population, and the people were very poor. In fact, what few people we met, we were called upon to feed from our scanty supply of food. If you don't care to starve you must take your own grub on a Mexican trip. We always found the people hospitable, but they had little or nothing to divide with us.

A Mexican will kill his last chicken for a wayfarer, and divide with him all he has, but the Mexican border people have been robbed by bandits and their own changeable government until they are poor beyond anything that we know on this side of the line.

I can't refrain from adding one last incident from our Mexican trip. Maybe it will serve in the cause of temperance in the tobacco habit.

One spring, during our severe drought time, we had to push our homeward-bound herd a long night drive of twenty miles without water. There were many calves in the herd and the cattle moved very slow. After hours of urging them along, the cowboys began to weaken and I saw they were getting desperate for a drink of water. I suggested that I would stay with the herd to try and keep them moving, while the others should go on ahead with the loose horses till they reached the first water. All were tobacco users but me, and I knew I had the ability to stand it longer without water. It was long after sunup the next day before they got back and brought me a drink. But I had not suffered from thirst, although I did get pretty dry. I offer this as a little sermon for smokers, but I doubt if it has any effect. It stands to reason that a smoker must injure his stamina, more or less, and I think that night's trial proves my case.

It would, however, seem a severe hardship if a cowboy were deprived of tobacco. He has many lonesome hours on his solitary rides on the range, and often a long winter alone with his saddle horse at a line camp. Often he has no company except maybe a fiddle and a cigarette or pipe to help drive dull care away. It is rare that one is found who has a book for a friend. But there is no better spot in the world in which to wade through and get pleasure from even a heavy treatise on some technical subject, or say, a copy of *Bacon's Essays,* than at a lonely cow camp reading by the light of a greasy rag fixed in a can of tallow. A "bitch" is the common name for this kind of light. One can wade through the heaviest tome under these conditions and enjoy every word of some ancient lore. Whereas, in a beautifully equipped library, the reader would shudder at even the sight of such a book.

Our southern border has always been an eyesore and I think our own government is much to blame. I think also that the cattlemen of the Southwest, and all residents within one hundred miles of Mexico, will uphold this statement. In comparison with the peace and goodwill along the entire length of our Canadian border, the condition along our southern border has always, you might say, been one of insecurity, if not to say lawlessness.

True, Mexico never has had a government free from more or less banditry and revolutionary movements in the making, if not actually visible, but with our big and strong government, we of the Southwest frontier felt that a better protection was due us, but it was not given. Even a late secretary of state went so far as to say that Americans should keep out of Mexico, that they had no business crossing the line.

Because of drift cattle, we cowpunchers had consider-

Rancher Pete Kitchen, who came to Arizona Territory in 1854.

This one room adobe structure, fortified against Apache raids, was built by Pete Kitchen. It was the first American ranch house in Arizona Territory.

able business in crossing the line. Otherwise we would soon lose much of our stock. But we knew how to take care of ourselves and acted accordingly.

Often, in crossing into Mexico on a cow hunt, it seemed to me that northern Mexico is in many respects an ideal spot, especially for ranch life. Mild, frostless winters with new land, and many places well watered. In fact, at first thought, it would seem an ideal place for the sturdy pioneer American type.

In course of time, I learned why the American white man had better keep out of Mexico. Old-timers about Tucson, in answer to that query, simply reply, "Do you know what Pete Kitchen[110] got in Sonora?"

Pete Kitchen was an old prospector who had roamed over much of Sonora in search of mineral wealth, and it occurred to him that he could make a fortune in raising hogs in Sonora when pork was always in demand, even at top prices. So he ventured with his hogs onto an ideal spot. A couple of years had passed when Pete again appeared in Tucson. To his friends query of, "Well, Pete, what did you get out of the hog business in Sonora?" his brief, but to the point answer was, "I got hell."

And that might be the answer to all American enterprise across the line in a country without law or security, as we know those two things on our side of the line. It is better to have only a Tucson blanket and your health in the U.S.

And what, you ask, is a Tucson blanket? Just the blue sky above. For much of the year that blue sky above is ample protection to the Tucson dweller.

(110) Legendary character Pete Kitchen was born in Kentucky in 1822. He came to Arizona Territory in 1854, where he established a ranch and farm at the junction of Potrero Creek and the Santa Cruz River, about seven miles north of Nogales. Determined not to succumb to maurading Apaches, he constructed a five-room adobe ranch house with walls two feet thick; the roof surrounded by a parapet on which a sentinel stood guard. The Apaches came and came again. His neighbors were driven off; his herder killed; his stepson murdered; cattle and hogs slaughtered. But Kitchen stood his ground. As his reputation spread, his ranch was considered the safest point between Tucson and Magdalena, Sonora. In time, the Apaches gave up and left Kitchen alone.

Known for the fine hogs he raised, Kitchen's ham, bacon, and lard could be found in stores as far distant as Fort Yuma, Santa Fe, and El Paso.

Kitchen's last years were spent in Tucson where he died August 5, 1895.

Faulk, *Arizona*, pp. 94–95.
Workers, *Arizona*, pp. 302–03.
Trimble, *Roadside*, pp. 45–46.

IN A FRONTIER LAND where there is no law in reach and where it is one hundred miles to the county seat, requiring two days of travel to reach, a quick decision as to the right thing to do is often necessary. But it might lead to embarrassing consequences. Such a crisis for brother Dick and myself happened one bright morning at the old Animas Valley Ranch.

Long before sunup, a stranger rode up and appealed to us for help. His story was that a well-armed bunch of Mexicans had appeared in the night at his camp at the old Double Dobies,[111] and had seized about one hundred head of cattle he was holding there while his partner had gone to Lordsburg[112] for grub. The Mexicans, he said, were now rushing these cattle back to over the border, and he asked us to help recover them.

We did not know the man, but the fact that he was white and a fellow American seemed in his favor, and a quick decision was necessary. We did not hesitate but agreed to go at once. We, of course, knew these cattle might have been stolen from the Mexicans and that they might only be taking justice into their own hands. But there was the other side to look at. A man of our own kind had appealed to us for aid. And we feared, too, that our horses might have been picked up on the way. If, on overtaking the herd, we found the Mexicans were only regaining their own stock which had been stolen, and had done no harm, we could turn back.

So we rode out to overtake the Mexicans, if possible, before they reached the border. We picked up four more cowboys at the Lang Ranch, who willingly joined us on hearing the story, and, seven strong, we dashed ahead.

We knew they must be heading for Deer Creek, the only possible pass that cattle could be driven through into Mexico. True enough, we soon saw the dust raised by the herd. As a precaution against an ambush, we took to the high ground on each side of the pass and, scattering out, we each fired a shot in the air to suggest to the Mexicans we might be a bigger force than we were.

This worked, for despite our waving our hats when we came in sight of the herders to show our "friendly interest," they fired a few shots which came close enough to alarm us. We dismounted and hid behind our mounts. Then we saw that the Mexicans had abandoned the herd and were speeding up their mounts in an evident attempt to get away. We had won the fight with our bluff, and the poor bunch of panting cattle were ours by conquest.

No loose horses were in the herd, and we suddenly

(111) Double Dobies was the nickname of the Double Adobes Ranch adjacent to the Gray Ranch in the Animas Valley of New Mexico. A stream there ran year round, and during the drought of the early 1890s, it was a sought after watering place for cattle.
Hilliard, p. 25.

(112) Lordsburg was a Southern Pacific Railroad town, established October 18, 1880, and named after an engineer in charge of construction. A post office was opened in 1881. It is the seat of Hidalgo Country, its economy based on mining and ranching.
Pearce, p. 90.

(113) Drought struck Arizona Territory in 1892 when less than half the usual amount of moisture fell during the rainy season. Ranges were filled to capacity with some 1.5 million head of cattle, and by the summer of 1893, countless animals had perished.
  Wilson, p. 189.

(114) Lick Observatory on Mount Hamilton was a gift to the University of California by James Lick (1796–1876), a Pennsylvania German who made a small fortune in South America. He came to California shortly before the gold rush, and enlarged his fortune through real estate speculation.
  Gudde, Erwin G. *California Place Names: The Origin and Etymology of Current Geographical Names.* Berkeley: University of California Press, 1965, p. 167.

(115) As the Central Pacific Railroad pushed east from the Pacific coast to meet the Union Pacific at Promontory, Utah, May 10, 1869, railroad towns sprang into existence. Some ninety miles from Reno, at a place early traders called French Ford and then French Bridge, a substantial station was built. By the time the first train came through on September 16, 1868, a small town called Winnemucca, named after the Paiute chief, had come into being.
  Best, Gerald M. "Rendezvous at Promontory: The 'Jupiter' and N. 119." *Utah Historical Quarterly,* Vol. 37, No. 1 (Winter, 1969), pp. 69–75.
  Elliott, Russell R. *History of Nevada.* Lincoln: University of Nebraska Press, 1987, p. 113.

(116) The town takes its name after nearby Los Banos Creek. A post office was established in 1874, and in 1889, after the arrival of the railroad, a townsite was laid out.
  Gudde, p. 173.

(117) In 1814, a Scotch sailor named John Gilroy was put ashore at Monterey becasue he had the scurvy—and thus it is that Gilroy became California's first permanent non-Spanish resident. He made his home in the Santa Clara Valley and married a woman who was grantee of a portion of the San Isidro land grant. A settlement sprang up around the rancho, first called San Isidro, later Gilroy.
  Gudde, p. 114.

(118) It would not have been a detachment of Coxey's Army that Gray encountered, but a local organization in sympathy with Jacob S. Coxey's ideas. Born in 1854, Coxey—after the Panic of 1893—introduced in Congress bills advocating the right of local governments to exchange noninterest-bearing bonds for Treasury notes to finance public works. He proposed a vast road-building program as a means to ease unemployment, and advocated a variety of measures to assist the poor.
  On March 25, 1894, what had come to be called Coxey's Army—a group of some 100 largely unemployed men—set out from Massillion, Ohio to Washington, DC. When the army arrived on May 1, it had grown to some 500. As they approached the capitol, they were stopped by police who clubbed fifty of the men. Coxey was arrested for carrying a banner and walking on the grass. He was sentenced to twenty days in jail. None of his ideas would come to fruition until years later when Franklin D. Roosevelt came to office and introduced the New Deal. Coxey died in 1951.
  The Encyclopedia Americana: International Edition. CT: Grolier, Inc., 1993, Vol. 8, p. 136.
  The New Encyclopedia Britannica. Chicago: Encyclopedia Britannica, Inc., 1995, Vol. 3, p. 700.

realized the rustler—which he then admitted to be—had worked us to a finish. But we otherwise took our medicine with good grace, feeling we could not have done otherwise from our point of view. And if again we were called upon to make a choice between a white man and a Mexican, and there were no known extenuating circumstances in favor of the Mexican, we would have to step to the side of our countryman. Such was the universal law on the border involving relations of the "gringo" and the "greaser."

MOST OF OUR SHIPMENTS of feeder cattle would go east on the Santa Fe to Colorado, Montana, or Kansas pastures, but occasionally we made a sale to California cattlemen. During the drought period, we were glad to have our shipments go west, as there was less danger of losses with poor cattle, and no cold weather such as we would meet with in the mountains of New Mexico and Colorado.

1893 was a drought year in Arizona and cattle were in poor shape on ranges.[113] The California range was good, and we made an effort to find buyers among the cattlemen of that state. Our stumbling block was the railroad. The Southern Pacific required us to pay freight, or guarantee it in advance of shipping, but we got around this by having the buyers assume this obligation. We finally obtained a special rate of $75 per car for trainload lots, provided cattle were billed to Winnemucca, Nevada. Rates to California points were much higher. The railroad figured that shipments to Winnemucca would later on have to be reshipped over their line to markets in California, and this gave them a second haul. But we saw our way out of this hole as new developments will show.

Our buyer had a ranch in Hall's Valley near Mount Hamilton, where the Lick Observatory stands.[114] If we shipped to San Jose—the logical railroad point—it would have cost $100 per car. So we billed our train load of cattle to Winnemucca[115] at $75 per car, and we unloaded at Los Banos Station in the San Joaquin,[116] driving our herd across the Coast Range through Pacheco Pass and down the Santa Clara Valley via Gilroy[117] and San Jose to Hall's Valley. The railroad agent at Los Banos protested, as our cattle were billed farther on into Nevada, but there was no law or reason that could compel us to ship farther. The railroad company had received payment of freight to Winnemucca, although we stopped 300 miles short of that point.

That was the year of Cox's Army,[118] and we met a big detachment of that army at Yuma when we unloaded to feed our stock. The following morning by sunup we had our cars loaded, and when the train pulled up to Yuma Station for orders, we found another load awaiting us.

The conductor told us there were 500 hoboes seeking passage into California. They had drifted into Yuma, but a close guard on the bridge across the Colorado River had kept them from crossing, so they had conspired to use our train for transportation. There were four of us cowboys and the trainmen thought we would help them keep these men off the cars. We told the trainman, however, that it was not our scrap and our only interest was to keep anyone from getting into cars with the cattle—so no effort was made to stop the army from riding on top of the cars.

The men rushed for places. Every car was soon loaded on top, and our twenty-two cars went out of Yuma virtually with flags flying, for many men held little banners above them. It was a lively crowd at the start.

It was a bright, sunny morning and we moved across the desert as if going on a picnic. But it gets hot on the Colorado Desert even in winter, and that was the 24th day of December. When we arrived at Salton Station, where the salt works were then in operation, the thermometer in the depot registered 120 degrees. Our top car passengers were a sorry looking sight—dust-covered and thirsty.

They rushed for the station, where one lone man held sway, and begged him for water. But he had to tell them he could not give them any. This man got his water shipped in by rail and he was down to about a gallon of the precious stuff as the tank car was long overdue.

We had to move on at once, and we pulled out of there with our thirsty hoboes still with us. Luckily, however, it was not far to Indio and our engine crew humanely speeded up that all might soon find relief, which they did at Indio Station.[119] The people at the Southern Pacific Hotel generously donated bread and cooked for these famished men. It was there, too, that they received the good news that there was a large encampment of Cox's Army at Colton,[120] who would welcome them upon their arrival.

So at Colton our passengers left us, and we saw at the edge of town, the camp fires around which were bivouacked Cox's Army of the unemployed. It had been a tough day on our hoboes but, all's well that ends well.

That night we crossed the Tehachapi Mountains by Bakersfield[121] and traveled down the San Joaquin to Los Banos, where we unloaded our cattle and found the buyers of Hall's Valley awaiting us with saddle horses. Soon we

(119) The Southern Pacific Railroad built a station here in May, 1876, naming it Indio—Spanish for Indian—for nearby Indian Wells.
Gudde, p. 143.

(120) Settled in 1873, when the Southern Pacific Railroad reached this point in 1875, the town was christened Colton for David D. Colton, financial director of the Central Pacific Railroad.
Gudde, p. 68.

(121) A civil and hydraulic engineer, Thomas Baker was a most ambitious man who sought, in the early 1860s, to create a navigable waterway from Kern Lake to San Francisco. He did not succeed, but in the process acquired a large parcel of land. He fenced it in and thereafter it was called Baker's field. A town sprang up and in 1868, took the name Bakersfield.
Gudde, pp. 18–19.

had the herd on the way for its long trek via Pacheco Pass into the Santa Clara Valley, and headed for Mount Hamilton. This trail proved easy going and a happy journey for us desert cowpunchers, who came from a land of long distances between drinks.

On the summit of Pacheco Pass at sunrise, we looked down on the big Santa Clara Valley with its endless squares laid out like a checkerboard of farms. Smoke rose from a thousand homes amidst green fields.

We desert cowboys gazed long at this panorama. As one remarked, it was "good for sore eyes." We drifted our herd down wide country roads. Grass was green and in abundance; hardly a mile was traversed without finding some pools of rain water along the way. At night we found beds and food for ourselves at some farm house or village hotel, and a pasture for our stock. In fact, as my fellow cowboys said on our return trip to Arizona, "It was sure good going—chicken and cream pies, feather beds, and lots of grass and water"—a cowboy's dream.

We came near to having a bad nightmare, however, before our journey's end.

After we arrived at the summit of Pacheco Pass, we began to meet the spring migration of sheep en route to pasturage in the Sierra Nevadas. The first flock had Basque herders and we warned them they had better not attempt to pass our herd on the highway, but to make a gap in the fence and turn the sheep into the adjoining field until we had our cattle by. The head Basque spoke but little English and seemed to think we were trying to impose on him, so despite our warning he kept the flock approaching us on the road. Maybe he thought of the natural antagonism of cattlemen for sheep herders, and felt he had as much right on the road as we.

We took precautions to have most of our cowboys keep behind our herd to prevent a stampede when the sheep advanced among them. All went well at first, and the sheep, though apparently frightened by the cattle, advanced in a close bunch to one side of the herd. But an old steer seemed to resent the looks of one of the sheep. Suddenly he lowered his head, lifted the sheep on the tips of his horns, and with the sheep's sudden bleat of alarm, the entire flock broke into a wild run. All we could see was a cloud of dust moving off down the road, with the herders vainly trying to keep in sight of them. And so, one more victory of cattlemen over sheepmen.

Afterward, we met quite a number of flocks headed east for the Sierras, but we found all of them sidetracked on the other side of the fence awaiting our passing. They had learned their lesson.

On our last day, a few miles from San Jose, we ran into a dense tule fog, as it is termed in California valleys. We had night-herded our cattle near Coyote Station[122] and we started early, before daybreak. Our cattle were strung out for probably a mile, drifting down the country road when we ran into this dense fog. We had one of the boys ride on ahead, and he was to watch closely for open gates. If he found any, he was to close them so our herd would not stray into gardens along the way. The cowboy must, however, have been dazed by some lure and neglected to close the gates leading into Edenvale,[123] a place of beautiful grounds and a fine house—the property of a religious cult. And when we reached that point and discovered to our horror that our lead cattle had entered these grounds, and saw they had created considerable havoc, we were fearful of the consequences. We hastily rode in, and with as little noise as possible, we routed our cattle out onto the road again.

I would hesitate to estimate the damage we had done, but a hasty glance showed that the cattle had almost ruined the garden. The water in the fountain pond was drunk dry, bushes were badly mauled about, and one big steer even had the impudence to be resting on the front porch.

We saw no one about, and got our herd strung out on the road again. We pushed them ahead for a mile or so and, luckily, reached the side road we were to take that led toward Mount Hamilton.

When the fog lifted, we turned off the road and struck across a steep mountain that lay between us and Hall's valley. We thought this would be a short cut, so took it instead of going by the longer but easier road. It was this road that probably saved us from further trouble over our invasion of Edenvale. Later on we learned the Edenvale people were hot on our trail, but luckily for us a small beef herd had followed ours, and it was this herd which was overtaken by the Edenvale people and accused of the damage. It took some time for these later herders to clear themselves of the charge, and that helped us get away.

After we had delivered our cattle to Hall's Valley and were on our way back to Arizona, we heard from our Hall's Valley rancher that the real culprits were never discovered by the Edenvale people. It was a close call and we dreaded to think what it might have cost us had we been apprehended. As it was, this trip was a jolly vacation for us Arizona cowboys.

(122) This station was near what had, as early as 1776, been called the Coyote River in Santa Clara County.
Gudde, p. 74.

(123) Located in Santa Clara County, Edenvale was given its name by the Southern Pacific Railroad at an unknown date, but prior to 1887. It appears, however, not to have been a town per se, but a 240-acre estate owned by Mary Hayes-Chynoweth, a spiritualist and mystic who founded the True Life Church. Wrote historian H.S. Foote in 1888 of the Hayes-Chynoweth estate, "... Along its front, and bordering the avenue, is a row of stately eucalyptus trees, which adorn the place without intercepting the view from the roadway ... An Evergreen bower, inclosing flower beds in many designs, occupies a portion of the space between the residence and the road front. The winding walks are also bordered with evergreens and roses. The building improvements, which are to be on an extensive scale, will require some time before the plans of the owners are realized. In 1887 the contract was let for the construction of the stable building, and the same year finished at a cost of $10,000. It is a handsomely designed structure, not excelled in the county .... Among its beauties may be mentioned five attractive sleeping-rooms for attendants. The crowning building improvement, however, is to be the palatial residence, which will be commenced and possibly completed in 1888, at a cost of between $50,000 and $75,000. Eastern architects are now engaged on the plans for the building."
Edenvale eventually was swallowed up by San Jose and in the mid-1900s, nineteen acres of this once palatial estate became an amusement park called Frontier Village. In 1985, the city of San Jose purchased the 41,000 square foot mansion, and in 1988 purchased the park "... to preserve its [the mansion and grounds] integrity as a historic landmark," wrote the San Jose *Mercury-News.* "The 64-room mansion, built by spiritualist Mary Hayes [Chenoweth], has three wings, several fireplaces, 15 bathrooms and servants' quarters on the third floor."
Gudde, p. 92.
Hoover, Mildres Brooke, Hero Eugene Rensh, Ethel Grace Rensch, revised by William N. Abelow, *Historical Spots in California*, Stanford: Stanford University Press, 1966, p. 431.
Sawyer, Eugene T., *History of Santa Clara County California with Biographical Sketches*, Los Angeles: Historic Record Company, 1922, pp. 334–338.
Foote, H.S., *Pen Pictures from the Garden of the World: Santa Clara County, California*. Chicago: The Lewis Publishing Company, 1888, pp. 254–255.
San Jose *Mercury-News*, July 11, 1990.

Ours was the first trail herd seen by Santa Clara Valley residents since the early days, and many watched us go by with curiosity. We had about one thousand head of stock and sometimes the herd extended a mile or more down the road, and to many it seemed much more numerous than it really was. One old-timer said he "reckoned we had five thousand head."

At one place where we stopped overnight, an old settler asked how far we had come. We gave him honest figures of eleven hundred miles, but he did not understand that most of it was by rail, so he studied a little and then replied, "My, you must have come 'a-flukin'"—his expression for speed.

Part of our cattle were to go to a young man who was deaf and dumb. His widowed mother was getting them for him. The young fellow met us at Los Banos to accompany us on our trip down the valley, and one day we had him leading the herd. Some passerby accosted him about the cattle, but he had to answer in sign language. The rest of us were strung along at different points of the herd and this stranger accosted the next man he met. This cowboy was quick to see a chance for fun, so he keep mum and simply moved his fingers in imitation of our deaf and dumb boy. The man shook his head and rode on to the next man where he got the same reception, and so on down the line. What he thought of this "deaf and dumb" bunch we could only guess, but we punchers enjoyed the joke and I guess I have heard the story told a hundred times around campfires after our return to the Arizona range.

THE ARIZONA COWBOYS were probably over-zealous in criticizing the U.S. Army during the Apache raids, but sometimes such criticism was well deserved. Often the bad acting of an army troop was due to the inexperience of its commanding officer. Frequently a cavalry troop was commanded by a green lieutenant recently graduated from West Point who might be a strict and able technician, but West Point was no place to learn Indian fighting or the ways of navigating the rough lands of Arizona. A green lieutenant might lead his command into serious trouble.

One day a cavalry company and pack train of mules marched in double file by our old Rucker Ranch house. We were sitting on our front porch after an early supper as the troop passed with the commanding officer at the head of the double file column. Usually a passing troop of cavalry would halt and the officers would dismount to extend

AHS #44694

Army pack trains were essential to the Apache campaigns.

greetings and inquire about a place to make camp. Such permission was always given by us, and without charge for wood and water for their camp.

But on this occasion, the officer at the head of the column sat stiffly in the saddle as though on parade at West Point. He seemed to be looking straight ahead, and not seeing, or ignoring us, marched on and soon was out of sight. We thought no more of the incident as troops often passed our ranch in those days.

The following day about dusk, the same troop rode up to the ranch house and stopped and dismounted this time—a bedraggled and tired looking bunch. The officer, rather worn looking, walked in and sat down on the porch, then told us all about his troubles. He had led his troop up the canyon, following an old road which ended at an abandoned sawmill, then apparently had attempted to keep on in the same direction, finally ending up in a box canyon with sides too steep for the horses and mules to make headway. They camped there for the night. The following day they once again attempted to move up the mountain, leading their horses and mules. After hours of scrambling over rough country, skinning the legs of their stock and tearing their own clothing on the brush, the officer gave up and ordered a retreat. The Lieutenant seemed a sadder, and it was hoped, wiser man.

We told him we would gladly have put him on the right road, but we supposed he knew what he was doing.

Often after that, we had his troop camp with us. He said, frankly, that he had learned his lesson. At heart he was quite a good fellow. It was simply his West Point training that needed a little wearing off by our Arizona rocks, cactus, and rough sledding.

Another case came up that left a bad taste with us. That was our finding a dead soldier near our horse camp in the San Simon. It was a case of another green lieutenant lately from West Point and put in charge of a cavalry company.

The reason for so many inexperienced officers just out of West Point being placed in charge of these troops was, no doubt, because the old officers side-stepped the Apache trouble by getting easier duties, a job at Washington or just a furlough.

Anyway, this lieutenant came to our cow camp from a trip to the Mexican border at the head of the Yaqui River, and told us he had had to discipline one of his men for getting drunk on Mescal. He had left him afoot with instructions to report to Fort Bowie. The lieutenant asked us to

A cavalry detachment moving out on patrol from Fort Bowie during the 1880s.

AHS #70127

keep on the lookout for this man and lend him a hand if we saw him.

The man had evidently attempted to walk back, and it was about fourteen days after that we found the dead body of the soldier—and that find was due to the curiosity of a little mule.

One of our cowboys had left camp to bring in our horse herd. In driving in this herd, a little mule used as a pack animal had run out to one side, attracted by something he had discovered, and the cowboy rode out to turn in the mule when he noticed the dead soldier, which was what had attracted the mule's attention in the first place.

The soldier had evidently become weakened and overcome by the hot weather, lack of food and water. He had tried to summon help, as he had fired his gun many times—the cartridge shells lying empty on the ground testifying to this fact. The body had simply dried up like a mummy in the hot sun, but no animal or vulture had touched it. It was probably preserved, too, by the alcohol in the drink of mescal he had consumed. I have heard my father say that coyotes and vultures would not touch the Mexican dead on the battlefields of the Mexican War. This was laid to the mescal drink of the Mexicans and the pepper they used in their food.

We sent word to Fort Bowie, and a detachment came out with a pack mule for the remains. The discipline of this man was probably according to army orders, but as a cowboy saw it, it was close to murder to turn even a drunk man loose afoot and alone on a hot, waterless desert to find his way out.

Another instance we remember is of a thoughtless soldier on courier duty who lost his way in crossing the south end of the San Simon Valley through the Malpais section. When his horse gave out, he took off the saddle and tied the animal to a stake pin and struck out afoot. Luckily, he found his way to a cow camp and food and water. But he never was able to locate the spot where he left his horse. It was several years later that a cowboy hunting cattle, ran onto the skeleton of a horse, attached by halter and rope to a driven stake pin, which was no doubt that soldier's mount.

What a pitiful comment on the thoughtless, not to say cruel, mind of a man. Why did he not turn his poor horse loose and at least give him a fighting chance for his life? His probable fear of discipline for the loss of a horse was in his mind, but the chances are that the horse, loose, would have found his way out and thus back to the government.

ONLY A FEW YEARS AGO I met an old-timer who had freighted in the 1860s over the old Santa Fe Trail. He said our government at one time paid sixty dollars for an Indian scalp and that he quit his freight team for a time and became a hunter for scalps. In the early Spanish rule, such rewards had been paid and probably this method had been followed by army officers of the U.S. If so, it was surely a great wrong done in the name of the United States, for it led to the murder of many Indians who had always been at peace with us.

As this freighter said, it was no trick to get Papago Indian scalps and pass them off for Apaches. The Papagos were always good, peaceful fellows, but a scalp hunter would hardly draw the line for the matter of sixty dollars. Maybe this "expense account" was never entered on the books at Washington. It is said that the Spanish troops paid such rewards as a desperate attempt to hold their authority over the Indians, who often had defeated them. Our troops, likewise, never won much glory against the Apaches. But this reward era will always be a bad chapter in the conquest of our frontier.[124]

General George Crook, seated right with hand in jacket. Called the "greatest Indian fighting general" in the army. Gray disagreed.

(124) A documented instance of scalp hunting involves John Glanton, an unsavory character who headed a band of outlaws at Yuma in the early 1850s. Glanton was hired by the Mexican government to gather Apache scalps at one hundred dollars for each man, fifty dollars for each woman, twenty-five dollars for each child. Glanton, however, did not discriminate and scalped Pimas, Opatas, and Mexicans as well. When the Mexican government caught onto his scheme, he fled the country.

Farrish, Thomas E. *History of Arizona*, Vol. 1. Phoenix: State of Arizona, 1915, pp. 235–236.

GENERAL CROOK was author of the plan to use Indians to hunt the renegade Apaches and he always had several companies of Indian scouts in the field. These scouts could ride if they furnished their own mounts, so we often had chances to sell them ponies. About thirty-five dollars was as high as a scout would go, for he drew only the private soldier's pay of thirteen dollars a month. On the ranch we always kept on hand a few thirty-five dollar horses for the

Indians, and that sum they would give without any question. A higher price would be met with refusal by the scout. Their idea of a good horse was one of thirty-five dollar value—that probably being the price of the first horse they bought, which always afterward seemed the proper value to them.

The scouts were always paid in silver dollars and they didn't seem to consider anything else as money. Outside of buying horses, I think they had little use for money, except to beat the dollars into silver buttons for bridle ornaments. After every payday they would ask for the use of our blacksmith shop, where they would diligently work with the anvil and hammer beating out buttons for ornaments.

At the same time, an Indian scout might be pretty shrewd. I remember that a soldier quartermaster would issue every evening a grain ration for their horses. On one occasion, I overheard the Q.M. sergeant ask an Indian, "How many horses?"—as some might have more than one. This Indian answered, "Seven horses." Of course that was too many horses for one man to have, and on further questioning it was revealed that the scout had named his one horse, "Seven Horses." This was in the hope of getting an abundance of grain for his mount.

Indian scout companies were usually in command of some civilian white man who could talk the Apache language, and who was experienced of the country's trails.

Al Sieber[125] was an old-time chief of scouts, and Tom Horn often brought his company of scouts to our ranch. These scouts were taken from some Apache tribe that had a good record at the San Carlos reservation.

There was always doubt among ranchers about the wisdom of arming Indians to fight the hostiles. They were all Apaches, and many times we were convinced that the scouts lost the trail purposely when it was getting too hot, or else led the white troops in the wrong way.

An Apache is a poor horseman and often when a scout would get a new pony at the ranch he would want to try it out. The result sometimes was that Mr. Indian was bucked off. But even most gentle ponies would resent the rough, homemade saddle used by the Indian. Then some cowboy would shame the Indian by riding the same pony bareback, and then his fellow scouts would yell with joy at their comrade's discomfort.

There was Mike Keating who had a little cow ranch near Galeyville. He evidently had walked into a pasture to drive up a horse or maybe a milk cow. He was not packing a gun. He was found dead, beaten to death by a rock on the

(125) Born in Mingolsheim, Germany, February 29, 1844, Albert Sieber was five-years-old when in 1849 his family, by then fatherless, migrated to Lancaster, Pennsylvania; then, about 1856, to Minneapolis. A few days following his eighteenth birthday in 1862, Sieber enlisted in the First Minnesota Volunteers, a distinguished unit that saw much action during the Civil War, including the battle of Gettysburg in which Sieber was badly wounded. Discharged in the summer of 1865, Sieber returned to Minneapolis, but his stay was brief. Early in 1866 he set about for San Francisco. He remained there several months, then took work cutting ties for the Central Pacific Railroad, which was building its great roadbed over the Sierra Nevadas. Later, he followed the mining boom to Virginia City, then to White Pine County. He first came to Arizona in 1868, and was hired as foreman of a ranch in the Williamson Valley northwest of Prescott where Indian attacks were frequent. It was there in April, 1870 that Seiber experienced what was probably his first real fight with Indians, the first of countless such encounters. During the summer of 1871, Lieutenant Willam J. Ross, General George Crook's quartermaster, hired Sieber to serve as scout at a salary of $125 a month; the beginning of a now legendary career. In time, he was appointed Crook's Chief of Scouts and played a pivotal role in the Apache wars. Sieber died February 19, 1907, his body crushed by a falling boulder.

Thrapp, *Sieber*, pp. 3–7, 15, 23–27, 29, 32, 38, 42, 53, 59, 62–63, 94, 400–01.

AHS #19624

Al Sieber, legendary Chief of Scouts.

head. Only a few miles away, on the old Galeyville grade, two miners, both old men, were found dead on their wagon seat, evidently shot by Apaches from ambush near the road. The only thing the men had worth the taking was the team of two work horses. One man was shot through his hatband, proving that his head must have been lowered as if against a driving rain, but if he had been looking ahead he must have seen the Indians before they shot.

Across the Chiricahua Mountains on the west side, another elderly man, living alone at a cabin, was found lying across the woodpile, shot through the body. These things all happened within a few days time on one Indian raid, and proves how easy one might fall before the Apache. In all probability, it happened in the early morning or the dusk of evening. A poor mongrel dog—the best friend of man—might have saved these lives. It could not have happened, and probably would not have been attempted, with the protection of a dog and the warning of its bark.

The Apache, and I venture to say, all our American Indians, could shoot with any accuracy only at short range. So they always got within a few yards before shooting. In other words, they took no chances of missing their victim.

One could fill pages of accounts of Apache murders of whites, but invariably these murders have been an ambush in some mountain area, or some lone rancher or prospector was shot from a concealed place when he was totally unaware of the danger. And that trait, it might be termed, made the Apache the most dangerous and deadly enemy of all our frontier people. He would not face one in the open and allow his enemy a fighting chance, as would the northern Indians, and even the Comanches of Texas. The only thing to do in the face of an Apache sneak was to use the Indian's tactics when possible—that is to keep off roads and trails at the critical times of daybreak and dust when the Indian was up to most of his devilment.

It was wise never to be without a good dog at camp,

and if it was necessary to travel alone with a wagon, to go at night. Two or more men could travel anytime with little danger, as the Apache was not apt to take a chance that he might not get both. The Apache felt that against one man, one shot did the work.

But do not think for a moment that we cowboys did not at times get the "jitters"—as we term a fit of the nerves today. Someone might come to our camp and spread the alarm that a bunch—which might mean from half a dozen to a hundred—of Apaches had left San Carlos, and their trail had crossed the tracks of the railroad at some mentioned point and headed south. Such news would put us on the jump. Our saddle horses would be in danger and we must gather them quickly and put them where they could be guarded from a raid.

If the warning came in time, we would rush our saddle stock to the nearest corral and stand night guard over them until we heard of the Indian trail being found further south. Always they would head for the high Sierra Madres in Mexico. That did not mean the danger was over, but it gave us a few days respite to hunt up any missing horses, as we knew the renegade Indians would soon return on a raid out of Mexico. In short, our side of the line was about the only profitable region for a raid, as border Mexico had little if anything worth the taking. But the lofty Sierra Madres made a good hiding place to which the Apache could retreat.

WE SELDOM STOP to think how much we owe to our friend and slave, the horse, who ranks with the dog as man's best animal friend. And especially is this true of the cow pony who seems more necessary and a part of this rider's daily life than any other horse in any other role.

Without his mount, a cowboy is helpless. With his trusty mount he becomes a ruler over the herds, faces all kinds of weather, and is as near a king in his own domain as it is possible for a human being to be. I would class the cow pony and rider as the centaur of our age. So much depends on the quick wit of the cow pony, as well as of the rider. Watch the well trained cutting horse in a roundup. Often before a cow makes a move, the cutting horse will give a quick jump in anticipation of the cow's move, and is at the spot in advance to check it.

Old cowboys can tell almost unbelievable stories of some "Old Faithful" who instinctively anticipated a cow's move and acted accordingly, to the wonder of the rider.

I had an old gray cow pony who served me fourteen

years as a top cutting horse. He had a trick which always seemed a marvel to all who witnessed it. That was his handling of a stubborn cow, steer, or even a heavy old bull that would refuse to be driven out of the roundup and if cut, would keep insisting on turning back. Give the old gray his head and he would hug up alongside the unruly animal, push his head and neck back of the horns, slowly pushing against his stubborn opponent to turn him back into the herd. Thus the old gray would pilot the stubborn animal to the cut before it was aware, and the deed was done.

At the task of loading cattle into cars at the railroad, often an animal would stall and refuse to move up the chute. Here, the old gray pony came to the rescue, seeming to love to crowd up behind and, by pure strength, push the stalled animal step by step into the car.

Once in reloading a train of mixed cattle at San Marciel,[126] New Mexico, we had a case of a big bull who refused to move up the car chute. Of course we had no old gray pony to help us. So after loading all but the stubborn bull, we called on the engineer in his cab to help us, and willingly he agreed. We ran the big tow cable from the engine through the car door on the off side of the chute, and then a rope to the bull's horns. With three sturdy fellows pushing the bull from behind and the engine slowly moving ahead, our bull, resisting every inch, moved forward and we soon had him in the car and our train merrily moving on its way east.

WE ARE NOT TRYING to criticize the methods of our government or those of the army, but to simply tell the story as we knew it. It was plain to us ranchers—and General Miles as much as admitted it—that the average soldier as then enlisted in our big cities, was next to worthless on the frontier. And whenever General Miles had an important message to send by courier, he invariably delegated a rancher or one of the rancher's cowboys for the task.

One cavalry troop which was stationed at Rucker all one summer could make the best bread you could wish for. They came from San Francisco where they had enlisted during a bakers' strike. But a cowboy once said they couldn't follow a wagon track and were constantly getting lost. Of course the army is vastly improved since, and during the World War, but when the pay was only thirteen dollars a month it could not be expected that the Army would get many desirable recruits. And you could not object to the customary phrase, "as ornery as a soldier."

(126) San Marciel was once a station of the Santa Fe Railroad.
Workers, *New Mexico*, p. 254.

There were some enlisted men who entered the service just to get out West. Some were adventurers and purposely enlisted just to win at cards the payday checks or money of their comrades. One of this latter kind I cannot refrain from mentioning, as he was in a way a clever, all around sharper. He accumulated most of the payday revenue of his troop until his comrades began to realize they were being robbed. Then they made it so hot for him he deserted, but he made the error of taking for his mount a fine saddle mare which was the property of an officer. This led to his early capture, as a big reward was offered by the owner of the mare. This soldier was sent for a limit-period to Alcatraz Island.

The late escape from this Island by two prisoners, and the general belief that nobody had ever escaped or could survive the rough bay waters surrounding the island, is disproved by this soldier. His stay at Alcatraz was short.

It was only a few months after this soldier was sent to Alcatraz that a fellow came to our ranch on foot and asked for work. In those days we would not have the heart to turn down a plea for work, especially if the man was afoot, and I remember the man remained a month or more at our place.

In the course of time, he told us that he was the deserter who had escaped from Alcatraz. He said he saw the opportunity to step into the water and escape attention until nightfall and then, with the incoming tide, he managed to swim to the San Francisco waterfront. He said it was an easy getaway from then on. As far as I know he was never recaptured.

In those days I doubt if any deserter was ever informed on by a rancher. It seemed a despicable thing to have a man arrested for the twenty-five dollar reward offered for deserters.

ONE WINTER THERE CAME to our horse camp at Mulberry Spring in San Simon, a rider leading an extra horse packing a small bedroll. As is the custom in the cow country, we never questioned his name, past performances, nor ask from whence he came. He gave his name as Hall and stayed on through the rest of the winter, accepting our usual hospitality and sharing our meals. We were building a pasture fence of barbed wire. Often the stranger would help with the work, and at other times stay at the camp and have supper ready for us.

At the time, Grant Wheeler was breaking several

young horses for the ranch, and being thrown a great deal in the company of this stranger, they became close friends—or rather, Grant was probably induced to join with Hall in a certain partnership which was a plotted scheme for making a strike.

As weather was becoming spring-like, Grant and Hall asked me to lend them a camp outfit for a few weeks, saying they were going on a prospecting trip. They left us with, ostensibly, this end in view. About two weeks later, I was driving a two-horse team and wagon across Sulphur Springs Valley on my way to Willcox for a load of grub, and I met a sheriff's posse of about twenty men riding at a fast gait toward me. The sheriff asked me at once where Grant Wheeler was, and then said the Southern Pacific passenger train had been held up the night before by two men and one of these men was Grant Wheeler.

They had boarded the westbound train as it pulled out of Willcox about dusk and had forced the engineer to stop about three miles west of Willcox, where two saddled horses were tied. There they robbed the express car by blowing up the safe.

The robbers had used a big consignment of Mexican dollars—a shipment for San Francisco—to lay on top of the dynamite charge which was put on top of the safe, and thus blew open the safe and got the contents. Mexican dollars were picked up every little while all over the prairie and it was reported about fifteen thousand of them had been scattered in that way.

How much actual money was taken by Grant Wheeler and Hall we never knew, but detective Thacker of the Express Company who came to Rucker Ranch on the hunt for the robbers, said the haul was small. A big consignment of Louisiana lottery tickets was in the safe, and evidently Grant and Hall, in the dark, thought this was currency, as they took it with them.

So far as I know no trace was ever found of Hall. I have a suspicion that he had used Grant as his tool and that they separated soon afterward, Hall taking most of the money. Grant Wheeler was trailed to Durango, Colorado. As the posse closed in on him, Grant turned and fired two shots from his pistol over their heads. Then with his last shot, he blew his own brains out. His money was all gone, so I doubt if he had ever received much for his night's work near Willcox.

Cowmen generally felt kindly toward Grant. He was a good rider and always a capable and willing cowhand. We blamed Hall for leading him astray. As Detective Thacker said, he never saw a case where an outlaw had such loyal friends. Although he offered a thousand dollars to anyone who could locate Grant's whereabouts, no one was found among those who had known Grant who would join in any way to help effect a capture. So Grant got clear away and took his own life when he saw no other way of escape.[127]

I think this was the only train holdup of the Southern Pacific line through Arizona during all the days of the rustler, for strange to relate, the rustler always steered clear of the railroads and only on one noted occasion was it known that they had planned a big coup. But there was a leak somewhere and it was frustrated.

That was a scheme to stop the train on which President Rutherford B. Hayes was a passenger to California. The plan was to kidnap the president and hold him prisoner in the high Sierra Madres of Mexico for ransom. They did not, apparently, figure on the heavy guard which always accompanies our presidents. The plan had leaked out, and in Texas a full company of soldiers was put aboard the train. The rustlers, of course, called it off.

IT SEEMED A NATURAL SEQUEL from the old pioneer days when the gun was as necessary as the axe—the latter to build the log cabin for shelter, and the former to kill game for food, as well as serve as protection. It was easy to lay aside the axe and make the gun alone serve your wants. Now in the present era, our firearms have become our greatest menace to civilization. It is unfortunate that we have allowed the practice of carrying guns, especially the quick-shooting and repeating pistols, to spread until the possession of a pistol is considered essential to many households. I venture to state that if firearms were prohibited to all except peace officers, that our present crime wave would be reduced by half, and probably more.

The adventures of most of the trigger men who attempt to live by their wits backed by quick shooting, are generally ended in a lonely mound on the prairie or as a number only, sewed on their shirts as their only identity at the penitentiary.

When the boys at camp heard the story of the end of Suggs,[128] their camp fellow of former days, it only tended to stiffen the backs of some who might have dreamed of the romance of a Robin Hood.

Poor, misguided Suggs had left the cow camp for a romantic adventure with a pal of his, when he figured life would roll on with little effort and some easy money. He

(127) According to Gray's account of the bungled holdup, Grant Wheeler's accomplice was a cowboy drifter named Hall. It is possible that Hall was used as an alias, that Gray did not know the man's real identity. Other accounts of this story—and they are legion—cite Wheeler's partner as Joe George, of whom little is known.

Detective Thacker, of whom Gray writes, was John N. Thacker, a leading detective for Wells, Fargo, who gained renown for arresting the notorious Black Bart (Charles E. Bolton), who had robbed some twenty-seven California stagecoaches between 1875 and 1883.

In his 1928 autobiography, Billy Breakenridge, deputy to Sheriff John Behan at the time of the Earp-Clanton feud, offers a most interesting account of the Wheeler-George debacle.

When, on January 30, 1895, the holdup occurred, Breakenridge was a special officer for the Southern Pacific Railroad, headquartered in Tucson. He does not mention Gray, but states that Wheeler and George were cowboys who worked in the Sulphur Springs Valley near Camp Rucker, which, of course, was Gray's Rucker Ranch.

In Willcox, the holdup men purchased dynamite, rifle and pistol ammunition, and said they were going prospecting near Dos Cabezas. Instead, they rode some five miles west, unloaded their purchases and staked their horses. Walking, they arrived back in town just as the train pulled into the depot.

They jumped aboard, drew pistols on the engineer and fireman, and ordered them to proceed some three miles distant. There they forced the fireman to uncouple the mail and express cars from the body of the train, then they went to the spot where their horses were staked.

Unbeknownst to them, however, the express messenger realized what was happening. He gathered up what valuables he could and fled the train. When the express car door was forced open, he was not to be found.

Several times did Wheeler and George attempt to blow open the safe. Each attempt failed. In desperation, they placed dynamite atop the safe, then placed heavy sacks atop the dynamite to act as ballast. They lit the fuse and in seconds an explosion rocked the car. Not only was the safe blown open, but eight thousand Mexican silver dollars were blown from the car and spread far and wide for some two or three hundred feet.

The disappointed robbers took what money and jewelry the express messenger had left behind (accounts vary from $200 to $1,500) and rode off toward the Chiricahua Mountains. Sheriff C.S. Fly (the noted Tombstone photographer whose studio figured in the shootout near the OK Corral), gathered a posse and gave chase, but lost the trail and was forced to turn back.

Breakenridge was brought over from Tucson, Thacker from San Francisco. They met in Tombstone. Because the safe was Wells, Fargo property, Thacker let it be known that he had jurisdiction in the matter and wanted no assistance from the Southern Pacific special officer. Breakenridge returned to Tucson.

Thacker trailed the bandits for several weeks to no avail. He returned to San Francisco.

On the night of February 26, 1895, the same pair held up the same train, but this time at Stein's Pass, New Mexico. They followed the same *modus operandi*, and they blundered as badly. They intended to uncouple both the mail and express cars and force the engineer to move them a few miles down track. But upon arrival at their destination they discovered the mail car only was attached to the locomotive. In disgust, they blew up their dynamite—harmlessly, this time—and rode away empty-handed.

Notified at Tucson, Breakenridge and his posse loaded horses into a boxcar, and were at Stein's Pass before daylight. But the unskilled robbers eluded them. Three weeks passed. When he was about to return home, a tip led the detective to Durango, Colorado where a woman had recognized Wheeler from a photograph. Breakenridge, in the company of Colorado lawmen, trailed the wanted man into a gulch. Told to throw up his hands, he refused. A gunshot rang out. Rather than surrender, Wheeler had placed the barrel of his pistol in his mouth and pulled the trigger.

George was never captured.

Hungerford, Edward. *Wells Fargo: Advancing the American Frontier.* NY: Random House, 1949, pp. 146–48.

Breakenridge, pp. 395–406.

(128) Apparently, no record exists of Suggs and his misadventure.

(129) Beginning in 1885, nine colonies were established in Chihuahua and Sonora, Mexico for Mormon polygamists seeking sanctuary from prosecution by the United States government. By 1912, at the height of Pancho Villa's reign of terror, most of the colonies had been abandoned.

Whetten, LaVon B. *The Mormon Colonies in Mexico: Commemorating 100 Years.* Deming, NM: Colony Specialties, 1985, pp. 5–9.

and his partner evidently made a start by raiding a small Mormon settlement in northern Chihuahua, Mexico,[129] making a getaway with several good horses. But they did not get far. An armed posse of the Mormon farmers took the trail, followed Suggs and his partner across the line into Animas Valley, New Mexico. There they overtook the horse thieves and killed them in their blankets without even awakening them, except with a fatal shot through the head. The shots were heard at a nearby cattle ranch, the dead men were found and so were reported to the sheriff. The sheriff took charge of burying the men at the spot where their bodies were found, accepting the story without further inquiry. That was a case of frontier justice.

The case of Suggs passed into oblivion. I don't doubt that the cowboys who had known Suggs took heed from his abrupt ending, resolving that honest work was not so bad after all.

There was Billy Leonard whom I have mentioned as one of the stage robbers—a man much above his fellow rustlers in intellect and education. He told me he came from New York City, was by trade a watchmaker, had developed lung trouble and came west for a cure. Naturally, he was chosen as captain of the rustlers and all seemed to look up to Billy as their leader.

This Leonard was a clever workman. Noticing that I had only a long-barreled Winchester, he asked if I wouldn't like it cut short into a carbine for a saddle gun. I was more than willing but couldn't see anything on the place that he could use for the necessary tools. But he said he could do the job with an ordinary table knife. This he made into a saw with the aid of a three-cornered file. With about an hour's work my long Winchester became a short saddle gun with the sights reset and all in proper shape. I knew he would not accept pay for his work, but I happened to have a book I thought would please him. It was the *Life of Bill Hickock,* the noted gunman of the Deadwood country of Dakota. I'm sure no small boy was ever more pleased with a new toy than was Billy with this book.

He lost no time in getting his little bunch of followers together, and then spent the rest of the day reading to them. Bill Hickock was the hero, henceforth, of the rustlers, and by present day standards that book ranked as the best seller of all time with the rustlers.

Why is this so? Why does such a man of ability as Ellsworth, the antarctic explorer, name his ship the *Wyatt Earp?* Maybe the answer can be given by the readers of Western story magazines, and by those who have made the moving picture, *Dodge City* so popular. Dodge City is a town where I think I saw more one-armed men and one-legged men in the early Nineties than any other town could boast of.

If my viewpoint in these memoirs seems to belittle some of these men who lived by their guns instead of by honest toil, I can only say I have tried to state the case as I saw and knew it, and if time has glossed over some of their deeds, my memory tells only of those old days as they appeared at the time and they are not being viewed as a distant era, which seems inclined to make heros out of desperadoes.

IN MOST MOUNTAIN REGIONS you can find some queer characters of men living in lonely cabins up some side canyon or gulch off the main traveled roads. These hermits are generally old men who have soured on the world. Occasionally there might be one who had outlawed himself in some community and had his back to the wall, thinking everyone his enemy.

About two miles up Rucker Canyon lived such a character, old Doc Monroe. In the days when Camp Rucker was a military post, the old doc probably fared pretty well, as his charcoal pits found a good market. He seemed to resent our coming with cattle to mar the solitude of the hills, for cows do not step about quite as noiselessly as wild creatures. An old cow may miss her calf and will seek it with low, drawn-out moos, and her calf will be persistent as a human baby in its cries for the mother. A bull, though usually genteel in behavior, will sometimes begin muttering as he moves along, and then suddenly let forth a screech loud and long, probably a note of defiance to all other bulls in reach of his voice. All such "cattle talk" seemed quite offensive to old Doc Monroe.

But we knew of no way to correct the situation and tried to make amends for the noises we brought to his neighborhood by gifts from mother's good cooking.

As the days went by, the resentment of old Doc Monroe for any neighbors seemed to grow. Occasionally we found a dead cow or bullock in the neighborhood with a bullet hole in the skull.

For awhile old Doc would make a regular weekly call on father and mother at Rucker, and on these occasions he was always in soldier's uniform with cap, brass buttons and all, evidently obtained from a soldier in the days of the government post there.

On his visits to our house, my mother always loaded him up with something good to take home, but on one of these visits the old Doc had a heated argument with my father. Suddenly he broke off his visit, bidding my father a dignified good day and adding, "Mik'el Gray, I neither fear ye, nor do I love ye," and he never called again.

But mother made it a habit to take a horseback ride by the old Doc's cabin at least once a week to leave a package of cooked food and see that he was not in want. As winter came on we knew these trips could not always be kept up, so mother persuaded the old man to think about going to a soldiers' home, as he claimed to be a G.A.R. man.

Luckily, we found a buyer willing to give the old Doc two hundred dollars for his squatter rights, and the price of a railroad ticket to Los Angeles. We put him on the westbound train at Willcox and bade him Godspeed.

He was a strange but interesting old man with much intelligence, but close mouthed. He could never be persuaded to tell us anything about his life prior to his advent about ten years previously at the little home place in the Chiricahua Mountains. I rather think he was a member of the Virginia Monroes. He had the appearance and dignity of good breeding, but the years had taken their toll.

Old Doc Monroe left on our hands his little black dog that had been his companion for years. He found dogs could not ride in the passenger car and he would not trust him to the express car, so he finally consented to leave him in our care. But despite all our efforts to make friends with the little dog, he resented everything we did. We left food for him for several days, but as time went on he seemed to grow still more resentful, and viciously came at anyone who tried to enter the small enclosure around his master's old cabin.

It was the only case we ever knew of this kind. This little animal seemed to have acquired from his old master an enmity for all mankind. It ended finally with our having to kill the little dog with a rifle bullet as he was slowly starving himself to death. This was undoubtedly a case of devotion to his old master, and the determination of that little dog to hold the fort until his master's return.

THERE WAS ANOTHER old hunter who often dropped in at Rucker for a piece of pie which he knew mother would have in the cellar. This man claimed his name was Rocky Mountain Beasley, and he lived up to his name as a man of the hills. He packed many a deer into Tombstone, and Rocky would tell of getting an even dozen wild turkeys in one night's hunt. He had found their roost in a high cottonwood tree, built up a blazing fire at the foot of the tree, and the foolish turkeys remained sitting on their roost while Rocky picked them off one by one as the firelight clearly made them out on the limb, until the last of the flock lay at his feet.

Another hunter who dropped in at Rucker for one of my mother's good dinners was Old Tex. He said he was born Alonzo Dionysius Whaley, but to his friends he was Old Tex. He had built himself a log cabin on the east slope of the pass leading into San Simon Valley. With his pack of hounds he hunted deer, antelope, and bear, occasionally making a ten-strike by getting a mountain lion. The latter's scalp would bring twenty-five dollars at the courthouse at Tombstone. Bear meat would bring fifty cents a pound in Tombstone, but the fifty mile trip was too far for Tex's burros in the summertime to get the meat to market.

Often we would hear old Tex's hounds baying in their chase of some wounded deer, and often I would manage to get in on these hunts. Almost invariably a deer, when wounded, goes downhill and seeks some water hole. In back of the Rucker Ranch house a long, hog-back hill sloped gradually from the summit, and invariably a deer, wounded high up in the hills, would try to follow this hog-back and thus get to some water hole in White Water River—or creek, as it really was.

It was my aim, whenever I heard the bay of the hounds getting nearer to hurry as fast as I could to the nearest point on this hog-back hill. Invariably the wounded deer would soon crash through the brush near me. I remember once a big seven-point buck almost ran over me, coming along on three legs with the other leg dangling from bullet wounds. I could almost touch him with my gun. To fool Old Tex, I hurried home as fast as I could with the deer and had him hanging to a tree limb at the ranch and was sitting on the porch when along came Tex, about winded from his strenuous chase. I asked him if he would recognize the deer if he met him again. Then I directed him to the side where the tree grew in which I had hung the deer. Old Tex was tickled to death as he recognized his game and I at once relinquished all claim to the buck, but he would always give me a quarter of the venison. This was only one of quite a number of deer I caught this way for Tex.

I don't think I ever met a hunter who enjoyed the sport more. Once I was on horseback on the summit pass leading to the San Simon and ran into Tex there. He was much excited over the dogs baying up on the mountain, and he was anticipating the coming of a deer. I waited with him and soon a beautiful, big white-tail buck jumped into view. Tex lost his nerve and made a wild shot. Again and again he pumped his old Winchester and pulled the trigger, but still the deer stood unhurt. Then the buck seemed to recover from his shock and went speeding away. Fearing we might lose him entirely, I let go with my gun and stopped the deer for Old Tex.

Poor Tex had had a bad case of buck ague and he was completely unnerved for a bit. It seemed funny to see an old hunter taken this way, but I guess we all lose our heads at times and do things reminiscent of the buck ague.

Our boys of today miss much of the old-time fun of hunting and do not seem to have the keenness of eyesight and hearing of us old-timers. Constant need of these senses in our daily life seemed to develop their keenness. Many a time I have sensed the nearness of a deer long before I could get sight of it.

Once in discussing deer hunting with a party of visitors from Tombstone, I recklessly offered to bet a dollar that I could start from the Rucker Ranch house porch, where we were then seated, and be back inside of half an hour with a deer. I was immediately challenged, but I made up my mind to stay with the bet and told the party to time me. I picked up my old Winchester and started for the creek across our little orchard and garden spot. It was midday and I trusted that a deer would be in for water. Sure enough, when I reached the fence in a brushy corner of the field and not twenty yards away, I heard a rustle and made ready with my gun resting on the top rail of the fence. Soon I caught sight of two long ears and the top of a doe's head. Fearful that I might frighten her into running before I could shoot, I quickly aimed at where I thought the deer's shoulder would be, and fired. Luckily, I guessed right. I jumped over the fence and picked up my deer, shot through the heart. I did not even wait to cut her throat, but hastened back to my company to claim my bet, finding my time was just under twelve minutes. I called that a piece of wonderful luck, but passed it off to my audience as nothing uncommon.

GOOD DOGS always seem to give more than they receive, and bad dogs, like some bad men, take where they can.

At the old OK Corral in Tombstone, often country folk on their way to town would sleep in the spare room next to John Montgomery's office. Montgomery was the OK Corral proprietor. This would save expense at a lodging house as all his customers were welcome to the sleeping room if they brought their own blankets.

A "bummer" dog had the habit of sneaking in at night if the door was left open, and stealing all the socks found on the floor. Then away he would scamper to parts unknown to the great aggravation of the lodgers. The reason for the dog's action was a mystery.

MY FATHER, Mike Gray, was born in the backwoods of Tennessee in 1827, and moved with his parents to Texas in 1831. They settled on the spot where the town of Huntsville has since grown into one of that state's big cities.

At the age of fourteen, he enlisted in the army being organized by General Sam Houston for the defense of that new country. He always remembered that date as it was then he donned his first pair of pants—a necessary covering required by a soldier. Previously, like all boys of that time and country, he had worn only a long-tail hickory shirt, and always went barefoot.

Father followed Colonel Jack Hayes throughout the Mexican War, and reached the rank of first lieutenant.

In 1849, his family joined the great migration of the covered wagon, starting from St. Joseph, Missouri for California. On this long trek, he and my mother first met. She, Sarah Ann Robinson, was also on her way with her parents in search of the promised land, leaving the old family home on the banks of the little St. Francis River in Missouri, with all its home comforts discarded forever, to follow that mirage of gold into the far West.

My mother often told us in later years that even the old folks had unbounded enthusiasm as they pulled out of St. Joe. But many of the elder ones fell by the wayside long before the journey ended, for it was mainly the young who could stand the strain of the hardships encountered.

The cholera swept across the plains taking its toll mainly on the old. The elder Gray was buried on the banks of the Platte in what is now western Nebraska, and my father carried on as captain of the wagon train. Mother's parents lived through the trip but did not live long after settling in California. Her two younger sisters and brother became her charge in that new land. It was a grievous mistake that the old folks ever left the old Missouri home. They crossed the Sierra Nevadas by the northern route, close to the present Oregon line, thus avoiding the dangers that befell the unfortunate Donner party in the high Sierras.[130]

I have often heard my mother say that it was one of

(130) In November, 1846, a wagontrain of emigrants traveling to California was trapped by heavy snow in the Sierra Nevada Mountains. By April, nearly half the party had succumbed to cold and starvation. In an effort to stay alive, some members of the company resorted to cannibalism.

Johnson, Kristin, ed. *Unfortunate Emigrants: Narratives of the Donner Party.* Logan: Utah State University Press, 1996, p. 1.

(131) Robert Bloomer Buchanan was born in Pennsylvania in 1822. As a child, he moved with his family to Wisconsin, then followed the Gold Rush to California in 1849. Buchanan was appointed the first sheriff of Yuba County, February 17, 1850, by the first *Alcalde* (a spanish word interchangable for justice of the peace or mayor) or Marysville. Buchanan also held a permit to operate a ferry across the Yuba River at Marysville.

Chamberlain, William Henry, *History of Yuba County, California*, Oakland: Thompson & West, 1879, p. 125.

(132) Buchanan died June 10, 1855. In the Yuba County Records Book is this entry from October 23, 1855: "Minerva E. Buchanan sold to Samuel R. Smith for the sum of $5,000.00 a ferry boat, rope, tackling, etc. now lying and being in and across the Yuba River opposite the public plaza of the city of Marysville . . . ."

Chamberlain, p. 125.

Miscellaneous Record Book I, Yuba County, California, pp. 190–91.

(133) Shortly after statehood in 1850, California passed exclusionary laws that forbade immigrant Mexicans from striking claims in the Sacramento gold fields. It was a most unpopular law among the immigrants, and Joaquin Murieta vowed vengence. It came in the form of a murderous rampage that climaxed in 1853 with Murieta's death by a posse lead by Captain Harry Love of the California Rangers. Murieta's horse was shot from beneath him, then he was shot dead. Love ordered—ostensibly for purposes of identification—that the outlaw's head be cut off and taken to authorities. It was. Later, it was put on public display.

Rush, Phillip S. *A History of the Californias*. San Diego: Neyenesch Printers, Inc., 1964, p. 140.

Nash, pp. 236–238.

(134) In all probability Gray was acting sheriff of Yuba County, but no record of his appointment is extant. The author is mistaken, however, in stating that his father served eight years as sheriff. Michael Gray served as Yuba County Sheriff from 1852 to 1856, when he was replaced by William B. Thornburg.

Chamberlain, p.120.

(135) Charles N. Felton served in the United States Senate from March 19, 1891 to March 3, 1893.

the happiest experiences of her life, riding most of the way horseback across that vast stretch of prairie and uninhabited land—uninhabited except for a few wandering Indian tribes. They had no trouble with these, probably because their train of covered wagons was well organized and had a large number of young men whom my father had organized into a scouting party which kept well in advance of the wagons.

The long trek ended when they arrived on the banks of the Feather River in California. Most of the party settled there on land that became part of the new Yuba County, which was formed the following year—1850—when California was admitted to the Union. Marysville was made the county seat, and it was there that Father and Mother were married.

The first sheriff of Yuba County was a Mr. Buchanan.[131] A short time after his taking office, one moonlit night he and a deputy went to what was known as "Spanish Town," about five miles out of Marysville, to arrest three Mexicans for whom he had warrants. This place was the resort of many Mexicans, and some were bad ones. The Sheriff was met by armed guards, the result being that he was shot through the body and for a long while his life hung in the balance.[132]

Spanish Town was one of the headquarters of the notorious bandit, Joaquin Murieta.[133]

My father became acting sheriff, then served eight years as sheriff of Yuba County.[134] He was known as one of the best shots in the West and this skill, combined with his frontier courage in facing any hazard, stood him in good stead. His undersheriff through all these years was Charles N. Felton,[135] in later years U.S. Senator from California, and a leader in the financial life of the West.

The old senator loved to tell of those early days and about Mike Gray being the "bravest man he ever knew." He said that on one occasion he saw Mike, as he familiarly called my father, overcome a prisoner. This man was seated in the sheriff's buggy and father had stepped out to adjust something about the horse's bridle. Evidently somebody had slipped a revolver to the man on the buggy seat. Charley Felton was looking on from the sheriff's office window when three shots rang out in rapid succession. Mike quietly held the horse's bridle in one hand, and with the other reached for a small derringer pistol in his coat pocket. He took deliberate aim over the horse's neck—and the only shot he had was enough.

On another occasion, the old senator told of an incident in Sacramento, where my father had gone on sheriff's business. A prisoner had escaped from the Sacramento jail, had jumped into the river and was apparently making a successful getaway. From the river bank they could see this man swimming for the farther shore and there seemed no way to stop his escape into the thickly wooded country on the other side. Just as the swimmer reached shallow water and raised an arm to grab hold of an overhanging branch to assist him, father's pistol rang out. The arm dropped instantly and the prisoner raised the other arm in a token of surrender.

IT IS DOUBTFUL that the true story of Joaquin Murieta will ever be known. He was without question the most colorful outlaw in California history. His field of operation extended from San Diego to Mount Shasta, and although hunted by every sheriff in the state, it was not until July, 1853, that he was finally run down and killed by that undaunted Texan, Harry Love in the Tulare Basin of the San Joaquin Valley.

Joaquin Murieta had many friends, especially among the Mexican population, and there was about him a charm of personality and daredevil quality which, coupled with the story that his life was devoted to the avenging of a wrong, led many to befriend him.

He was born of a good family of some wealth in Sonora, Mexico. As a boy of eighteen he came to San Francisco in 1848, where a brother had preceded him. In 1849, he and his brother struck out for the gold fields somewhere upon the Mokelumne River. In those days there were many rough characters in the various diggings, and it is told that these Mexican brothers met with a very harsh reception. They were warned by some of the harder whites that Mexicans were not wanted, and were told to get out at once.

Joaquin—who had his young wife, Carmen, with him—and his brother refused to go. Soon after he found his brother hanged by the neck to a tree limb, and his young wife killed in his cabin. This double crime has been put forth as the cause of Joaquin Murieta becoming the most murderous and revengeful villain of all California. He organized gangs of faithful followers— some whites, but mostly Mexicans—all over

THE LIFE OF JOAQUIN MURIETA

THE Brigand Chief of California

BUTLER & CO.
PUBLISHERS OF THE "CALIFORNIA POLICE GAZETTE,"
SAN FRANCISCO.

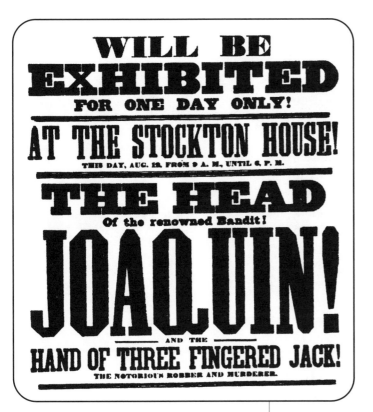

WILL BE EXHIBITED FOR ONE DAY ONLY!

AT THE STOCKTON HOUSE!

THIS DAY, AUG. 12, FROM 9 A. M., UNTIL 6, P. M.

THE HEAD

Of the renowned Bandit!

JOAQUIN!

AND THE

HAND OF THREE FINGERED JACK!

THE NOTORIOUS ROBBER AND MURDERER.

the state, operating under his self-appointed lieutenants. The years of 1851, '52, and '53, became almost a reign of terror.

My father often said that many crimes committed by other outlaws were attributed to Murieta. Joaquin had a certain amount of genius in organizing his followers. He seemed to have local companies to raid different sections, and he, himself, kept a roving command that swept all over the state. And, evidently, all were loyal to Joaquin Murieta until the end.

Often alone, or with a few followers, he would stop for days in the larger towns of the state. It was said his headquarters were in a house in Los Angeles on the little Mercantile Street, which has now been built over and is known as the Arcade, between Broadway and Spring.

One day, in riding leisurely along through Stockton, Joaquin passed a corner where he was attracted by some large posters nailed up. He stopped and read, "500 Dollars Reward To The One Who Delivers Joaquin Murieta, Dead Or Alive." Joaquin dismounted, and in pencil wrote underneath, "I will give $10,000—Joaquin." Then he rode away.

But with all his life of robbery and murder, then carousal and wastage of his plunder, there seemed a certain method. It was learned that he had sent great herds of stolen horses back to his native Mexico together with much gold dust accumulated in his robberies, and that he was fomenting a vast filibustering scheme to recapture California for Mexico. With his friends in this state, and the hope for backing from Mexico, it was not a danger to be laughed at, had not Harry Love ended Joaquin's career.

It seems that but one of his followers was ever captured alive, and he was placed in Martinez jail for safekeeping. One night the doors of the jail were broken open by an armed band of Mexicans, and the Mexican prisoner was taken out and hanged. These Mexicans were undoubtedly Joaquin's followers and possibly ranchers who had befriended him. They, no doubt, wished to prevent any compromising revelations being forced from the prisoner.

Harry Love and his twenty loyal followers, who finally ran down Joaquin Murieta, well deserved all the rewards offered throughout the state, but to get these it was necessary to prove beyond a doubt that they had killed Murieta.

So Harry Love had Joaquin's head placed in alcohol and then it started on a tour of the various towns of California.

My father said he had the painful duty of escorting a young Mexican, a woman who was a sister of Joaquin, from Marysville to Sacramento, and walk with her by a drug store window in which the head of Joaquin was on display, so that she might identify him. And she did.

Today that seems a revolting method of identification, but possibly it was the only way to satisfy the people who had suffered so much at the hands of the desperado. However, the final use of Joaquin's head was totally unjustified, for it fell into the hands of a showman, as this notice would indicate: "Joaquin's head is to be seen at King's Corner, Halleck and Sansome Streets, opposite the American Theatre. Admission One Dollar."

IN THOSE EARLY DAYS of sheriffing, father and mother lived at the old Plumas Ranch on the banks of the Feather River. In later years we children were always most interested in hearing about the old Newfoundland dog, Mack, who would run to the river whenever the up steamer whistled, and swim industriously into the river to rescue the bag of mail which would be tossed overboard for him.

It was from this home that my mother's sister Martha was married to the California Stage Company's secretary, Harry A. Charles, who in after years became a well-known stockbroker in San Francisco.

Mother was a typical pioneer woman, following wherever the wanderlust of father seemed ever leading him. And he was one of those restless pioneers who could not stay in one place for long.

When the Civil War broke out, father, being a Southerner by birth, was naturally in sympathy with the Confederacy. That feeling, and the prevailing Union sentiment in California, as well as what he thought was a better chance to aid the South, led father off on a mining venture to the west coast of Mexico. In the following winter of 1861 and '62, Mother followed him there with myself, then a year-old baby, and my older sisters of three and five years. At Guaymas in 1862, my younger brother was born. He was christened Dixie Lee in honor of the South and its heroic leader.

With us on the trip was our constant and faithful attendant, the colored girl, Nannie. I mention her with a tender feeling for her memory. My father had brought her from Texas as a small child in the 1849 trek across the plains to California. Nannie became a member of my mother's family, grew up with us children, and spent her whole life in a faithful, undivided affection for the family. She never married and her ever-loyal devotion to our family remained during all her good life. For, though colored, she was just one of those women that Booker T. Washington tells about, who ever remained loyal to their old white masters—"Nursing them in sickness, feeding them in want, and burying them in death." What would the South after the war have done without them?

We lived during most of our Mexican venture in Mazatlan. Father was mining in the back country and doing well. Then the Maximillian war came on and upset that land. His mules and freight wagons on the road to the mine would be confiscated first by French troops and then by Mexicans. It became impossible to make a move without serious trouble. So, one day, when the Panama steamer touched Mazatlan on its northward trip, Father bundled us all aboard the old side-wheeler, Brother Jonathan, and off we went to San Francisco.

Mother regretted leaving her old clay-bank horse she had ridden all over that country, and at the last moment she sold him to the old Montgomery Queen Circus then on stand at Mazatlan. Strange to say, nearly ten years later, while we were living in Gilroy, California, the Montgomery Queen Circus came to town and Mother took us children to see it. And, galloping out to slow music, there came Mother's old clay-bank horse. She knew him at once and rejoiced in knowing he had had such good care.

Then came 1872, the year of the famous hoax, mostly a forgotten incident now. It was the diamond discovery on the San Juan River in northeast Arizona. William T. Ralston and Colonel Harpington, both always ready to back adventure, sent for my father. Soon he was off on another wild goose chase, as Mother termed them.

An old prospector had laid before Ralston and Harpington a fabulous tale about the whereabouts of a lone peak standing out on the desert. This peak was virtually a solid pile of silver ore. He told his story so well that the two men fell for it, and put up twenty thousand dollars. They then asked father to head an expedition of twenty men to follow this prospector—Jones was his name—to the bonanza. It so happened that this Jones' mine was in the same San Juan country that the tale of the diamonds came from, and though not ostensibly in search of diamonds, Ralston evidently had some faith in the story and was enthusiastic about both.

My father prepared at once for the venture. He had no trouble picking twenty men who volunteered for the trip. Nobody was to get any compensation, but all were to share alike in half of what they found; the financial backers to get the other half.

My father chose as one of the party a Dr. Bryant, who later became a distinguished physician in San Francisco. The party went by rail to Denver, where they outfitted with saddle and pack mules, and purchased supplies for the long trip. From there they struck out through a then unknown country, Jones guiding them on.

So vividly did Jones go into the detailed description of his original discovery that none of the party ever seemed to doubt its truth. But the days went into weeks and weeks went into months, and they had not yet located the mountain of silver. They passed through the Navajo tribes and beyond, into a land that even the Indian seemed to avoid, where they found difficulty getting water and feed for the mules.

By this time, my father was beginning to doubt the sanity of Jones. It was always a little farther on to the fleeting mountains. Soon there was heard muttering among the men that Jones must make good soon, and threats of what they would do to him if he failed in his search.

One night, when all the others were asleep, Father took Jones to one side and told him the time had come for a showdown. Jones then broke down and said he was lost, begging that his life be spared. My father told him he couldn't answer for the morrow, as the men were getting desperate, but that there would be one chance for Jones to escape that night.

Jones was given his saddle mule and a few days rations, all that could be spared. He slipped away into the night and was never heard of further, as far as Father knew.

The next morning the men were worked up to a pitch that some proposed to trail Jones down and punish him. But Father told them that he was in charge and that he would not consent to have the mules used for that purpose, and that they were almost out of grub. Their only chance was, he pointed out, to strike out for the Colorado River, and he promised to safely lead them there. This he did, and they followed the river down to Yuma where they sold the pack and saddle outfit and all took transportation on the old steamer, *Esmeralda,* which plied between Yuma and Los Angeles by way of the Gulf, and around Cape San Lucas.

This ended Father's adventure. His total assets were two extra fine Navajo blankets. The diamond excitement had exploded into thin air long before my father reached the scene of the San Juan River. No doubt a few low grade diamonds had been salted there, but the builders of the hoax had fallen out among themselves and the story had been exposed before any claims could be sold or any money realized.

In 1876, Father picked up his prospector pick and struck out for Mexico. He was in Sonora when he heard of Ed Schieffelin's find at Tombstone, so he saddled his mule and was among the first on the ground.

And in 1879, Mother and my sister and brother answered his call. In those days, the end of steel was Yuma, so from there they took passage in the trail wagon of a twenty-mule team that plodded along at about fifteen miles a day for the four hundred miles of mostly desert land between there and Tombstone. It takes patience and also a good command of language to follow day after day the slow progress of the mule.

I once heard the late David Starr Jordan describe most vividly the method of a mule skinner. He said—and this talk was in Trinity Church in San Francisco—that the most eloquent man he ever heard was on the road between Maricopa Wells and Phoenix in the days before the railroad joined those places. On meeting a freight outfit, they had to drive their stage to one side of the road and await the passing of the mule team.

It was heavy pulling for the mules and the driver was on foot with his long blacksnake whip busy. A string of language, mostly cuss words, came in loud tones from the driver. Professor Jordan said that he and his fellow passengers simply sat spellbound at that wonderful flow of words without a single intermission, ever floating out over those mules, and the way those dumb listeners put their shoulders to the collar and moved their heavily loaded wagons was all most marvelous.

"Never," said Professor Jordan, "have I heard such eloquence or seen such unanimous response given, as on this occasion." It was not blasphemy. The driver used that language probably as the most handy to his tongue, and he used it with an art that was beyond criticism.

Why a man becomes a mule skinner might puzzle one to answer, but once on the job it becomes a fixture, as is said of a fellow trade, "once a stage driver, always a stage driver." And I know the famous freighter for the Tombstone mines, Jimmy Carr, had drivers who had been with him for years.

Mule driving is almost one of the lost arts now. Who of us could take care of, hitch up and drive, a string of twenty mules from daylight to dark in all kinds of weather, day after day, cooking our own meals by the roadside, sleeping out under the stars, sometimes in rain. All this for a small paycheck which a modern street sweeper would turn down.

But handling the jerkline was one accomplishment at which my father was an expert. I remember once taking a trip with him in a buckboard into the San Joaquin Valley from Gilroy about the year 1875, when the San Joaquin was a valley of magnificent distances between ranches. We met a twenty-horse team drawing three loaded wagons of flour about ten miles out of Visalia headed, I think, for Bakersfield. The outfit was stuck in a sandy wash. The driver was almost in tears. He was alone with over twenty tons of flour and he couldn't get a pull out of those horses. It was a fine looking team of big horses and able to move the load if only they would pull together.

We drove alongside him. Father offered to try his hand with the team and the young driver was more than willing. The horses were nervous from their treatment by the driver in trying to whip them into pulling. Father, noting this, spent several minutes going from one to the other, stroking their coats and speaking quietly to them. Then he mounted the saddled wheel horse, took hold of the jerkline, pulled the leaders off the road, first to one side, then the other. When back in the road again he urged them on as did Professor Jordan's mule skinner, with a flow of language of which I could hardly believe him capable. But those horses moved off together, as their driver told us, better than he had ever before seen them pull, and in a few moments all the wagons were out of the wash and on good smooth road. This feat has become one of the lost arts now.

IN A DIM OLD PHOTO of the Rucker Ranch house, my mother can be seen standing just inside the gate. Always was she ready to welcome the stranger at the gate. Wherever her lot was cast, she made that place seem like home to all. That she did this, none can deny.

Even the many army officers who passed Rucker in the Apache days seldom missed a chance to accept Mother's hospitality, for her good cooking was known to all. Even newly fledged West Pointers, always the most fastidious in their wants and habits, would praise the bounteous dinners at Rucker, even though they were shocked at first to see the pie come with the soup.

In those days free hospitality to all was the unwritten law of the cattle ranges, and if a new settler would levy on a traveler, it was soon made plain to him that the offense must not be repeated. This open house habit probably led to the roving chuckline rider who was really a tramp on horseback, passing over the country ostensibly in search of work, but well satisfied in not finding it. He grew to be quite a numerous class, but the cowman could always find some onerous work to offer, which would induce the chuckline rider to move on.

One would travel from Tombstone to El Paso in those days and never go hungry or without a bed to sleep in, even if he hadn't a dollar to his name. I wonder if it could be done now.

AT RUCKER in those early days, was a girl—for Emma Fish was always a girl even when the years might convince one that she had reached old maidhood—who was a natural born entertainer. She played the guitar and could sing with a charm and sweetness that we never wearied of. If I should be asked if Em was a pretty girl, I would have to answer, "I don't know." But she was always cheerful. Once I overheard a Texas cowpuncher say, "There's a girl at Rucker just as pretty as a red wagon"—and everybody likes a red wagon.

Emma had been a member of our family since she was ten years old. She was one of those rare spirits who dance through life with a smile. Though she had suitors galore, she was always friendly to all but partial to none, always remaining a young old maid.

MY FATHER was one of those old line Democrats who would always mention the opposing party as "black Republicans"—their war time appellation. He was a member of the lower house of the Arizona Territorial Legislature for so many years that he was termed, "the Father of the House."[136]

AND NOW AT THE END of the trail it is time to say, *"Adios, amigo."* The stern old mountains have changed none in the years, but there is something missing. Probably you might term it the romance of the old life, which is gone with the

(136) Apparently no record is extant of Michael Gray having been called the "Father of the House." He was, however, a member of the Territorial House of Representatives for eight years, between 1887 and 1901, serving unconsecutive terms. In 1887, his place of residence is listed as Benson; in 1893, Rucker; in 1899 and again in 1901, Pearce (a mining town that is today a ghost town), all in Cochise County.

Wagoner, Jay J. *Arizona Territory, 1863–1912: A Political History.* Tucson: University of Arizona Press, 1970, pp. 518, 521, 524–25.

Kelly, George H. *Legislative History of Arizona, 1864–1912.* Phoenix: State of Arizona, 1926, pp. 131, 166, 204, 219.

passing of Geronimo and the Kid. It would seem strange to wander again down the old trails, free from the fear of the lurking Apache who used to be looked for at every corner or bushy spot. But we who are left of the old cowpunchers of those days can feel a certain satisfaction in having had a part, however small, in seeing it through.[137]

END

(137) John Plesent Gray died in a Los Angeles hospital, January 11, 1943. He was eighty-two years old.
      State of California, Department of Health Services, Certificate of Death.

Editor's note: What today is known the world over as the Gunfight at the OK Corral, to which John Plesent Gray stood witness, occurred October 26, 1881. The next day, the Tombstone Epitaph *reported the shooting. With no editing to grammar or spelling, this is what was written:*

YESTERDAY'S TRAGEDY

————

Three Men Hurled Into Eternity in the Duration of a Moment.

————

Stormy as were the early days of Tombstone, nothing ever occurred equal to the event of yesterday. Since the retirement of Ben Sippy as marshal and the appointment of V.W. Earp to fill the vacancy, the town has been noted for its quietness and good order. The fractious and formerly much dreaded cowboys when they came to town were upon their good behavior, and no unseemly brawls were indulged in, and it was hoped by our citizens that no more such deeds would occur as led to the killing of Marshal White, one year ago. It seems that this quiet state of affairs was but the calm that precedes the storm that burst in all its fury yesterday, with this difference in results, that the lightning's bolt struck in a different quarter than the one that fell one year ago. This time it struck with its full and awful force upon those who, heretofore, have made the good name of this country a byword and a reproach, instead of upon some officer in the discharge of his duty or a peaceable and unoffending citizen.

Some time Tuesday Ike Clanton came into town and during the evening had some little talk with Doc Holliday and Marshal Earp, but nothing that caused either to suspect, further than their general knowledge of the man and the threats that had previously been conveyed to the Marshal that the gang intended to clean out the Earps, that he was thirsting for blood at this time, with one exception, and that was that Clanton had told the Marshal, in answer to a question, that the McLowrys were in Sonora. Shortly after this occurred some one came to the Marshal and told him the McLowrys had been seen a short time before, just below town. Marshal Earp, not knowing what might happen and feeling his responsibility for the preservation of the peace and order of the city, staid on duty all night and added to the police force his brother Morgan and Holliday. The night passed without any disturbance whatever, and at sunrise he went home and retired to rest and sleep. A short time afterward one of his

147

brothers came to his house and told him that Clanton was hunting him, with threats of shooting him on sight. He discredited the report and did not get out of bed. It was not long before another of his brothers came down and told him the same thing, whereupon he got up, dressed and went with his brother Morgan up town. They walked up Allen street to Fifth, crossed over to Fremont and down to Fourth, where, upon turning up Fourth toward Allen, they came upon Clanton, with a Winchester rifle in his hand and a revolver on his hip. The Marshal walked up to him, grabbed the rifle and hit him a blow at the same time on the head, stunning him so that he was able to disarm him without further trouble. He marched Clanton off to the police court, where he entered complaint against him for carrying deadly weapons, and the court fined Clanton $25 and costs, making $27.50 altogether. This occurrence must have been about 1 o'clock in the afternoon.

The After-Occurrence

Close upon the heels of this came the finale, which is best told in the words of R.F. Coleman, who was an eye-witness from the beginning to the end. Mr. Coleman says: I was in the O.K. Corral at 2:30 p.m., when I saw the two Clantons (Ike and Bill), and the two McLowry boys (Frank and Tom), in earnest conversation across the street, in Dunbar's corral. I went up the street and notified Sheriff Behan, and told him it was my opinion they meant trouble, and that it was his duty, as Sheriff, to go and disarm them; I told him they had gone to the West End Corral. I then went and saw Marshal Virgil Earp, and notified him to the same effect. I then met Billy Allen, and we walked through the O.K. Corral, about fifty yards behind the Sheriff. On reaching Fremont street I saw Virgil Earp, Wyatt Earp, Morgan Earp and Doc Holliday, in the center of the street, all armed. I had reached Bauer's meat market; Johnny Behan had just left the cowboys, after having a conversation with them. I went along to Fly's photograph gallery, when I heard Virg. Earp say, "Give up your arms, or throw up your arms." There was some reply made by Frank McLowry, but at the same moment there were two shots fired simultaneously by Doc Holliday and Frank McLowry, when the firing became general, over thirty shots being fired. Tom McLowry fell first, but raised and fired again before he died. Bill Clanton fell next, and raised to fire again when Mr. Fly took his revolver from him. Frank McLowry ran a few rods and fell. Morgan Earp was shot through and fell. Doc Holliday was hit in the left hip, but kept on firing. Virgil Earp was hit in the third or fourth fire in the leg, which staggered him, but he kept up his effective work. Wyatt Earp stood up and fired in rapid succession, as cool as a cucumber, and was not hit. Doc Holliday was as calm as if at target practice, and fired rapidly. After the firing was over Sheriff Behan went up to Wyatt Earp and said, "I'll have to arrest you." Wyatt replied, "I won't be arrested today; I am right here and am not going away. You have deceived me; you told me those men were disarmed; I went to disarm them."

This ends Mr. Coleman's story which in the most essential particulars has been confirmed by others. Marshal Earp says that he and his party met the Clantons and McLowrys in the alleyway; he called to them to throw up their hands, that he had come to disarm them. Instantaneously Bill Clanton and one of the McLowrys fired, and then it became general. Mr. Earp says it was the first shot from Frank McLowry that hit him. In other particulars his statement does not materially differ from the statement above given. Ike Clanton was not armed and ran across to Allen street and took refuge in the dance hall there. The two McLowrys and Bill Clanton all died within a few minutes after being shot. The Marshal was shot through the calf of the right leg, the ball going clear through. His brother, Morgan, was shot through the shoulders, the ball entering the point of his right shoulder blade, following across the back, shattering off a piece of one vertebrae and passing out the left shoulder in about the same position that it entered the right. This wound is dangerous but not necessarily fatal, and Virgil's is far more painful than dangerous. Doc Holliday was hit upon the scabbard of his pistol, the leather breaking the force of the ball so that no material damage was done other than to make him limp a little in his walk.

Dr. Matthews impaneled a coroner's jury, who went and viewed the bodies as they lay in the cabin in the rear of Dunbar's stables on Fifth street, and then adjourned until 10 o'clock this morning.

The Alarm Given

The moment the word of the shooting reached the Vizina and Tough Nut mines the whistles blew a shrill signal, and the miners came to the surface, armed them-

selves, and poured into the town like an invading army. A few moments served to bring out all the better portions of our citizens, thoroughly armed and ready for any emergency. Precautions were immediately taken to preserve law and order, even if they had to fight for it. A guard of ten men were stationed around the county jail, and extra policemen put on for the night.

Earp Brothers Justified

The feeling among the best class of citizens is that the Marshal was entirely justified in his efforts to disarm these men, and that being fired upon they had to defend themselves, which they did most bravely. So long as our peace officers make effort to preserve the peace and put down highway robbery—which the Earp brothers have done, having engaged in the pursuit and capture, where captures have been made, of every gang of stage robbers in the country—they will have the support of all good citizens. If the present lesson is not sufficient to teach the cow-boy element that they cannot come into the streets of Tombstone, in broad daylight, armed with six-shooters and Henry rifles to hunt down their victims, then the citizens will most assuredly take such steps to preserve the peace and will be forever a bar to further raids.

Editor's note: A coroner's jury convened October 28, and issued its verdict the following day. In its October 31, 1881 issue, the Tombstone Epitaph *had this to say:*

CORONER'S JURY

The coroner's jury after deliberating for two hours in regard to the late killing of William Clanton, Frank and Thomas McLowry, brought in a verdict that the men named came to their deaths in the town of Tombstone on October 26, 1881, from the effects of pistol and gunshot wounds inflicted by Virgil Earp, Morgan Earp, Wyatt Earp and one Holliday commonly called "Doc" Holliday. The verdict does not seem to meet with general approval, as it does not state whether the cowboys were killed by the marshal and his party in the discharge of their duty, or whether the killing was justifiable.

On Saturday warrants for the arrest of Wyatt, Virgil and Morgan Earp and J.H. (Doc) Holliday were placed in the hands of the sheriff but as Morgan and Virgil Earp were confined to their beds through wounds received in the late street fight, the warrants were not in their cases served and only Wyatt Earp and Holliday were placed under arrest. When these persons were taken before Justice Spicer he at first denied bail, but upon showing of the facts by affidavits bail was granted and fixed in the sum of $10,000 each, being justified in the sum of $20,000 each for each of the defendants, which amount was furnished.

Today Holliday and Wyatt Earp were before Justice Spicer to answer the charge. The investigation was conducted with closed doors. No one, except the officers of the court, and the witness whose testimony was being taken up, were allowed inside. The investigation is not yet concluded and will probably occupy the court for several days.

Editor's note: A hearing before Judge Wells Spicer, to determine if the defendants should be bound over for grand jury action, got underway at 3:00 p.m., October 31, 1881, and concluded November 29.

THE TESTIMONY FOR THE PROSECUTION

Sheriff John H. Behan

Was sworn for the prosecution and testified as follows: About 2:30 I was in the barber's shop and heard of trouble between the Clantons and Earps. I went over to Hafford's corner. I asked Virgil Earp, the marshal, what was the excitement. He said there was a lot of——in town looking for a fight. He mentioned no names. I said to Earp, "You had better disarm the crowd." He said he would not, but would give them a chance to make a fight. I said, "It is your duty as a peace officer to disarm the parties." I meant any parties connected with the cowboys who had arms. Morgan Earp and Holliday were the ones I was talking to at the intersection of Allen and Fourth. Virgil Earp had a shotgun. I saw no arms on the others. I then went down Fourth street to the corner of Fremont and crossed to the opposite side of Fourth street and saw Frank McLowry holding a horse and in conversation with somebody. I told McLowry I would have to disarm him; that there was likely to be some trouble in town and I proposed to disarm everybody that had an arm. He said he would not give up his gun; that he didn't intend to have any trouble. I insisted. About that time I saw Ike Clanton and Tom McLowry down the street below Fly's building. I said to Frank, "Come with me." We went to where Ike Clanton and Tom McLowry were standing. I said to them, "Boys, you must give up your arms." Billy Clanton and William Claiborne, alias Billy the Kid, were also there. Frank McLowry demurred. Ike Clanton told us he was unarmed. I put my arm around his waist and found he was not armed. I saw five standing there and asked how many there were of their party. They said four. Claiborne said he was not one of them; that he was there wanting them to leave town. I said, "Boys, you must go up to the sheriff's office, lay aside your arms, and stay till I get back." I told them I was going to disarm the other party. At that time I saw the Earps and Holliday coming down the south side of Fremont street. They came by the postoffice and Bauer's shop. I mean Morg Earp and Doc Holliday. I said to the Clanton party, "I see them coming down; wait here; I will go up and stop them." I walked twenty-two or twenty-three steps up the street and met them as they were coming out from under the awning of Bauer's shop, and told them not to go any further, that I was there for the purpose of disarming the Clanton party. They did not heed me. I said, "Go Back: I am not going to allow any trouble if I can help it." They brushed past me, and I turned and went with them or followed them, expostulating. When they arrived within a few feet of the Clantons and McLowrys, I heard one of them say, I think it is Wyatt Earp, "You s—s of b—s, you have been looking for a fight, and now you can have it." About this time a voice said, "Throw up your hands." During this time pistols were pointed. I saw a nickle-plated pistol in particular. It was in the hands of the Earp party, I think Doc Holliday. It was pointed, I think at Billy Clanton. I am not certain that Holliday had it. When the order was given to "throw up your hands," I heard Billy Clanton say, "Don't shoot me; I don't want to fight." At the same time, Tom McLowry threw open his coat and said: "I have nothing," or "I am not armed," or words to that effect, making the same remark and gesture he had previously made to me. I don't remember the position of Billy Clanton's hands. My attention was directed on the nickel-plated pistol for a couple of seconds. The nickel-plated pistol was the first fired, and almost instantaneously came two shots right together. The first shots could not have been from the same pistol; they were too close together. The nickel-plated pistol was fired by the second man from the right. After the first two or three shots were fired very rapidly, the firing was general. The first two shots were fired by the Earp party. I thought the next three shots came from the same side, but was not certain. It is only my impression. After the words "throw up your hands," immediately the nickel-plated pistol went off. I saw Frank McLowry with one

hand to his belly and with his right hand shooting toward Morgan Earp. As he started across the street, I heard a couple of shots from the direction in which Frank McLowry went. I looked and saw him running and a shot was fired and he fell over on his head. I heard Morg Earp say, "I got him." There may have been a couple of shots afterward, but that was the end of the fight. I did not see the effect of the two first shots that were fired; the only parties I saw fall were Frank McLowry and Morgan Earp. I saw no effects from the next three shots. The first man I thought was hit was Frank McLowry. I saw him staggering and bewildered shortly after the first five shots. I never saw any arms in the hands of anybody of the McLowry party except Frank McLowry and Billy Clanton. I saw Frank McLowry on the sidewalk a few feet from the line of the front of the lot. I think that eight or ten shots had been fired before I saw arms in the hands of any of the McLowry or Clanton party. Frank McLowry was the first man in whose hands I saw a pistol. After the first few shots, Ike Clanton broke and ran. I saw him at the back corner of Fly's house running into the back building.

When Ike Clanton broke and ran I did not know where he went. I found him afterward in Emanuel's building on Tough Nut street. I saw a shotgun with Holliday before the fight commenced, as they were coming down the street. He had it under his coat. I did not see the gun go off, and if I heard the report I did not distinguish it from a pistol. I afterward examined Billy Clanton, before he died, as he was lying in the street. After he was taken in the house all I heard him say was to go away and let him die. I saw him when he was lying on the sidewalk, and saw him when he shot Morgan Earp. A number were in the room when Billy Clanton was carried in. Dr. Gilberson said it was no use to give him anything. I left before Billy

Clanton died. He was gasping when I left. Tom McLowry's body was in the same room.

Wesley Fuller

Was sworn for the prosecution, and testified as follows: I live at Tombstone. My occupation is that of a jeweler. Was here, in Tombstone, on October 26, 1881. I saw a difficulty between the Earp party and the McLowry and Clanton party. It occurred on Fremont street, near the corner of Third. The parties engaged were Doc. Holliday, Morgan, Virgil and Wyatt Earp, on one side, and Tom and Frank McLowry and Billy and Ike Clanton on the other. At the time the difficulty occurred I was just back of Fly's photograph gallery, in the alley, next to and west of Fly's gallery. I was about seventy-five feet from Fremont street, and about ten feet from Fly's gallery. I was going down Allen street, and saw the parties standing on Fremont street and went down the alley to see Billy Clanton, and tell him to get out of town. I saw Billy Clanton, Frank McLowry and Johnny Behan on Fremont street. I couldn't see anybody else from where I was. I saw the Earp boys and Holliday, armed: that was why I went and told Billy Clanton to get out of town. The Earps and Holliday were on the corner of Fourth and Allen streets when I saw them armed. Virgil Earp had a shotgun, double barreled; the others had six-shooters. I did not go close enough to tell Billy Clanton anything before the difficulty. I saw the Earps through the alley, just as they got there. I heard some one say "Throw up your hands!" Billy Clanton threw up his hands and said, "Don't shoot me; I don't want to fight!" At the same time the shooting commenced. I did not see Ike Clanton at that time; I did not see Frank McLowry. The Earp party fired the first shot; two shots were fired right away; they were almost together; I think they were both pistol shots. Both parties then commenced firing rapidly. Billy Clanton staggered and fell at the end of the house. I think five or six shots were fired by the Earp party before Billy Clanton and Frank McLowry commenced shooting. They were the only ones of the Clanton-McLowry party I saw fire. At the time the first shots were fired by the Earp party, Billy Clanton's hands were up level with his head. When firing commenced Frank McLowry was standing by and holding his horse. He was doing nothing. I saw his hands; saw no weapon in them; would have seen it if he had one. The first two shots fired were directed at, and that one shot took effect on, Billy Clanton. I saw he was hit; he put his hand down against his stomach, and wheeled around. I saw no other effect at that time on anybody else. I saw Frank McLowry draw a weapon, and he was firing during the fight. When he drew his weapon I cannot tell where he was. I think he was a little past the middle of the street. When the first two shots were fired Frank McLowry was at the point marked "11" on the diagram. Several shots were fired by the Earps and Holliday prior to the time I first saw Frank McLowry draw his pistol—about seven or eight. I saw Tom McLowry and Ike Clanton during the fight. I saw Tom McLowry after the firing had been going on, pass through an open space in Fly's building. Fly's gallery has an open space between two buildings—between the second building as you go out of the door of the first. I did not see him afterward. I saw Ike Clanton pass through ahead of him. When I saw Tom McLowry between the buildings he as walking along slow; he appeared to be hurt; he was staggering. I don't know how long after that it was before he was brought into the house. It was probably ten minutes. He was dying. He was shot in the right side. I don't know who carried him in. Billy Clanton was in the room. Others were there. Kehoe was in there. I examined Tom McLowry after he was brought in. He had no arms on him at that time. I saw no cartridge belt on him. At no time during the shooting did I see Ike Clanton with any arms. I did not observe a shot gun at any time during the shooting. After the shooting was over, I saw Billy Clanton lying at the end of the next house below Fly's gallery. He was rolling around in agony. I picked him up and helped him in the house. He says, "Look and see where I am shot." I saw he was shot twice, once in the belly about here (above and to the right of the navel) and another shot below the left nipple. I told him he couldn't live. He says, "Get a doctor and give me something to put me to sleep." That was all I recollect of his saying. I did not leave until he died. During the shooting I saw Billy Clanton fire shots. I saw him when he first drew his weapon; it was a pistol. When he first drew his weapon he was in a crouched position against the corner of the house; he pulled his pistol with his left hand. When Billy Clanton first drew his pistol about six or seven shots had been fired by the Earps and Holliday. Billy Clanton was shot through the right wrist. At the time I first saw Frank McLowry draw his pistol, his appearance and action indicated he was shot. He was staggering and dizzy. I saw horses there during the shooting. Billy Clanton had one and Frank McLowry had the other. I saw arms on the horses. I suppose they were rifles but couldn't tell. I am positive there were arms on one; can not say about the other. It was on Frank McLowry's horse I saw one rifle. I saw no one use it. I did not see the horse after the shooting was over. When Frank McLowry left the horse the rifle was on the horse. Frank McLowry made an attempt to get possession of the gun that was on Frank McLowry's horse

during the shooting. He was trying to get the gun out of the scabbard, but there was so much shooting the horse kept jumping around and finally got away from him. About seven or eight, probably more, shots had been fired by the Earp brothers and Holliday before Frank McLowry commenced to try and get the gun.

William F. Clairborne

Sworn for prosecution. I reside in Hereford. Occupation, driving buggy and working for Colonel Herring of Neptune Mining company. I was here October 26. I know defendants. I knew Tom and Frank McLowry, Billy and Ike Clanton. I saw a little shooting between defendants and Frank McLowry, and Billy Clanton. Nobody else did any shooting. Tom McLowry and Ike Clanton were there. The day the shooting commenced I was standing there with Ike and Billy Clanton, Tom and Frank McLowry, and Johnny Behan. We were standing between the photograph gallery and a little building west of there. I was talking to Billy Clanton, and Sheriff Behan was talking to Tom McLowry, Ike Clanton and Frank McLowry. Behan turned his back and walked up Fremont street, and in a moment or two I looked up street, and saw defendants coming down street. Behan met them. Something was said between Behan and the Earp party, I think it was, "Hold on, boys, don't go down there." They brushed by and made no reply. They came to the corner of Fly's building to about ten feet from where we were standing. When they got to the corner of Fly's building they had their six-shooters in their hands, and Wyatt Earp said, "You s—s of b—s, you have been looking for a fight and now you can have it." Marshal Earp said, "Throw up your hands." Billy Clanton threw up his hands, Ike

Clanton threw up his, Frank McLowry threw up his. Frank said, "I have not got anything, I am disarmed." Then the shooting commenced—right then, at an instant—by Doc Holliday and Morgan Earp; the shots were so close that a person could hardly distinguish them. I saw them shoot; Holliday shot at Tom McLowry, Morgan Earp shot at Billy Clanton. When Doc Holliday fired that shot Tom McLowry staggered back; Billy Clanton fell up against the corner of the window and laid himself down on the ground. Frank McLowry had hold of a horse about the corner of the post. Ike Clanton was dodging and trying to get away when I saw him. About six or eight shots were fired rapidly by the Earp party, counting the first two shots. Billy Clanton, while lying on the ground, jerked his six-shooter and sitting up fired across his knee. Frank, at that time was out in the middle of the street with his six-shooter. I didn't see him draw it, I saw it in his hand. This was after the first six or eight shots were fired. From the middle of the street he went across the street. He left after Billy and Tom were killed. I mean after they were shot down; finally he was killed. Frank McLowry was not exactly running but was getting around lively when he was shot the last time. He was inclining away from the Earp party. I do not know how many times he was shot. I saw wounds on his person; one on the head, one on the belly. Billy Clanton was shot about the left nipple. That was the only wound I saw. I saw none on his hands or arms. He fell between the corner and the window. Morgan Earp pushed his pistol toward him and shot him. I saw the shot enter the body. I saw it hit him. Morgan Earp was at one corner, Billy Clanton at another. Morgan Earp's pistol was not near a foot from Billy Clanton's left nipple when he fired. I saw Billy Clanton fall up against the window. I—mean that Billy Clanton was on one side and Morgan Earp on the other

side of the same corner of the house and about three feet apart. Virgil Earp was shooting all the time from the time the first shot was fired. I saw him shoot. Doc Holliday, after the first shots were fired, was shooting at Frank McLowry on the street, Wyatt Earp was shooting at Frank McLowry. I did not see Tom McLowry have any weapons. I don't know who brought Tom McLowry into the house. He had no arms or belt. Saw no arms in hand or on belt of Ike Clanton before he ran into the photograph gallery. I don't know where Ike Clanton's arms were at the time of the shooting. I was not at Judge Wallace's court the day of the shooting. Did not see Ike Clanton's arms that day in the possession of any of the Earps before the shooting. Don't know where Tom McLowry's arms were. Immediately before or during the progress of the shooting I saw Frank McLowry and Billy Clanton with a horse each. I first saw them standing in front of Mr. Brown's hotel on Fourth street. There was a Winchester rifle on Frank McLowry's horse fixed down in the scabbard. During the shooting the horse was in the middle of the street. After the shooting I don't know what became of it. Frank McLowry had hold of the bridle rein during the shooting.

Frank McLowry separated from his horse nearly in the middle of the street after about eight or ten shots were fired. Frank McLowry went straight across the street. When I saw him last he was on the opposite side of the street, bent over this way [illustrating]. This was during or near the last part of the shooting. The way I happened to be with the Clanton party, was that I met Billy Clanton and Frank McLowry on the street. I knew them quite a while and was with them because I met them. I met them at Brown's hotel. I went to Johnny Behan's corral with Billy Clanton; then we went through Benson's corral. We went from there to where this difficulty occurred and was there until it did happen. The motive of the McLowrys' and Clantons' going down there was that the McLowrys had business at the butcher shop. The Clantons went to get their horses to go out home. I don't know if any of them had ordered their horses. I was on the ground until it was all over except a couple of shots which were fired after I left. One bullet struck me in the knee of my pants. I was put into the photograph gallery by Behan just before the last two shots were fired. About sixteen or eighteen shots were fired before I went into the photograph gallery; about two were fired afterward. When Behan was with the McLowry and Clanton party I seen him examine Ike Clanton to see if he had any arms, and Tom McLowry threw open his coat and showed that he had none. The sheriff found no arms on Ike Clanton to my knowledge. I had no arms upon my person at any time during the day of the shooting.

Joseph I. Clanton

Sworn for prosecution. I reside four miles above Charleston on the San Pedro river. My occupation is stock raising.

Q. Where were you on the 26th of October, 1881?

A. Here in Tombstone.

Q. Do you know the Earps and J.H. Holliday?

A. Yes, sir.

Q. Did you know Tom and Frank McLowry and Billy Clanton?

A. Yes, sir.

Q. Are they living or dead, and when did they die?

A. They are dead; they died October 26, 1881, on Fremont street, between Third and Fourth, Tombstone, Cochise county,

Arizona. They died a violent death; they were killed.

Q. Were you present at the time they were killed?

A. I was.

Q. Who else was present at the time, that you saw?

A. Holliday, Morgan, Virgil and Wyatt Earp, Sheriff Behan, William Claiborne; no one else that I remember seeing at the time of the killing.

Q. Who was engaged in the killing of those parties?

A. Wyatt, Morgan and Virgil Earp and Holliday.

Q. Begin at the commencement of the difficulty and tell all you saw about it.

A. I, the McLowry brothers, and William Clanton and Billy Claiborne were standing talking in a vacant lot, west of the photograph gallery on Fremont street, between that and the building next to it. The sheriff—Behan—came down and told us he had come to arrest and disarm us [objected to and objection overruled]. I asked the sheriff what for. He told me to preserve the peace. I told him I had no arms. Then Wm. Clanton told him he was just leaving town. The sheriff then said if he was leaving town all right. He then told Frank and Tom McLowry that he would have to take their arms. Tom McLowry told him he had none. Frank McLowry said that he would go out of town, but did not want to give his arms up until the parties that had hit his brother were disarmed. The sheriff told him that he should do it and take his arms up to his—the sheriff's—office and lay them off. Then Frank McLowry said he had business in town that he would like to attend to, but he would not lay aside his arms and attend to his business unless the Earps were disarmed. The sheriff then put his arms around me and felt if I was armed. Tom McLowry said, "I am not armed either," and opened his coat this way, [witness throws back the lapels of his coat]. The sheriff then looked up Fremont street, and ordered us to stay there until he came back.

The Earp party and Holliday just then appeared. Billy Clanton and I remained because the sheriff ordered us to. [Defendants move to strike out last answer as being part of a conversation already excluded by the court; motion denied.] Behan met the Earps, held up his hands and told them to stop, that he had our party in charge. They never stopped, but passed on and came by where we were. It was about twenty paces from where we were standing to the point where Behan met the Earps and Holliday, as they got where we were they pulled their pistols and Wyatt and Virgil Earp said, "You s—s of b—s, you have been looking for a fight," and at the same time ordered us to throw up our hands. We threw up our hands and they commenced shooting. The first two shots were fired by Holliday and Morgan Earp. Wyatt and Virgil Earp fired next in quick succession. Morgan shot before Wyatt did. The first two shots were fired so close together that I could not tell who fired first. Almost immediately after, perhaps a couple of seconds, Virgil Earp fired. Morgan Earp shot William Clanton. I don't know which of the McLowry boys Holliday shot at, but at one of them. I know Morgan Earp shot Billy Clanton because I saw his pistol pointed within two or three feet of his bosom and saw Billy stagger and fall against the house and put his hand on his breast where he was shot. When Billy Clanton staggered and fell against the house he was holding his hands up level with the top of his head with the palms of his hands out. When those first shots were fired Frank McLowry was holding his hands up level with the top of his head with the palms out. I was holding my hands in the same way. Tom McLowry

threw open his coat by the lapels and said he had no arms. I was never armed at any time during the shooting. Morgan Earp had taken my arms a short time before that and left them behind the Grand hotel bar. He took a Colt's forty-five caliber pistol and a Winchester carbine. During the shooting I did not see Tom McLowry with any arms. His Winchester was in Tuttle's stable below the shooting, on the other side of Fremont street. I don't know of my own knowledge where his other arms were. I came into town with Tom McLowry the day previous to the shooting, about 11 o'clock in the forenoon, in a spring wagon. He brought in with him a Winchester carbine and a six-shooter. The carbine at the stable is the same one he brought in. The pistol is the same as that formerly testified to by A.J. Mehan; I know it from the guard being sprung and from its general appearance. At the time when the Earp Party came up to where Billy Clanton and I were standing, Wyatt Earp shoved his pistol against my belly and told me to throw up my hands and said, "You s— of a b—, you can have a fight." I turned on my heel, taking hold of Wyatt and his pistol with my left hand and grabbed him around the shoulder with my right hand and held him for a few seconds. While I was holding him he shot. I pushed him around the corner of the photograph gallery and I jumped into the door of the photograph gallery. I went right on through the hall and out the back way. I went on across to Allen street and into a dancehall. As I jumped into the door of the photograph gallery I heard one or two bullets pass by my head. I ran across Allen street and seen no more of the fight. As I went through an opening, going toward Allen street, I heard bullets whiz by again; I heard shots strike the building ahead of me, the right of the rear of Fly's gallery. Four or perhaps five shots were fired by the Earp party before I left the ground where the shooting occurrd. Up to that time no shots had been fired by the Clantons or McLowrys, and no weapons drawn by them; they all had their hands up. There were two horses on the ground while the shooting occurred; Frank McLowry was holding a horse; Billy Clanton had a horse also. I never noticed the horses after the shooting commenced. There was a Winchester rifle on each horse. My reason for being there was I was going down for mine and Tom McLowry's team. By mutual understanding Frank and Billy Clanton were going out of town with us. I had given orders, as had Tom McLowry, to hitch our team up. At the time the Earp party approached us, at the time the shooting occurred, we were making no disturbance or noise, and were peaceable and quiet. There was a previous difficulty between Holliday, Morgan Earp and I the night before, at a lunch stand on Allen street close to the Eagle Brewery saloon. About 1 o'clock in the morning Doc. Holliday came in and commenced cursing me and said that I had used his name. He said I was a son of a b— of a cowboy. He told me to get my gun and get to work. I told him I had no gun. He said that I was a d—d liar and that I had threatened the Earps. I told him I had not; to bring whoever said that I had threatened the Earps to me and I would convince them I had not. He told me again to pull out my gun and if there was any grit in me to go to fighting. All the time he was talking with me, he was standing over me with his hand on his pistol or in his bosom. That is, he had his hand in his bosom and I suppose it was on his pistol. I looked behind me and saw Morgan Earp with his feet on the lunch counter. He had his hand in his bosom also. He was looking at me. I then got up and went out on the sidewalk. Doc. Holliday said, as I walked out, "You son of a b—, if you ain't heeled go heel yourself." Just at

that time, as I stepped on the sidewalk, Morgan Earp stepped out on the sidewalk and said, "Yes, you son of a b—h, if you want a fight, you can have all the fight you want now." I thanked him, and told him I didn't want any of it now, that I wasn't heeled. Virgil Earp was then ten or fifteen feet from me, down the sidewalk. Just about this time Wyatt Earp came out of the door while we were still standing there.

As I came out on the sidewalk, about this time or a minute later, Wyatt Earp came up, but did not say anything. Morgan Earp told me if I was not "heeled" then, when I came back on the street to be "heeled." I walked off and asked Morgan Earp not to shoot me in the back. I did not see Morgan Earp nor Doc Holliday any more that night to speak to them. Half an hour later I came back to the saloon on the west, either the Alhambra or Occidental, I think. I set down and played poker until nearly morning in that saloon, until daylight. Tom Corrigan was tending bar in the saloon in which I played poker, with Virgil Earp, Tom McLowry and another man, whose name I do not recollect, and Sheriff Behan. In the row between myself and Holliday, on the sidewalk, in front of the Alhambra, Virgil Earp told Doc Holliday and Morgan Earp to let me alone while Jim Flinn, the policeman, was there. When the poker game broke up, in the morning, after daylight, and Morgan Earp left, I saw Virgil Earp take his six-shooter out of his lap and stick it in his pants. I got up and followed him out doors, on the sidewalk. He was going down Allen Street, in front of the Cosmopolitan hotel. I walked up to him, and told him that, from his acts the night before and in regard to what he said to the policeman, and playing poker with a six-shooter in his lap, that I thought he stood in with the parties that tried to murder me the night before. I told him, if that was so, that I was in town. He said that he was going to bed. I went back and passed my chips in to the poker game, and had no more talk with the Earps that morning. About halfpast 1 o'clock, as I was walking up Fourth street, between Allen and Fremont, from Fremont to Allen street, Virgil and Morgan Earp came up behind me, I don't know where they came from. Virgil Earp struck me on the side of the head, behind the right ear, with a six-shooter. Morgan Earp cocked his pistol, and aimed at me. Virgil Earp took my six-shooter and Winchester rifle away from me. I did not then see Virgil or Morgan Earp before I was struck, or know they were about there until after I was struck. They pulled me along and said, "You d—d son of a b—, we will take you up here to Judge Wallace." When I got there and was behind the railings Wyatt Earp came in and told me I could have all the shooting I wanted. This was while I was a prisoner. He called me a thief and a son of a b—, and told me to name my style of fighting and when and where, that I could have all the shooting that I wanted; and that he could outwhip me or outshoot me. I told him I would fight him anywhere and anyhow. Wyatt Earp spoke up and said, "Yes, we will give it to you pretty plenty now." Morgan Earp said that he would pay my fine if I would fight them. Wyatt Earp offered me my rifle; put it down in front of me and told me to take it. As he presented it I saw Wyatt Earp put his hand into his bosom. Morgan Earp stood up on a bench over and behind at the same time. Wyatt Earp stood at my right and in front of me, and then I told him I did not want it that way. That was all the talk there. I don't know whether Judge Wallace was present, I think not. The door was full of people. I was fined, paid my fine and was released. This was close on to 1 o'clock; just before 1 o'clock. All occurred on the 26th October and about an hour and a half before the killing. When I was released Morgan Earp had taken my arms in charge. I got my arms a couple of days after that from Billy Soule the jailor. At the time Doc. Holliday charged me with having threatened the Earps I had never, in fact, threatened the Earps or Doc. Holliday.

Thomas Keefe

Sworn for the prosecution: I reside in this city; occupation, carpenter. I was in this city October 26, 1881. On that day I saw a difficulty between Wyatt Earp and Tom McLowry, on Fourth street, about fifty feet from Allen street, between there and Wallace's court, about noon. McLowry was walking from the Justice's court, on Fourth street, near Allen. Wyatt Earp was going toward Wallace's court, when they met; I didn't understand what they said, but the fight commenced. I saw Mr. Earp knock down McLowry with a pistol, twice. I saw him fall twice. McLowry threw his arms up to keep the blows down. Earp then put his pistol up and walked away. But two blows were struck with the pistol. McLowry then got up and kind of staggered, and walked toward the sidewalk, and picked up a scabbard or roll, and put on his hat that was knocked off. That was the last I saw of him for half an hour. I saw no other blows than those struck with the pistol. I heard no words; was about twenty-two or twenty-three feet from them. Others were nearer than I. I was at the scene of the difficulty after the killing occurred. No shots were fired after I got there. Heard the shooting. When the first shot was fired I was standing at the corner of Fourth and Allen streets; when I heard the firing I ran down Allen street to Third, and on Third to the corner of Fremont. My attention was drawn to a man dying but not dead laying along side of the house, on the corner of Third and Fremont streets. I called two or three men and said, "We will pick this man up and fetch him in the house before he dies"; we brought him in the house, and got a pillow, and laid him on the carpet, and made him as easy as we could. I asked him if he had anything to say before he died; he made no answer; he could not speak. I unbuttoned his clothes and pulled his boots off; gave him some water. The other young man, Clanton, was hallooing so with pain, I sent for a doctor to inject morphine into him. The doctor arrived, and I helped him inject morphine into him, alongside of the wound. He was turning, twisting, and kicking in every manner with pain. He said, "They have murdered me! Clear the crowd away from the door and give me air; I have been murdered!" The last words he said before he died were, "Drive the crowd away!" I staid there until the coroner came. It was eight or nine minutes after when the coroner came. Don't know who it was that assisted me in carrying Tom McLowry into the house. When I got to Tom McLowry there were four or five persons about him. I couldn't say who they were. I saw no arms about the person of Thomas McLowry at that time or afterwards. I examined his person when I took him in and looked for the wounds, found no arms, but found money on him. The men about McLowry's body got there about the time I did. I found no weapon on the ground where Tom McLowry was lying or on his person; no ammunition on or about him. When I took Tom McLowry into the house Billy Clanton was in there. Wesley Fuller, Mr. Noble and Campbell, clerk of supervisors, were there; another man, who used to stop at Boyle's, was holding Billy Clanton's head and attending to him. I examined Billy Clanton; he was shot through the right wrist; his arm was broke right there [points to inside right wrist]. He

was shot on the left side of the body; he was shot below the left nipple and the lungs were oozing out of the wound; he was shot through the pants on the right leg above his boot; did not touch the skin. I knew he was shot through the right wrist because I examined it and ran my finger in the wound. The ball passed through the arm, about two inches above the knuckle joint of the wrist.

J.H. Batcher

Sworn for the prosecution. I reside in Tombstone; am bookkeeper for P.W. Smith. On the morning of the 26th of October I saw a difficulty between Judge Wallace's office and the corner of Fourth and Allen street, on Fourth street; Wyatt Earp hit Tom McLowry with his pistol. I first saw Wyatt Earp at Judge Wallace's office; as he left the office I started for the corner store, following about fifteen feet behind Wyatt Earp. Tom McLowry was coming down Fourth street, toward Wallace's office; Mr. Wyatt Earp addressed Tom McLowry, said something to him, and I left; I cannot swear positively to what Wyatt Earp said. I heard Tom McLowry say to Earp that he didn't know what he had against him; that he had never done anything against him; that he was always a friend of his, or words to that effect. After some conversation, Tom McLowry addressed him in some manner and said whenever he wanted to fight he was with him. As he said that, Wyatt pulled his gun and said, "Are you heeled?" I don't know what Tom McLowry replied; he said something, I don't know whether he said he was or was not. Wyatt then struck Tom McLowry first with the palm of his hand, then he hit him with his right hand, with his pistol, on the side of the head, once; Tom McLowry fell down; Wyatt Earp walked off; Tom McLowry then got up and left.

Appolincar Bauer

Sworn for the prosecution. I reside in Tombstone; am in the butcher business. Was here October 26, 1881. I saw a difficulty between Tom McLowry and Wyatt Earp, after dinner, in the middle of the day. I can't tell if it was Wyatt; it was one of the Earps; the gentleman sitting at the table (Wyatt Earp) looks like him. The difficulty occurred on Fourth street between Wallace's court room and Allen street. When I crossed Allen street to go toward Judge Wallace's court, Mr. Earp walked ahead of me three or four steps. I was in company with Billy Hines, a cattlemen. Me and Mr. Hines both saw Tom McLowry coming from Wallace's court toward us, and Mr. Earp was walking toward him. They both said something, which I did not understand. Mr. Earp raised his left hand fistlike and said, "Are you heeled or not?" Tom McLowry said, "No, I am not heeled. I have nothing to do with anybody." Mr. McLowry backed off from Mr. Earp; Mr. Earp followed him, pulling a pistol out of his coat pocket and knocked him with it on his head. Mr. McLowry fell in about the middle of the street, and raised his left hand and held it to his left ear. Mr. Earp had struck Mr. McLowry two or three blows with his pistol. When Mr. Earp left Mr. McLowry lying down, he said "I could kill the s— of a b—".

APPENDIX D

THE TESTIMONY FOR THE DEFENSE

Wyatt Earp

Q. What is your name and age?

A. Wyatt S. Earp; age, 32 last March.

Q. Where were you born?

A. Monmouth, Warren County, Illinois.

Q. Where do you reside and how long have you resided there?

A. Tombstone; since Dec. 1st, 1879.

Q. What is your business or profession?

A. Saloon keeper; have also been employed as a deputy sheriff, and also as a detective.

Q. Give any explanation you may think proper of the circumstances appearing in the testimony against you, and state any facts which you think will tend to your exculpation.

A. The difficulty between deceased and myself originated first when I followed Tom McLowry and Frank McLowry, with Virgil and Morgan Earp and Captain Hearst and four soldiers, to look for six government mules which were stolen. A man named Eustis told me, at Charleston, that we would find the mules at McLowry's ranch, that the McLowrys were branding them "D.8" over U.S. We tracked the mules to McLowry's ranch, where we also found the brand. After

we arrived at McLowry's ranch there was a man named Frank Patterson who made some kind of compromise with Captain Hearst. Captain Hearst came to us boys and told us he had made this compromise and by so doing he would get his mules back. We insisted on following them up. Hearst prevailed upon us to go back to Tombstone, and we came back. Hearst told us two or three weeks afterwards that they would not give up the mules to him after we left, saying they only wanted to get us away; that they could stand the soldiers off. Captain Hearst cautioned me and Virgil and Morgan to look out for those men; that they had made some hard threats against our lives. About one month after that, after those mules had been taken, I met Frank and Tom McLowry in Charleston. They tried to pick a fuss out of me, and told me that if I ever followed them up again as close as I did before that they would kill me.

Shortly after the time Budd Philpot was killed by those men who tried to rob the Benson stage; as a detective I helped trace the matter up, and I was satisfied that three men, named Billy Leonard, Harry Head and Jim Crane were in that robbery. I knew that Leonard, Head and Crane were friends and associates of the Clantons and McLowrys and often stopped at their ranches. It was generally understood among officers, and those who have information about criminals, that Ike Clanton was a sort of chief among the cow-boys; that the Clantons and McLowrys were cattle thieves, and generally in the secrets of the stage robbers; and that the Clanton and McLowry ranches were the meeting places, and places of shelter for the gang.

I had an ambition to be sheriff of this county next election, and I thought it would be a great help to me with the people and business men if I could capture the men who killed Philpot. There were rewards offered of about $1,200 each for the robbers. Altogether there was about $3,000 offered for their capture. I thought that this amount might tempt Ike Clanton and Frank McLowry to give away Leonard, Head and Crane; so I went to Ike Clanton and Frank McLowry when they came to town. I had an interview with them in the back yard of the Oriental saloon. I told them what I wanted. I told them I wanted the glory of capturing Leonard, Head and Crane; if I could do so, it would help me make the race for sheriff next election. I told them if they would put me on the track of Leonard, Head and Crane—tell me where these men were hid— I would give them all the reward, and would never let anybody know where I got the information. Ike Clanton said he would be glad to have Leonard captured, that Leonard claimed a ranch that he claimed, and if he could get him out of the way he would have no opposition about the ranch. Ike Clanton said that Leonard, Head and Crane would make a fight, that they would never be taken alive, and that I must first find out if the reward would be paid for the capture of the robbers dead or alive. I then went to Marshall Williams, the agent of Wells, Fargo & Co., in this town, and at my request he telegraphed to the agent of Wells, Fargo & Co., at San Francisco, to find out if the reward would be paid for the robbers dead or alive. He received in June 1881 a

telegram which he gave me, promising that the reward should be paid dead or alive. I showed this telegram soon after I got it to Ike Clanton, in front of the Alhambra and afterwards told Frank McLowry of its contents. It was then agreed between us that they were to have all the 3,600 dollars reward, outside of necessary expenses in horse hire in going after them, and that Joe Hill should go to where Leonard, Head and Crane were hid, over near Yreka, in New Mexico, and lure them in near Frank and Tom McLowry's ranch near Soldier's Hole, 30 miles from here, and I would be on hand with a posse and capture them. I asked Joe Hill, Ike Clanton and Frank McLowry what tale would make them get over here. They said they had agreed upon a plan to tell them there would be a paymaster going from Tombstone to Bisbee, to pay off the miners, and they wanted them to come in and take them. Ike Clanton sent Joe Hill to bring them in.

He was gone about ten days and returned with the word he got there a day too late—that Leonard and Harry Head had been killed the day before by horse thieves. I learned afterwards that the horse thieves had been killed subsequently by members of the Clanton and McLowry gang. After that Ike Clanton and Frank McLowry said I had given them away to Marshall Williams and Doc Holliday, and when they came in town they shunned us, and Morgan and Virgil Earp and Doc Holliday and myself began to hear of their threats against us. I am a friend of Doc Holliday's because, when I was city marshal of Dodge City, Kansas, he came to my rescue and saved my life, when I was surrounded by desperadoes. A month or so ago Morgan and I assisted to arrest Stillwell and Spence, on the charge of robbing the Bisbee stage. The McLowrys and Clantons have always been friendly with Spence and Stillwell, and they laid the whole blame of their arrest on us though the fact is, we only went as a sheriff's posse. After we got in town with Spence and Stillwell, Ike Clanton and Frank McLowry came in. Frank McLowry took Morgan into the middle of the street, where John Ringgold, Ike Clanton and the Hicks boys were standing, and commenced to abuse Morgan Earp for going after Spence and Stillwell. Frank McLowry said he won't never speak to Spence again for being arrested by us. He said to Morgan, "If ever you come after me you will never take me." Morgan replied that if he ever had occasion to go after him he would arrest him. Frank McLowry then said to him, "I have threatened you boys' lives, and a few days ago I had taken it back, but since this arrest it now goes." Morgan made no reply, and walked off.

Before this and after this, Marshall Williams and Farmer Daly, and Ed Burns and three or four others, told me at different times of threats made to kill us, by Ike Clanton, Frank McLowry, Tom McLowry, Joe Hill and John Ringgold. I know that all these men were desperate and dangerous, cattle thieves, robbers and murderers. I knew of the Clantons and McLowrys stealing six government mules. I heard of Ringgold shooting a man down in cold blood near Camp Thomas. I was satisfied that Frank and Tom McLowry killed and robbed Mexicans in the Skeleton canyon two or three months ago, and I naturally kept my eyes open, and I did not intend that any of the gang should get the drop on me if I could help it.

Three or four weeks ago Ike Clanton met me at the Alhambra, and told me that I had told Holliday about this transaction, concerning the capture of Head and Leonard. I told him I never told Holliday anything. I told him when Holliday came up from Tucson I would prove it. Ike Clanton said that Holliday had told him so. When Holliday came back I asked him if he said so. I told him that Ike Clanton had said so.

On the 25th of October Holliday met Ike Clanton in the Alhambra saloon and asked him about it. Clanton denied it, and they quarreled for three or four minutes. Holliday told Ike Clanton he was a d—d liar, if he said so. I was sitting eating lunch at the time. They got up and walked out on the street. I got through and walked out, and they were still talking about it. I then went to Holliday, who was pretty tight, and took him away. Then I came back alone and met Ike Clanton. He called me to one side and said his gun was on the other side of the street at the hotel. I told him to leave it there. He said he would make a fight with Holliday any time he wanted to. I told him Holliday did not want to fight, but only to satisfy him this talk had not been made. I then walked away and went to the Oriental, and in a few minutes Ike Clanton came over with his six-shooter on. He said he was not fixed right; that in the morning he would have man for man; that this fighting talk had been going on for a long time, and it was about time to fetch it to a close. I told him that I wouldn't fight no one if I could get away from it. He walked off and left me, saying, "I will be ready for all of you in the morning." He followed me into the Oriental, having his six-shooter in plain sight. He said, "You musn't think that I won't be after you all in the morning." Myself and Holliday walked away, and we went to our rooms.

I got up next day, October 26th, about noon. Before I got up, Ned Boyle came to me and told me that he met Ike Clanton on Allen street, near the telegraph office that morning; that Ike was armed; that he said, "As soon as those d—d Earps make their appearance on the street today the ball will open." That Ike said, "We are here to make a fight; we are looking for the sons of b—s."

Jones came to me after I got up and went to the saloon, and said, "What does all this mean?" I asked him what he meant. He says, "Ike Clanton is hunting you Earp boys with a Winchester rifle and a six-shooter." I said, "I will go down and find him and see what he wants." I went out, and on the corner of Fourth and Allen streets I met Virgil Earp, the marshal. He told me how he had heard that Ike Clanton was hunting us. I went up Allen street, and Virgil went down Fifth street and then Fremont street. Virgil found Ike Clanton on Fourth street in an alley. He walked up to him and said, "I hear you are hunting for some of us." Ike Clanton then threw his Winchester rifle around towards Virgil. Virgil grabbed it and hit Clanton with his six-shooter and knocked him down. Clanton had his rifle, and his six-shooter was exposed in his pants. By that time I came up, and Virgil and Morgan took his rifle and six-shooter away (and took them to the Grand Hotel after examination), and took Ike Clanton before Justice Wallace. Before the investigation Morgan Earp had Ike Clanton in charge, as Virgil Earp was out. A short time after I went into Wallace's court and sat down on a bench. Ike Clanton looked over to me and says, "I will get even with all of you for this. If I had a six-shooter I would make a fight with all of you." Morgan then said to him, "If you want to make a fight right bad I will give you this one," at the same time offering Ike Clanton his (Ike's) own six-shooter. Ike Clanton started to get up to take it, when Campbell, the deputy sheriff, pushed him back on his seat, saying he wouldn't allow any fuss. I never had Ike Clanton's arms at any time as he has stated.

I would like to describe the positions we occupied in the court room at that time. Ike Clanton sat down on a bench, with his face fronting to the north wall of the building. I myself sat down on a bench that was up against the north wall right in front of Ike. Morgan Earp stood up against the north wall with his back against the north wall, two or three feet to my right. Morgan Earp had Ike Clanton's Winchester in his left hand and his six-shooter in his right hand; one end of the rifle was on the floor. Virgil Earp was not in the court room any of this time, and Virgil Earp came there after I walked out.

I was tired of being threatened by Ike Clanton and his gang. I believed from what they had said to others and to me, and from their movements, that they intended to assassinate me the first chance they had, and I thought if I had to fight for my life against them, I had better make them face me in an open fight. So I said to Ike Clanton, who was then sitting about eight feet away from me, "You d—d dirty cur thief, you have been threatening our lives, and I know it. I think I should be justified in shooting you down any place I should meet you, but if you are anxious to make a fight, I will go anywhere on earth to make a fight with you, even over to the San Simon among your own crowd." He replied, "all right, I will see you after I get through here. I only want four feet of ground to fight on." I walked out, and just then outside the court room, near the justice's office, I met Tom McLowry. He came up to me and said to me, "if you want to make a fight I will make a fight with you anywhere." I supposed at the time that he had heard what had first transpired between Ike Clanton and me. I knew of his having threatened me, and I felt just as I did about Ike Clanton, that if the fight had to come, I had better have it come when I had an even show to defend myself, so I said to him, "All right make a fight right here," and at the same time I slapped him in the face with my left hand, and drew my pistol with my right. He had a pistol in plain sight on his right hip, but made no move to draw it. I said to him, "jerk your gun and use it." He made no reply and I hit him on the head with my six shooter and walked away, down to Hafford's corner. I went into Hafford's and got a cigar, and came out and stood by the door. Pretty soon after I saw Tom McLowry, Frank McLowry and William Clanton. They passed me and went down Fourth street to the gunsmith shop. I followed down to see what they were going to do. When I got there Frank McLowry's horse was standing on the sidewalk with his head in the door of the gun shop. I took the horse by the bit, as I was deputy city marshal, and commenced to back him off the sidewalk. Frank and Tom McLowry and Billy Clanton came to the door, Billy Clanton had his hand on his six shooter. Frank McLowry took hold of the horse's bridle. I said "you will have to get this horse off the sidewalk." He backed him off on the street. Ike Clanton came up about that time and they all walked into the gunsmith's shop. I saw them in the shop changing cartridges into their belts. They came out of the shop and walked along Fourth street to the corner of Allen street. I followed them as far as the corner of Fourth and Allen streets and over to Dunbar's corral. Virgil Earp was then city marshal; Morgan Earp was a special policeman for six weeks, wore a badge and drew pay. I had been sworn in Virgil's place to act for him while Virgil was gone to Tucson on Stillwell's trial. Virgil had been back several days, but I was still acting. I knew it was Virgil's duty to disarm these men. I expected he would have trouble in doing so, and I followed up to give assistance if necessary, especially as they had been threatening me, as I have already stated. About ten minutes afterwards, and while Virgil, Morgan, Doc Holliday and myself were standing on the corner of Fourth and Allen streets, several persons said, "there is going to be trouble with those fellows," and one man named Coleman said to Virgil Earp, "they mean trouble. They have just gone from Dunbar's corral into the O.K. corral, all armed. I think you had better go and disarm them." Virgil turned around to Doc Holliday, Morgan Earp and myself and told us to come and assist him in disarming them. Morgan Earp said to me, "they have horses; had we not better get some horses ourselves, so that if they make a running fight we can catch them?" I said "No, if they try to make a running fight we can kill their horses, and then capture them." We four then started through Fourth to Fremont street. When we turned the corner of Fourth and Fremont streets we could see them standing near or about the vacant space between Fly's photograph gallery and the next building west. I first saw Frank McLowry. Tom McLowry, Billy Clanton and Sheriff Behan standing there. We went down the left-hand side of Fremont street. When I got within about 150 feet of them I saw Ike Clanton and Billy Claiborne and another party. We had walked a few steps further when I saw Behan leave the party and come toward us, every few steps he would look back as if he apprehended danger. I heard Behan say to Virgil Earp, "For God's sake don't go down there or you will get murdered." Virgil replied "I am going to disarm them" he, Virgil Earp, being in the lead. When I and Morgan came up to Behan he said, "I have disarmed them." When he said this I took my pistol, which I held in my hand under my coat, and put it in my overcoat pocket. Behan then passed up the street and we walked on down. We came up on them close—Frank McLowry, Tom McLowry and Billy Clanton standing all in a row against the east side of the building on the opposite side of the vacant space west of Fly's photograph gallery. Ike Clanton and Billy Claiborne and a man I did not know were standing in the vacant space about half way between the photograph gallery and the next building west. I saw that Billy Clanton, and Frank McLowry and Tom McLowry had their hands by their sides, and Frank McLowry's and Billy Clanton's six-shooters were in plain sight. Virgil said, "Throw up your hands, I have come to disarm you." Billy Clanton and Frank McLowry laid their hands on their six-shooters. Virgil said, "Hold! I don't mean that; I have come to disarm you." They—Billy Clanton and Frank McLowry—commenced to draw their pistols at the same time Tom McLowry threw his hand to his right hip and jumped behind a horse. I had my pistol in my overcoat pocket where I had put it when Behan told us he had disarmed the other party. When I saw Billy and Frank draw their pistols I drew my pistol. Billy Clanton levelled his pistol at me but I did not aim at him. I knew that Frank McLowry had the reputation of being a good shot and a dangerous man, and I aimed at Frank McLowry. The two first shots which were fired were fired by Billy Clanton and myself; he shot at me, and I shot at Frank McLowry. I do no know which shot was first; we fired almost together. The fight then became general. After about four shots were fired Ike Clanton ran up and grabbed my left arm. I could see no weapon in his hand and thought at the time he had none, and so I said to him, "The fight has now commenced; go to fighting or get away;" at the same time I pushed him off with my left hand. He started and ran down the side of the building and disappeared between the lodging house and the photograph gallery. My first shot struck Frank McLowry in the belly. He staggered off on the sidewalk but first fired one shot at me. When we told them to throw up their hands Claiborne held up his left hand, and then broke and ran. I never saw him afterwards until late in the afternoon, after the fight. I never drew my pistol

or made a motion to shoot until after Billy Clanton and Frank McLowry drew their pistols. If Tom. McLowry was unarmed I did not know it. I believe he was armed, and that he fired two shots at our party before Holliday, who had the shotgun, fired at and killed him. If he was unarmed there was nothing in the circumstances, or in what had been communicated to me, or in his acts or threats, that would have led me even to suspect his being unarmed. I never fired at Ike Clanton, even after the shooting commenced, because I thought he was unarmed. I believed then, and believe now, from the acts I have stated, and the threats I have related, and other threats communicated to me by different persons, as having been made by Tom. McLowry, Frank McLowry and Isaac Clanton, that these men, last named, had formed a conspiracy to murder my brothers Morgan and Virgil, and Doc Holliday and myself. I believe I would have been legally and morally justifiable in shooting any of them on sight, but I did not do so or attempt to do so: I sought no advantage. When I went as deputy marshal to help disarm them and arrest them, I went as a part of my duty and under the direction of my brother the marshal. I did not intend to fight unless it became necessary in self-defense, and in the performance of official duty. When Billy Clanton and Frank McLowry drew their pistols I knew it was a fight for life, and I drew and fired in defence of my own life, and the lives of my brothers and Doc Holliday.

I have been in Tombstone since December 1, 1879. I came here from Dodge City, Kansas, where, against the protest of business men and officials, I resigned the office of City Marshal, which I held there from 1876. I came to Dodge City from Wichita, Kansas. I was on the police force in Wichita, from 1874 until I went to Dodge City.

The testimony of Isaac Clanton that I had anything to do with any stage robbery, or any criminal enterprise, is a tissue of lies from beginning to end. Sheriff Behan made me an offer in his office on Allen street, and in the back room of a cigar store, that if I would withdraw and not try to get appointed sheriff of Cochise county, that we would hire a clerk and divide the profits. I done so, and he never said another word to me afterward in regard to it. The reasons given by him here for not complying with his contract, are false.

Myself and Doc Holliday happened to go to Charleston the night that Behan happened to go down to subpoena, Ike Clanton. We went there for the purpose of getting a horse that had been stolen from us a few days after I came to Tombstone. I had heard several times that the Clantons had him. When I got there that night I was told by a friend of mine that the man that carried the dispatch from Charleston to Ike Clanton's ranch had rode my horse. At this time I did not know where Ike Clanton's ranch was. A short time afterward I was in the Huachucas, locating some water rights. I had started to Tombstone, and had got within twelve or fifteen miles of Charleston, when I met a man named McMasters. He told me if I would hurry up I would find my horse in Charleston. I drove to Charleston, and saw my horse going through the streets toward the corral. I put up for the night at another corral. I went to Barnett's office, to get out papers to recover the horse. He was not at home, having gone to Sonora to see some coal fields that had been discovered. I telegraphed to Tombstone, to James Earp, and papers were made out and sent to Charleston, that night. While I was in town, waiting for the papers, Billy Clanton found out I was there. He went and tried to take the horse out of the corral. I told him that he could not take him out; that it was my horse.

After the papers came he gave the horse up without the papers being served, and asked me "if I had any more horses to lose." I told him I would keep him in the stable after this, and not give him a chance to steal him.

In one of the conversations I had with Ike Clanton about giving away Leonard, Head and Crane, I told him one reason why I wanted to catch them was to prove to the citizens of Tombstone that Doc Holliday had nothing to do with it, as there were some false statements circulated to that effect. In following the trail of Leonard, Head and Crane, we struck it at the scene of the attempted robbery, and never lost the trail or hardly a footprint from the time that we started from Drew's ranch, on the San Pedro, until we got to Helm's ranch, in the Dragoons. After following about eighty miles down the San Pedro river and capturing one of the men, named King, that was supposed to be in with them, we then crossed the Catalina mountains within fifteen miles of Tucson, following their trail around the front of the mountain after they had crossed over to Tres Alamos, on the San Pedro river. We then started out from Helm's ranch and got on their trail. They had stolen fifteen or twenty head of stock so as to cover their trail. Wyatt Earp, Morgan Earp, R.H. Paul, Breckenridge, Johnny Behan and one or two others still followed the trail up into New Mexico. Their trails never led south from Helm's ranch, as Ike Clanton has stated. We used every effort we could to capture these men. I was out ten days. Virgil Earp and Morgan Earp were out sixteen days and we done all we could to capture these men, and I safely say if it had not been for myself and Morgan Earp, they would not have got King, as he started to run when we rode up to his hiding place, and was making for a big patch of brush on the river, and would have got in it if it had not been for us.

Virgil W. Earp

Sworn for the defense. I reside in Tombstone, Arizona. On October 25th and 26th last was chief of police of Tombstone, Cochise county, A.T., and deputy U.S. Marshal; was acting as chief of police on October 25th and 26th last. Morgan Earp was sworn in as special policeman on those days and wore a badge; he was such special policeman for over a month. Wyatt Earp had been sworn in to act in my place while I was absent at Tucson, and after I returned a saloon had been opened, and I appointed him special, with power to keep the peace and make arrests. I also specially called on him to assist me to disarm Isaac Clanton, Billy Clanton, Frank McLowry, and Tom McLowry. On October 26th last I called on J.H. Holliday to help disarm the Clantons and McLowrys. On the morning of October 26th, about 6 or 7 o'clock, I started to go home when Ike Clanton stopped me and wanted to know if I would carry a message for him to Doc Holliday. I asked him what it was. He says, "The d—d s— of a b— has got to fight!" I says: Ike, I am an officer and I don't want to hear you talk that way at all. I says: I am going home now to go to bed and I don't want you to raise no disturbance while I am in bed. I started to go home, and when I got about ten feet away from him he says, "You won't carry the message?" I says, "No, of course I won't." I made 4 or 5 steps and he says: "You may have to fight before you know it." I made no reply, but went home and went to bed; I don't know how long I had been in bed; it must have been between 9 and 10 o'clock, when one of the policemen came down and told me to get up, that there was liable to be hell. I didn't get up right away, for perhaps half an hour; I can't be positive as to the time, it was between 10 o'clock and noon. I came up on the street; met a man named Lynch, who

told me—[Objected to.] I found Ike Clanton on Fourth street between Allen and Fremont with a Winchester rifle in his hand and a six-shooter stuck down in his breeches. I walked up and grabbed his rifle with my left hand; he let go of it and started to draw his six-shooter. I hit him over the head with mine, knocked him on his knees and took his six-shooter from him. I asked him if he was hunting for me; he said he was, and if he had seen me a second sooner he would have killed me. My attention was called next to them—Frank McLowry, Tom McLowry, Ike Clanton and Billy Clanton. I arrested Ike Clanton for carrying firearms inside the city limits; took him to Judge Wallace's court; the judge was not there; left him in charge of special officer Morgan Earp while I went out to look for the judge. After examination I asked him where he wanted his arms left? He said: "Anywhere where I can get them, for you hit me over the head with a six-shooter." I told him that I would leave them at the Grand hotel bar; I did leave them there. I heard no quarrel at that time Between Wyatt Earp and Ike Clanton. Next time I saw them was in the gunshop on Fourth street—Spangenberg's. I saw Billy and Ike Clanton and Frank and Tom McLowry; saw Wyatt Earp shoving a horse off the sidewalk, and I went down and saw them all, viz, the two Clantons and the two McLowrys, filling up their belts with cartridges and looking at guns and pistols. A committee of three or four men waited on me then and called me to one side. I turned to Wyatt Earp and told him to keep peace and order until I came back, and to move the crowd off the sidewalk so as not to have it blockaded. When I saw the party of Clantons and McLowrys again they were all going into Dunbar's corral; they did not remain long, but crossed over and into the O.K. corral. I called on Johnny Behan to go and help me disarm them. He refused to go with me, saying that if he went along there would be a fight for sure; that they would not give up their arms to me. He says "They won't hurt me, and I will go down alone and see if I can not disarm them. I told him that was all I wanted them to do—to lay off their arms while they remained in town. Shortly after he left I was notified that they were on Fremont street. I called on Wyatt and Morgan Earp and Doc Holliday, to go and help me disarm the Clantons and McLowrys. We started down Fourth street to Fremont, and turned down Fremont street toward Fly's lodging house and art gallery. When we got about to Bauer's meat market—before we got there—I discovered Ike and Billy Clanton, Tom and Frank McLowry, Behan and the "Kid," standing in the vacant lot west of the lodging house. Johnny Behan saw myself and party coming down towards him. He left the Clanton and McLowry party, and came on a fast walk, meeting us, and every once in a while he would turn around as if he expected danger of some kind. He kept looking back at the party he had left. He met us close to Bauer's butcher shop. He threw up both his hands and said, "For God's sake don't go down there, or they will murder you!" I says to him, "Johnny, I am going down to disarm them." By this time I had passed him a step, but I heard him make the remark, "I have disarmed them all." When he said that—I had previously had a walking stick in my left hand, and my six shooter, which was sticking on my waist, in front of me—I then, at his remark, shoved my six shooter around to my left hip, and changed my walking stick to my right hand. As soon as Behan left them they walked in between the two buildings, out of sight of us; all about we could see was the head of the horse. They was all standing in a row; Billy Clanton and Frank McLowry had their hands on their six-shooters. I don't know how Ike Clanton was standing; I don't

think he had his hand in any attitude where I could suppose he had a gun. Tom McLowry had his hand on the Winchester rifle, in the scabbard on the horse's saddle. As soon as I saw them I says, "Boys, throw up your hands; I want your guns," or, "I want your arms," I don't know which. I meant to disarm them. With that Frank McLowry and Billy Clanton drew their six-shooters, and I could hear the click, click, of their cocking them. Ike Clanton threw his hand on his breast. At that I threw both my hands up, having my cane in my right hand, and says, "Hold! I don't want that." As I said that, Billy Clanton threw his six-shooter down at arms length at full cock. I was standing at the left of my party, and he was standing a little to the left of Tom and Frank McLowry. I seen that he was not aiming at me, that the aim of his pistol was past me; two shots went off right together; Billy Clanton's was one of them. At that time I changed my cane to my left hand, drew my six-shooter, and went to fighting; the shooting then became general. At the crack of the first two pistol shots, the horse jumped to one side, and Tom McLowry failed to get the Winchester. He threw his hand back, and followed the movement of the horse around, keeping him as a kind of breastwork. He fired once if not twice over the horse's back.

Albert C. Bilicke

Sworn for the defense. I reside in Tombstone, my occupation is that of a hotel keeper. I knew Thomas McLowry by sight in his time. I saw him walking down the south side of Allen street, and enter Everhardy's butcher shop; shortly afterwards he came out again, and walked down the street a few steps further, and crossed Allen obliquely to the corner of Fourth and Allen street, and walked down Fourth street. This was between half-past 1 and half-past 2, probably about two o'clock. I saw no arms on him, either when he went in the butcher shop, nor when he came out. When he went into the butcher shop his right-hand pants pocket was flat and appeared as if nothing was in it; when he came out his pants pocket protruded, as if there was a revolver therein.

H.T.Boyle

Sworn for the defense. Employed as barkeeper at Oriental saloon.

Q. Did you, on the morning of the 26th of October, hear Ike Clanton make use of any threatening language against Wyatt, Virgil, Morgan Earp and Doc Holliday? And if so, state where, and the threats made and the language used. (Objection by the prosecution: overruled).

A. After I went off watch at 8 a.m. I met Ike Clanton in front of the telegraph office; his pistol was in sight and I covered it with his coat; and I advised him to go to bed, and he said that as soon as Earp and Doc Holliday showed themselves on the streets the ball would open and that they would have to fight.

H.F. Sills

Sworn for the defense. Locomotive engineer on furlough and visiting Tombstone.

On October 26, 1881, saw four or five men standing in front of O.K. Corral. They were talking of some trouble they had with Virgil Earp; made threats they would kill him on sight; someone of the party said they should kill the whole party of Earps. I made enquiries to know who Virgil Earp was; a man pointed out Virgil Earp as the town marshal: I called Mr. Earp to one side and

told him of the threats I had heard; said one of the men in the party had a bandage around his head. A few minutes later I saw a party start from Fourth street; followed them as far as the post office; then saw the party I had heard making the threats. I saw the marshal and his party go up and speak to the other party; I saw them pull their revolvers immediately. The marshal had a cane in his right hand. He threw it up and spoke. By that time Billy Clanton and Wyatt Earp had fired their guns; the marshal changed his cane to his other hand and pulled his revolver out. He seemed to be hit and fell down; got up and went to shooting. The shooting became general. I know it was Billy Clanton because I saw him after he was dead and recognized him as the one who fired at Wyatt Earp.

Mrs. Addie Borland

Was sworn and testified for the defense as follows. I live on Fremont street. A dressmaker by occupation. I live immediately opposite Fly's house. I saw five men opposite my house on the afternoon of October 26, leaning against the small house west of Fly's, and one of them was holding a horse, the man with the horse standing outside. I saw four men coming down the street toward them. A man with a long coat walked up to the man with the horse and put a pistol to his stomach, and then the man with the long coat stepped back about three feet. I was sitting in my house at the window when I saw this. Then the shooting commenced in a very few seconds after this. I don't know which party fired first; it was impossible to tell. I was looking at both parties, but no one in particular. I did not know the man with the long coat at the time of the shooting. (Witness points to Doc Holliday as the man with the long coat on).

Q. Did you notice what kind of weapon he had in his hand?

A. It was a very large pistol, dark bronze.

Q. Was it or was it not a nickle-plated pistol?

A. It was not a nickel-plated pistol.

Q. Did you see, at the time of the approach of the party on Fremont street, any of the cowboys throw up their hands?

A. I did not.

Q. Did you hear any conversation or exclamation between the two parties after they met and before the firing commenced?

A. I did not, for my door was closed. I continued to look at the parties until the firing commenced, when I got up and went in my back room. The first thing the cowboys did when the other party approached them was to raise up and come out to meet them from the side of the house. I cannot tell how many shots were fired before I left the window. By the time I left the window it looked as if all were shooting. I saw no parties fall by the time I left the window.

Editor's Note: Spicer issued his verdict December 1, 1881.

THE VERDICT

Opinion of Justice Wells Spicer Releasing the Defendants.

In Justice's Court, Township No. 1, Cochise County, A.T.—Before Wells Spicer, J.P.—Territory of Arizona vs. Morgan Earp et al.

Defendants Wyatt Earp and John H. Holliday, two of the defendants named in the above entitled action, were arrested upon a warrant issued by me on the 29th day of October on a charge of murder. The complaint filed upon which the warrant was issued, accuses said defendants of the murder of Wm. Clanton, Frank McLowry and Thos. McLowry on the 26th day of last month, at Tombstone, in this county.

The case has now been on hearing for the past thirty days, during which time a volume of testimony has been taken, and eminent legal talent employed by both sides.

The great importance of the case, as well as the general interest taken in it by the entire community, demand that I should be full and explicit in my findings and conclusions, and should give ample reasons for what I do.

From the mass of evidence before me—much of which is upon collateral matters—I have found it necessary, for the purposes of this decision, to consider only those facts which are conceded by both sides or are established by a large preponderance of testimony.

Viewing it in this manner, I find that on the morning of the 26th day of October, 1881, and up to noon of that day, Joseph I. Clanton or Isaac Clanton, the prosecuting witness in this case, was about the streets and in several saloons of Tombstone, armed with revolver and Winchester rifle, declaring publicly that the Earp brothers and Holliday had insulted him the night before when he was unarmed, and now he was armed and intended to shoot them or fight them on sight. These threats were communicated to defendants Virgil Earp and Wyatt Earp. Virgil Earp was at this time chief of police of the City of Tombstone, and charged, as such officer, by the city ordinances, with the duty of preserving the peace, and of arresting, with or without warrant, all persons engaged in any disorderly act whereby a breach of the peace might be occasioned; and to arrest and disarm all persons violating the city ordinances which declare it to be unlawful to carry on the person any deadly weapon within the city limits without first obtaining a permit, in writing.

Shortly after noon of October 26th, the defendant, Virgil Earp, as chief of police, assisted by Morgan Earp, who was also at that time a special policeman in the pay of the city and wearing his badge, arrested and disarmed said Isaac Clanton, and in such arrest and disarming inflicted upon the side of his head a blow from a pistol. Whether this blow was necessary or not is not material here to determine. Isaac Clanton was then taken to Justice or Recorder Wallace, where he was fined, and his arms consisting of a revolver and Winchester rifle, taken from him and deposited at the Grand hotel subject to his order.

While at Justice Wallace's court, and awaiting the coming of Judge Wallace, some hot words passed between Isaac Clanton and Wyatt Earp—Earp accusing Clanton of having previously threatened to take his life, and then proposed to make a fight with him anywhere, to which Isaac Clanton assented, and then declared that "fight was his racket," and that when he was arrested and disarmed, if Earp had been a second later "there would have been a coroner's inquest in town." Immediately subsequent to this, a difficulty occurred in front of Judge Wallace's court room between Wyatt Earp and the deceased Thomas McLowry, in which the latter was struck by the former with a pistol and knocked down.

In view of these controversies between Wyatt Earp and Isaac Clanton and Thos. McLowry, and in further view of the quarrel the night before between Isaac Clanton and J.H. Holliday, I am of the opinion that the defendant Virgil Earp, as chief of police, by subsequently calling upon Wyatt Earp and J.H. Holliday to assist him in arresting and disarming the Clantons and McLowrys, committed an injudicious and censurable act; and although in this he acted incau-

tiously and without proper circumspection, yet, when we consider the condition of affairs incident to a frontier country; the lawlessness and disregard for human life; the existence of a law-defying element in our midst; the fear and feeling of insecurity that has existed; the supposed prevalence of bad, desperate and reckless men who have been a terror to the country, and kept away capital and enterprise, and considering the many threats that had been made against the Earps, I can attach no criminality to his unwise act. In fact, as the result plainly proves, he needed the assistance and support of staunch and true friends, upon whose courage, coolness and fidelity he could depend in case of an emergency.

Soon after the conclusion of proceedings at Judge Wallace's court, Isaac Clanton and Thomas McLowry were joined by William Clanton and Frank McLowry, who had arrived in town. In the afternoon these parties went to a gunshop, where they were seen loading their guns and obtaining cartridges. These proceedings were seen by Wyatt Earp, who reported same to Virgil Earp, chief of police, said Wyatt Earp at the time being a sworn policeman.

After this the Clantons and McLowrys went to the Dexter stables, on Allen street, and shortly after crossed the street to the O.K. corral and passed through Fremont street.

With what purpose they crossed through to Fremont street will probably never be known. It is claimed by the prosecution that their purpose was to leave town. It is asserted by the defendants that their purpose was to make an attack upon them, or, at least, to feloniously resist any attempt to arrest or disarm them that might be made by the chief of police and his assistants.

Whatever their purpose may have been, it is clear, to my mind, that Virgil Earp, the chief of police, honestly believed (and from information of threats that day given him, his belief was reasonable) that their true purpose was, if not to attempt the death of himself and brothers, at least to resist with force and arms any attempt on his part to perform his duty as a peace officer by arresting and disarming them.

At this time Virgil Earp was informed by one H.F. Sills, engineer from the A., T & S. F. R. R., then absent from duty on a lay-off furlough, and who had arrived in town only the day before and totally unacquainted with any person in town or the state of affairs existing here, that he (Sills) had overheard armed parties, just then passing through the O.K. corral, say, in effect, that they would make sure to kill Earp, the marshal, and would kill all the Earps.

At the same time several citizens and a committee of citizens came to Virgil Earp, the chief of police, and insisted that he should perform his duty as such officer, and arrest and disarm these cow-boys, as they termed the Clantons and McLowrys.

Was it for Virgil Earp, as chief of police, to abandon his clear duty as an officer because its performance was likely to be fraught with danger? Or, was it not his duty, that, as such officer, he owed to the peaceable and law-abiding citizens of the city, who looked to him to preserve peace and order and their protection and security, to at once call to his aid sufficient assistance and proceed to arrest these men?

There can be but one answer to these questions, and that answer is such as will divert the subsequent approach of the defendants toward the deceased of all presumptions of malice or illegality.

When, therefore, the defendants, regularly or specially appointed officers, marched down Fremont street to the scene of the subsequent homicide, they were going where it was their right and duty to go; they were doing what it was their right

and duty to do; and they were armed, as it was their right and duty to be armed, when approaching men whom they believed to be armed and contemplating resistance.

The legal character of this homicide must, therefore, be determined by what occurrd at the time, and not by the precedent facts.

To constitute the crime of murder there must be proven, not only the killing, but the felonious intent. In this case the corpus delicti, or fact of killing, is in fact admitted, as will be clearly proven. The felonious intent is as much a part to be proven as the corpus delicti, and in looking over this mass of testimony for evidence upon this point I find that it is anything but clear.

Witnesses of credibility testify that each of the deceased, or at least two of them, yielded to a demand to surrender. Other witnesses of equal credibility testify that Wm. Clanton and Frank McLowry met the demand for surrender by drawing their pistols, and that the discharge of fire-arms from both sides was almost instantaneous. There is a dispute as to whether Thomas McLowry was armed at all, except with a Winchester rifle that was on the horse beside him. I will not consider this question, because it is not of controlling importance. Certain it is that the Clantons and McLowrys had among them at least two six-shooters in their hands and two Winchester rifles on their horses; therefore, if Thomas McLowry was one of a party who were thus armed, and were making felonious resistance to an arrest, and in the melee that followed was shot, the fact of his being unarmed, if it be a fact, could not of itself criminate the defendants, if they were not otherwise criminal. It is beyond doubt that William Clanton and Frank McLowry were armed, and made such quick and effective use of their arms as to seriously wound Morgan Earp and Virgil Earp.

In determining the important question of whether the deceased offered to surrender before resisting, I must give as much weight to the testimony of persons unacquainted with the deceased or the defendants, was to the testimony of persons who were companions and acquaintances, if not partisans of the deceased, and I am of the opinion that those who observed the conflict from a short distance and from points of observation that gave them a good view of the scene, to say the least, were quite as likely to be accurate in their observations as those mingled up in or fleeing from the melee. Witnesses for the prosecution state unequivocally that Wm. Clanton fell or was shot at the first fire, and Claiborne says he was shot when the pistol was only about a foot from his belly. Yet it is clear that there were no powder burns or marks on his clothes, and Judge Lucas says he saw him fire or in the act of firing several times before he was shot, and he thinks two shots afterward.

Addie Borland, who saw distinctly the approach of the Earps and the beginning of the affray from a point across the street where she could correctly observe all their movements, says she cannot tell which fired first, that the firing commenced at once from both sides upon the approach of the Earps, and that no hands were held up; that she would have seen them if there had been. Sills asserts that the firing was almost simultaneous; he cannot tell which side fired first.

Considering all the testimony together, I am of the opinion that the weight of evidence sustains and corroborates the testimony of Wyatt and Virgil Earp, that their demand for a surrender was met by William Clanton and Frank McLowry drawing their pistols. Upon this hypothesis my duty is clear. The defendants were officers charged with the duty of arresting and disarming brave determined men who were experts in the use of firearms, as quick as thought and certain as death, and who previously declared their intentions not to be arrested nor disarmed. Under the statutes (sec. 32, page 74, of Comp. Laws), as well as the common law, they had a right to repel force by force.

In coming to this conclusion, I give great weight to several particular circumstances connected with the affray. It is claimed by the prosecution that the deceased were shot while holding up their hands in obedience to the demand of the chief of police, and on the other hand, the defense claim that William Clanton and Frank McLowry at once drew their pistols and began firing simultaneously with the defendants. William Clanton was wounded on the wrist of the right hand on the first fire, and thereafter used his pistol with his left. This wound is such as could not have been received with his hands thrown up, and the wound received by Thomas McLowry was such as could not have been received with his hands on his coat lapels. These circumstances being indubitable facts, throw great doubt upon the correctness of the statement of witnesses to the contrary.

The testimony of Isaac Clanton that this tragedy was the result of a scheme on the part of the Earps to assassinate him, and thereby bury in oblivion the confessions the Earps had made to him about "piping" away the shipment of coin by Wells, Fargo & Co., falls short of being a sound theory, because of the great fact most prominent in the matter, to wit, that Isaac Clanton was not injured at all, and could have been killed first and easiest. If it was the object of the attack to kill him, he would have been the first to fall; but, as it was, he was known or believed to be unarmed, and was suffered and, so Wyatt Earp testifies, told to go away, and was not harmed.

I also give just weight in this matter to the testimony of Sheriff Behan, who said on one occasion, a short time ago, Isaac Clanton told him that he (Clanton) had been informed that the sheriff was coming to arrest him, and that he (Clanton) armed his crowd with guns and was determined not to be arrested by the sheriff, or words to that effect. And Sheriff Behan further testifies that a few minutes before the Earps came up to them that he, as sheriff, had demanded of the Clantons and McLowrys that they give up their arms and that they demurred, as he said, and did not do it, and that Frank McLowry refused and gave as a reason that he was not ready to leave the town just then, and would not give up his arms unless the Earps were disarmed, that is, that the chief of police and his assistants should be disarmed.

In view of the past history of the country, and the generally believed existence at this time of desperate, reckless and lawless men in our midst, banded together for mutual support, and living by felonious and predatory pursuits, regarding neither life or property in their career, and at this time for men to parade the streets armed with repeating rifles and six-shooters, and demand that the chief of police of the city and his assistants should be disarmed, is a proposition both monstrous and startling. This was said by one of the deceased only a few minutes before the arrival of the Earps.

Another fact that rises up preeminent in the consideration of this sad affair, is the leading fact that the deceased from the very first inception of the encounter were standing their ground and fighting back, giving and taking death with unflinching bravery. It does not appear to have been a wanton slaughter of unresisting and unarmed innocents, who were yielding graceful submission to the officers of the law, or surrendering to, or fleeing from their assailants, but armed and defiant men, accepting the wager of battle and succumbing only in death.

The prosecution claim much upon the point, as they allege, that the Earp party acted with criminal haste; that they precipitated the triple homicide by felonious anxiety and quickness to begin the tragedy; that they precipitated the killing with malice aforethought, with the felonious intent then and there to murder the deceased, and that they made use of their official character as a pretext.

I cannot believe this theory, and cannot resist the firm conviction that the Earps acted wisely, discreetly and prudently to secure their own self-preservation—they saw at once the dire necessity of giving the first shot to save themselves from certain death. They acted; their shots were effective, and this alone saved all the Earp party from being slain.

In view of all the facts and circumstances of the case; considering the threats made, the character and position of the parties, and the tragical results accomplished, in manner and form as they were, with all surrounding influences bearing upon the result of the affair, I can not resist the conclusion that the defendants were fully justified in committing these homicides; that it was a necessary act, done in the discharge of an official duty.

The evidence taken before me in this case would not, in my judgement, warrant a conviction of the defendants by a trial jury of any offense whatever. I do not believe that any trial jury that could be got together in this territory would, on all the evidence taken before me, with the rules of law applicable thereto given them by the court, find the defendants guilty of any offense.

I conclude the performance of the duty imposed upon me by saying, in the language of the statute, "There being no sufficient cause to believe the within named" Wyatt S. Earp and John H. Holliday, "guilty of the offense mentioned within," I order them to be released.

WELLS SPICER
Magistrate

APPENDIX F

Editor's note: President Arthur made public his concern about lawlessness in the Arizona Territory with issuance of this statement to the United States Senate and House of Representatives, April 26, 1882:

PRESIDENT CHESTER A. ARTHUR'S
MESSAGE TO CONGRESS

By recent information received from official and other sources, I am advised that an alarming state of disorder continues to exist within the Territory of Arizona, and that lawlessness has already gained such a headway there as to require a resort to extraordinary means to repress it.

The Governor of the territory under date of the 31st ultimo, reports that violence and anarchy prevail, particularly in Cochise County and along the Mexican border; that robbery, murder and resistance to law have become so common as to cease causing surprise, and that the people are greatly intimidated and losing confidence in the protection of the law. I transmit his communication herewith and call especial attention hereto.

In a telegram from the General of the Army, dated at Tucson, Arizona, on the 11th instant, herewith transmitted, that officer states that he hears of lawlessness and dis-

order which seem well attested, and that the civil officers have not sufficient force to make arrests and hold the prisoners for trial or punish them when convicted.

Much of this disorder is caused by armed bands of desperadoes known as "cowboys," by whom depredations are not only committed within the territory, but it is alleged predatory excursions are made therefrom into Mexico. In my message to Congress, at the beginning of the present session, I called attention to the existence of these bands and suggested that the setting on foot within our own territory of brigandage and armed marauding expeditions against friendly nations and their citizens be made punishable as an offense against the United States. I renew this suggestion.

To effectively oppress the lawlessness prevailing within the territory a prompt execution of the process of the courts and vigorous enforcement of the laws against offenders are needed. This the civil authorities there are unable to do without the aid of other means and forces than they can now avail themselves of. To meet the present exigencies the Governor asks that provision be made by Congress to enable him to employ and maintain temporarily a volunteer militia force to aid the civil authorities, the members of which force to be invested with the same powers and authority as are conferred by the laws of the territory upon peace officers thereof.

On the ground of economy was well as effectiveness, however, it appears to me to be more advisable to permit the co-operation with the civil authorities of a part of the army as a posse comitatus. Believing that this, in addition to such use of the army as may be made under the powers already conferred by section 5298, Revised Statutes, would be adequate to secure the accomplishment of the ends in view, I again call attention of Congress to the expediency of so amending section 15 of the act of June 18, 1878, chapter 263, as to allow the military forces to be employed as a posse comitatus to assist the civil authorities within the territory to execute the laws therein. This use of the army, as I have in my former message observed, would not seem to be within the alleged evil against which that legislation was aimed.

(signed)
Chester A. Arthur

Editor's note: On May 3, 1882, seven days after his message to both houses of congress, President Chester A. Arthur issued his controversial proclamation to the citizens of the Arizona Territory.

THE PRESIDENTIAL PROCLAMATION

Whereas it is provided by the laws of the United States that—whenever, by reason of unlawful obstructions, combinations, or assemblages of persons or rebellion against the authority of the Government of the United States, it shall become impracticable, in the judgement of the President to enforce by the ordinary course of judicial proceedings the laws of the United States within any state or territory, it shall be lawful for the President to call forth the militia of any or all the states as he may deem necessary to enforce the faithful execution of the laws of the United States or to suppress such rebellion, in whatever state or territory thereof the laws of the United States may be forcibly opposed or the execution thereof forcibly obstructed.

And whereas it has been made to appear satisfactorily to me, by information received from the Governor of the Territory of Arizona, and from the general of the army of the United States and other reliable sources, that in consequence of unlawful combinations of evil-disposed persons who are banded together to oppose and obstruct the execution of the laws it has become impracticable to enforce by the ordinary course of judicial proceedings the laws of the United States within that territory, and that the laws of the United States have been therein forcibly opposed and the execution thereof forcibly resisted; and

Whereas the laws of the United States require that whenever it may be necessary, in the judgement of the President, to use the military forces for the purpose of enforcing the faithful execution of the laws of the United States, he shall forthwith, by proclamation, command such insurgents to disperse and retire peaceably to their respective abodes within a limited time:

Now, therefore, I, Chester A. Arthur, President of the United States, do hereby admonish all good citizens of the United States, and especially of the Territory of Arizona, against aiding, countenancing, abetting, or taking part in any such unlawful proceedings; and I do hereby warn all persons engaged in or connected with said obstruction of the laws to disperse and retire peaceably to their respective abodes on or before noon of the 15th day of May.

In witness whereof, I have hereunto set my hand and caused the seal of the United States to be affixed.

Done at the city of Washington, this 3rd day of May, A.D. 1882, and of the Independence of the United States, the one hundred and sixth.

(signed) Chester A. Arthur.
By the President:
Frederick T. Freylinghuysen
Secretary of State.

SELECTED BIBLIOGRAPHY

BOOKS

Altshuler, Constance Wynn. *Cavalry Yellow & Infantry Blue: Army Officers in Arizona Between 1851 and 1886.* Tucson: Arizona Historical Society, 1991.

Bakarich, Sara Grace. *Gunsmoke—The True Story of Old Tombstone.* Tombstone, Arizona: Tombstone Press, 1954.

Ball, Eve. *Indeh, An Apache Odyssey.* Provo, Utah: Brigham Young University Press, 1980.

Ball, Larry D. *The United States Marshals of New Mexico and Arizona Territories: 1846–1912.* Albuquerque: University of New Mexico Press, 1978.

Barnes, Will C. *Arizona Place Names.* Tucson: University of Arizona Press, 1936.

Barrett, Stephen Melvil. *Geronimo's Story of His Life.* New York: Duffield and Company, 1906.

———. *Sociology of the American Indians.* Kansas City, Missouri: Burton Publishing Company, 1946.

Betzinez, Jason. *I Fought with Geronimo.* Edited by Wilbur Sturtevant Nye. Harrisburg, Pennsylvania: Stackpole, 1959.

Bond, Ervin. *Cochise County, Arizona: Past and Present.* Douglas, Arizona: the author, 1984.

Bourke, John G. *An Apache Campaign in the Sierra Madre.* New York: Charles Scribner's Sons, 1958.

———. *On the Border with Crook.* New York: Ckharles Scribner's Sons, 1891.

Boyer, Glenn. *I Married Wyatt Earp: The Recollections of Josephine Sarah Marcus Earp.* Tucson: University of Arizona Press, 1976.

Brandes, Ray, and Ralph A. Smith. *Frontier Military Posts of Arizona.* Globe, Arizona: Dale Stuart King, 1960.

Breakenridge, William M. *Helldorado: Bringing the Law to the Mesquite.* Lincoln: University of Nebraska Press, 1992.

Burns, Walter Noble. *Tombstone—An Iliad of the Southwest.* New York: Doubleday & Company, 1927.

Burrows, Jack. *John Ringo: The Gunfighter Who Never Was.* Tucson: University of Arizona Press, 1987.

Carmony, Neil, ed. *Whiskey, Six-guns & Red-light Ladies: George Hand's Saloon Diary, Tucson, 1875–1878.* Silver City, New Mexico: High-Lonesome Books, 1994.

Chamberlain, William Henry. *History of Yuba County, California.* Oakland: Thompson & West, 1879.

Chaput, Donald. *Virgil Earp: Western Peace Officer.* Encampment, Wyoming: Affiliated Writers of America, 1994.

———. *Nellie Cashman and the North American Mining Frontier.* Tucson: Westernlore Press, 1995.

Cunningham, Eugene. *Triggernomentry: A Gallery of Gunfighters.* Caldwell, Idaho: The Caxton Printers, Ltd., 1947.

Davis, Britton. *The Truth About Geronimo.* New Haven: Yale University Press, 1929.

Debo, Angie. *Geronimo: The Man, His Time, His Place.* Norman: University of Oklahoma Press, 1976.

———. *A History of the Indians of the United States.* Norman: University of Oklahoma Press, 1970.

Dodge, Fred. *Undercover For Wells Fargo: The Unvarnished Recollections of Fred Dodge.* Edited by Carolyn Lake. Boston: Houghton Mifflin Company, 1969.

Duncklee, John. *Good Years for the Buzzards.* Tucson: University of Arizona Press, 1994.

———. *Coyotes I Have Known.* Tucson: University of Arizona Press, 1996.

Elliott, Russell R. *History of Nevada.* Lincoln: University of Nebraska Press, 1987.

Farish, Thomas Edwin. *History of Arizona,* 8 vols. Phoenix: State of Arizona, 1915.

Faulk, Odie B. *Arizona: A Short History.* Norman: University of Oklahoma Press, 1970.

————. *Tombstone: Myth and Reality.* New York: Oxford University Press, 1972.

Foote, H.S. *Pen Pictures from the Garden of the World: Santa Clara County, California.* Chicago: The Lewis Publishing Company, 1888.

Garza, Phyllis de la. *The Apache Kid.* Tucson: Westernlore Press, 1995.

Gudde, Erwin G. *California Place Names: The Origin and Etymology of Current Geographical Names.* Berkeley: University of California Press, 1965.

Hilliard, George. *A Hundred Years of Horse Tracks: The Story of the Gray Ranch.* Silver City, New Mexico: High-Lonesome Books, 1996.

Hoover, Mildred Brook, and Hero Eugene Rensch, Ethel Grace Rensch, revised by William N. Abeloe. *Historic Spots in California.* Stanford: Stanford University Press, 1966.

Hungerford, Edward. *Wells Fargo: Advancing the American Frontier.* New York: Random House, 1949.

Johnson, Kristin. *Unfortunate Emigrants: Narratives of the Donner Party.* Logan, Utah: Utah State University Press, 1996.

Kelly, George H., ed. *Legislative History: Arizona, 1864–1912.* Tucson: University of Arizona Press, 1926.

Lake, Stuart N. *Wyatt Earp: Frontier Marshal.* New York: Houghton Mifflin Company, 1931.

Lockwood, Frank C. *Pioneer Days in Arizona.* New York: The Macmillan Company, 1932.

Martin, Douglas. *Tombstone's Epitaph.* Albuquerque: University of New Mexico Press, 1951.

McClintock, James H. *Mormon Settlement in Arizona.* Phoenix: State of Arizona, 1921.

Miles, Nelson A. *Personal Recollections.* Chicago and New York: The Werner Company, 1897.

————. *Serving the Republic.* Freeport, New York: Books for Libraries Press, 1971.

Myers, John Myers. *The Last Chance: Tombstone's Early Years.* New York: E.P. Dutton & Company, Inc., 1950.

————. *Doc Holliday.* Boston: Little, Brown and Company, 1955.

Myrick, David F. *Railroads of Arizona.* 3 vols. Berkeley: Howell-North Books, 1975.

Nash, Jay Rogers. *Encyclopedia of Western Lawmen & Outlaws.* New York: Paragon House, 1992.

O'Neal, Bill. *Encyclopedia of Western Gunfighters.* Norman: University of Oklahoma Press, 1979.

Parsons, George Whitwell. *The Private Journal of George Whitwell Parsons.* Phoenix: Statewide Archival and Records Project, 1:286 (November 1939).

Patterson, Richard. *Historical Atlas of the Outlaw West.* Boulder: Johnson Books, 1985.

Pearce, T.M., ed. *New Mexico Place Names: A Geographical Dictionary.* Albuquerque: University of New Mexico Press, 1965.

Rosa, Joseph. *The Gunfighter: Man or Myth?* Norman: University of Oklahoma Press, 1969

Rush, Phillip S. *A History of the Californias.* San Diego: Neyenesch Printers, Inc., 1964.

Sawyer, Eugene T. *History of Santa Clara County California with Biographical Sketches.* Los Angeles: Historic Record Company, 1922.

Sheridan, Thomas E. *Arizona: A History.* Tucson: University of Arizona Press, 1995.

Smith, Henry Nash. *Virgin Land: The American West as Symbol and Myth.* Cambridge: Harvard University Press, 1970.

Sonnichsen, C.L. *Billy King's Tombstone.* Caldwell, Idaho: The Caxton Printers, Ltd., 1942.

————. *Tucson: The Life and Times of an American City.* Norman: University of Oklahoma Press, 1982.

Sweeney, Edwin R. *Cochise: Chiricahua Apache Chief.* Norman: University of Oklahoma Press, 1991.

Thrapp, Dan L. *Al Sieber: Chief of Scouts.* Norman: University of Oklahoma Press, 1964.

————. *The Conquest of Apacheria.* Norman: University of Oklahoma Press, 1967.

Trimble, Marshall. *Roadside History of Arizona.* Missoula: Mountain Press Publishing Company, 1986.

————. *Arizona: A Cavalcade of History.* Tucson: Treasure Chest Publications, 1989.

Wagoner, Jay J. *Arizona Territory, 1863–1912: A Political History.* Tucson: University of Arizona Press, 1970.

————. *Early Arizona: Prehistory to Civil War.* Tucson: University of Arizona Press, 1977.

Walker, Henry P., and Don Bufkin. *Historical Atlas of Arizona.* Norman: University of Oklahoma Press, 1979.

Walters, Lorenzo D. *Tombstone's Yesterday.* Tucson: Acme Printing Company, 1928.

Waters, Frank. *The Earp Brothers of Tombstone: The Story of Mrs. Virgil Earp.* New York: Clarkson N. Potter, Inc., 1960.

Whetten, LaVon B. *The Mormon Colonies in Mexico: Commemorating 100 Years.* Deming, New Mexico: Colony Specialties, 1985

Wilson, John P. *Islands in the Desert: A History of the Uplands of Southeastern Arizona.* Albuquerque: University of New Mexico Press, 1995.

Wood, Leonard. *Chasing Geronimo: The Journal of Leonard Wood–September 1886.* Albuquerque: University of New Mexico Press, 1970.

Workers of the Writers' Program of the Work Projects Administration. *Arizona, The Grand Canyon State: A State Guide.* New York: Hastings House Publishers, 1940.

Workers of the Writers' Program of the Work Projects Administration. *New Mexico: A Guide to the Colorful State.* New York: Hastings House Publishers, 1940.

PERIODICALS

Albert, S. R. "History of Camp John A. Rucker." *Arizona Cattlelog,* 30, no. 10 (October 1974), 18–27; 30, no. 11 (November 1974), 24–27.

Ames, Charles R. "Along the Mexican Border—Then and Now." *Journal of Arizona History,* 18, no. 4 (Winter 1977), 431–46.

Chapel, William L. "Camp Rucker: Outpost in Apacheria." *Journal of Arizona History,* 14, no. 2 (Summer 1973), 95–112.

Clum, John P. "It All Happened in Tombstone." *Arizona Historical Review,* 2 (October 1929), 46–72.

Gatewood, Charles B. "The Surrender of Geronimo." *Journal of Arizona History,* 27, no. 1 (Spring 1986), 53–70.

Knox, Mertice Buck. "The Escape of the Apache Kid." *Arizona Historical Review,* 3, no. 4 (1931), 77–87.

Loomis, Noel M. "Early Cattle Trails in Southern Arizona." *Arizoniana,* 3, no. 4 (Winter 1962), 18–24.

Martin, E.R. "Old Camp Rucker: Its Place in History." *Periodical 11,* 1, no. 39 (1979), 42–49.

Noonan, Buddy. "Camp Rucker, the Army's Forgotten Outpost." *Desert,* 43, no. 10 (October 1980), 18–20.

Robinson, Charles M. III. "Lieutenant Henry Flipper: Guilty." *True West,* February 1994, 20–25.

Spude, Robert L. "A Land of Sunshine and Silver: Silver Mining in Central Arizona, 1871–1885." *Journal of Arizona History,* 26, no. 1 (Spring 1975), 29–76.

Underhill, Lonnie E. "The Tombstone Discovery: Recollections of Ed Schieffelin & Richard Gird." *Arizona and the West,* 21, no. 1 (Spring 1979), 37–75

Walker, Henry P. "Arizona Land Fraud: Model 1880; The Tombstone Townsite Company." *Arizona and the West,* 21, no. 1 (Spring 1979), 5–36.

Warner, Ezra J. "A Black Man in the Long Gray Line." *American History Illustrated,* January 1970, 30–38.

West, Elliott. "The Saloon in Territorial Arizona." *Journal of the West,* 13 (July 1974), 61–73.

DOCUMENTS

Miscellaneous Record Book I, Yuba County, California.

State of California Department of Health Services, Certificate of Death, John P. Gray.

PHOTO CREDITS

All photos, unless otherwise stated, are from the author's personal collection.

INDEX

References can be found in either text or sidenotes.

ABOUT THE EDITOR

photo credit: Penny Duncklee

After a career of more than twenty years as a broadcast journalist, W. Lane Rogers left the industry in 1987 to pursue historical research and writing full-time. A prolific author, he has since published more than 600 articles in worldwide publications, served as book review editor of the *Tombstone Epitaph,* and is an historical columnist for *Arizona Capitol Times.* Rogers was the 1995 recipient of the Arizona Historical Society's C.L. Sonnichsen Award for best article in the presitigious *Journal of Arizona History.* His most recent book is *Crimes & Misdeeds: Headlines From Arizona's Past* (Northland Publishing, 1995). He is the author of *Deadly Intent: The Utah Murders; Bad Folks, Bullets & Badges;* and *The California Snatch Racket.* He is currently at work on a photographic history of Tucson.

Rogers' abiding interest in Western history was stimulated by grandparents who were pioneers in both northern and southern Arizona, and in Chihuahua, Mexico. The father of four grown children, he and his wife Patricia—along with five dogs and seven cats—live in a turn-of-the-century adobe home in one of Tucson's historic districts.

The editor welcomes comments and suggestions
for subsequent editions of *When All Roads Led to Tombstone.*
Please write c/o
Tamarack Books, Inc., PO Box 190313, Boise, ID 83719-0313.

Additional copies of *When All Roads Led to Tombstone*
can be found in bookstores nationwide
or directly from the publisher.

If ordering direct,
please include a check for $23.95
(book @ $19.95 plus a shipping/handling charge of $4.00).
Please add sales tax if applicable.
Idaho residents should send $24.95
(book @ $19.95, ID State Tax $1.00, and shipping/handling of $4.00).

Send your name, address, and check to:

Tombstone
Tamarack Books, Inc.
PO Box 190313
Boise, ID 83719-0313

To place orders using MasterCard or Visa, please call
1–800–962–6657.